Instant Pot
Cookbook For Beginners

600 Delicious and Easy Pressure Cooker Instant Pot Recipes for Your
Family Everyday

By Dannie Smith

Table of Content

Introduction

You may have been hearing a lot about Instant Pot lately and maybe you are wondering what they are. Well, you aren't the only one who is curious about Instant Pot! Everyone is looking into this new and exciting appliance and finding out how amazing it is. It's time you jump on the band wagon and get started on your Instant Pot adventure too!

Let's begin at the very beginning and discover what an Instant Pot actually is. An Instant Pot is a multifunctional programmable pressure cooker. The Instant Pot can act as a slow cooker, a pressure cooker a steamer, a rice cooker, a warming pot and even a yogurt maker. Sounds like it does a whole lot for one machine! The beauty of the Instant Pot is its ability to act as numerous appliances and to cook food easily.

Chapter 1 The Instant Pot Basics

The 7-in-1 Functions of Instant Pot

Pressure Cooking

The pressure cooker function is the task that the Instant Pot is most well-known for and that many people are drawn too. This function is also how the Instant Pot got its name! Essentially, you can add all the ingredients for a recipe, seal the pot and let it rise to a high-pressure temperature which will cause the food to be cooked quickly. Meals that use to take hours to cook on the stove top, can be done in a matter of minutes with this amazing machine. It does sound ideal, doesn't it?

Of course, all the other functions of the Instant Pot are also desirable. Homemade yogurt is quite simple to make as well as quickly cooking perfect rice. You can get rid of your traditional slow cooker and make any of your favorite slow cooker recipes right in the Instant Pot. Essentially, this machine does it all. Intrigued? Keep reading, it just gets better!

One Pot Cooking

If you have seen an Instant Pot or just read about them thus far, you already know that the Instant Pot is just one big pot. Cooking in the Instant Pot means that everything is made inside of this one pot, all together, with no other cooking pans needed. This is perfect for ease of cooking as everything is simply placed inside one pot rather than juggling multiple pans and dishes.

Cooking in one pot also makes cleaning up afterward so much easier. When you cook in just one pot, you only have one pot to clean! Cooking *and* cleaning is faster with an Instant Pot! The Instant Pot liner is also dishwasher friendly so you can just throw the pot into the dishwasher and call it a day.

Fast Cooking

When you hear the name Instant Pot, you likely think that your food will be ready quickly, even instantly. While it still does take a few minutes to cook anything in and Instant Pot, it is much faster than other traditional methods of cooking. The reason why is the pressure that builds inside the machine.

Pressure cooking is when a food is sealed inside a vessel with just a little bit of water or liquid. The machine heats up, the liquid inside quickly boils and then the steam released by the boiling liquid is trapped inside the machine. This process causes the internal temperature to rise quickly and reach a higher temperature than is typically possible when cooking on a stovetop where the maximum possible temperature is 212 degrees F (the boiling point of water).

The high-pressure cooking option on the Instant Pot definitely will cook your favorite foods quickly and give you the same results as if you have been cooking for hours. This is perfect for anyone who wants to cook something in a hurry, when you forgot to start that slow cooker to tenderize a tough piece of meat or if you just want to make dinner in a faster way. In Instant Pot is where you should turn when you need to cook quickly.

Healthy Cooking

You may now be wondering if cooking in the Instant Pot is a healthy way to cook. The simple answer is yes, it is definitely a healthy cooking method and here is why. To begin, pressure cooking helps maintain foods natural taste, texture and nutrients. When food is cooked quickly and in a sealed compartment, nothing escapes the pot and nutrients are not lost. All the goodness of your food is trapped inside the Instant Pot and stays part of the food rather than being cooked off and dissipating into the air.

When cooking in an Instant Pot, you are able to use less water or cooking liquid which also helps preserve nutrients in each food. The beneficial parts of the food you cook are not dissolved in the water but they are retained in the food as it cooks- the nutrients have nowhere to go!

Instant Pot cooking requires a whole lot less fats than cooking foods on a stovetop. When you pan sear a food or sauté a meal, you need to use some kind of fat to prevent the food from sticking to the bottom of the pan. Instant Pot cooking requires little to no fats as this method of cooking is more similar to steaming, where the steam prevents food from sticking. Less cooking fat, of course, means that you are eating less unhealthy fats! Another win for the Instant Pot!

Cooking in an Instant Pot has also been shown to help make grains and legumes more digestible as the proteins and phytic acids are broken down as they cook. When these beneficial grains and legumes are cooked under pressure, your body is able to absorb all the good nutrients associated with them meaning you are getting the fully benefits of eating such healthy foods.

As you can see, cooking in an Instant Pot is extremely healthy and may be one of the best methods of cooking out there when it comes to maintaining the healthful benefits of foods. Just one more reason to keep that Instant Pot on your counter all the time- you are going to want to use it on a daily basis!

Pre-Set Cooking Time

Wouldn't it be nice to come home after a long day at work to a hot, perfectly cooked meal?

Well, that dream can come true when you use your Instant Pot! Many Instant Pots come with the great feature of being programmable so you can add all your ingredients to the pot, seal it up and then set a timer for when you would like the food to cook. After that, the Instant Pot will do all the work for you! Your food will be ready whenever you need it!

This is ideal for anyone who has a hectic schedule and may have a few minutes to spare in the middle of the day to throw some things into the Instant Pot rather than rushing at night to prepare dinner. It is great for people who are away at work all day and don't want to worry about cooking a fresh meal after a hard day of work. Essentially, the pre-set cooking timer is ideal for, well, anyone! Just another fun little feature to make you really want an Instant Pot that much more!

The Benefits of Instant Pot

Environmentally Friendly

When you think about what to cook and how to cook your meals, the impact on the environment may be a consideration. You don't want to be using any appliances that will damage the ozone layer or create grease and smoke that can have a negative environmental impact. Luckily, the Instant Pot is a very environmentally friendly appliance.

When you cook with an Instant Pot, you are cutting your cooking time in half (or more!) which means that you are using less electricity. Less electricity means you are saving energy and cooking in a "greener" manner. In fact, studies have shown that the Instant Pot uses about 70% less energy to cook food than an oven or stove top.

That sounds like a definite environmental win!

When the Instant Pot cooks, it releases no smoke or harmful vapors into the air. Everything is sealed right inside so there are actually no emissions at all. Compare this to the harmful smoke created when you grill foods or the gas needed to run a gas functional appliance and you are definitely on a more environmentally friendly track when you opt to use an Instant Pot.

Easy to Use

After reading all about the benefits of an Instant Pot, you now may be questioning if such an amazing appliance is actually easy to use. To make food quickly, perfectly cooked, and in an environmentally friendly way, it must be hard, right?! Not at all! In fact, Instant Pots are one of the easiest appliances to use that you will ever find in the kitchen.

The majority of Instant Pot recipes only have a few simple steps to follow. You begin by putting all the ingredients for your recipe inside of the Instant Pot bowl and then placing the top of the Instant Pot on, turning it to the lock position and setting the steamer valve to the "seal" position. Then, all you have to do to start cooking is press a few buttons and walk away- the Instant Pot does the rest of the work for you!

Since the Instant Pot has preprogrammed cooking times and settings, the pot knows how long to cook certain foods and at what temperature the foods should be cooked. For example, if you are making stew and press the "stew" button, your Instant Pot knows when to raise and lower the temperature inside the pot to cook the stew to perfection. If you are making yogurt, the Instant Pot knows what temperature the yogurt should be to be made safely and properly.

The fact is, you don't need to know much about cooking at all to use an Instant Pot as the machine is already programmed for you! All you need to do is measure some ingredients, push a few buttons and you are done! No culinary degree needed here! Instant Pots are as easy to use as they are quick to make food.

Safety

Many people hear the words "pressure" cooker and get a little nervous about using this appliance. Stories of stovetop pressure cookers "exploding" may be stuck in your brain and the idea of a machine that builds so much pressure inside your kitchen can be a little intimidating. However, those horror stories are about pressure cookers of the past. The Instant Pot is a totally different machine!

Instant Pots are equipped with safety latches and seals that ensure they do not "explode". The steam release valves help steam escape from the Instant pot in a controlled, slow manner which is ideal to bring the pot back to normal pressure. The lid of the Instant Pot is also full of sensors and detection systems that make sure the lid is properly attached. If it is not on correctly, the Instant Pot won't even turn on!

In addition to building and releasing pressure safety, the instant Pot is also equipped with an overheat protection system which means your food will not burn. If there is not sufficient cooking liquid in the pot or the heat inside is not evenly distributing, the Instant Pot will lower its heat output to prevent burning. A machine that helps you never to burn food? What a great appliance!

Instant Pots are also fitted with an electrical fuse and a thermal fuse which will cut the power to the machine off if electrical currents or internal temperatures are too high or out of range. Just another safety control that makes the Instant Pot very safe to use for even the most beginner chefs.

Start Cooking with Instant Pot

As you can see, Instant Pots are quite amazing in what they can do and how they function. Gone are the days of unsafe, hard to use pressure cookers that were unreliable and didn't make food as perfectly as you may hope. Gone are the days of needing several different large appliances, each of which only cooked foods in one way. Gone are the days when a new, deluxe appliance was out of your price range or too advanced for your cooking abilities. The Instant Pot changed all of that.

Instant Pots are definitely one of the best and most useful kitchen appliances you can purchase. With their multi-functional abilities, quick cooking times and ease of use, it is a machine that you will find yourself using all the time. So, weather you are looking for a new way to make healthier foods, want to start making delicious foods faster or are just super excited for this new trendy kitchen tool, you need to get an Instant Pot as soon as possible. It is a purchase you will not regret.

Grab that Instant Pot you have been eyeing in the store and find a nice spot for it on your counter (you are going to want it out all the time!). Now, open up this cookbook and get ready to create some fantastic meals that will surprise and delight you. The hardest part about using the Instant Pot is deciding what to make first!

Happy cooking!

Chapter 2 Breakfast Recipes

Diced Turmeric Eggs

(Prep Time: 5 Mins |Total Time: 15 Mins | Serves: 3)

Ingredients:
- 6 Eggs
- ½ tsp Turmeric Powder
- ¼ tsp dried Parsley
- Pinch of Pepper
- 1 ½ cups Water

Cooking Direction
1. Pour the water into your Instant Pot and lower the trivet.
2. Grease a baking dish and crack the eggs into it, but make sure not to break the yolks.
3. Place the baking dish on the trivet and put the lid on.
4. Turn clockwise to seal and set the IP to MANUAL.
5. Cook on HIGH for 4 minutes.
6. Do a quick pressure release and remove the baking dish from the IP.
7. Transfer the egg 'pie' onto a cutting board.
8. Sprinkle the spices over and dice the eggs finely with a knife.
9. Serve and enjoy!

Nutrition Values

(Calories 130| Total Fats 8g | Carbs: 2g | Protein 10g | Dietary Fiber: 0g)

Smoked Salmon Eggs

(Prep Time: 3 Mins |Total Time: 10 Mins |Serves: 4)

Ingredients:
- 4 Eggs
- 1 tbsp Olive Oil
- 4 slices of Smoked Salmon
- 1 tsp chopped Chives
- 1 cup of Water

Cooking Direction
1. Pour the water into your Instant Pot and lower the trivet.
2. Grease 4 ramekins with the olive oil.
3. Place a slice of salmon inside each of the ramekins.
4. Crack an egg on top.
5. Sprinkle with the chives and cover the ramekins with foil.
6. Place the ramekins on the trivet.
7. Put the lid on and seal.
8. Set your Instant Pot to MANUAL and cook on HIGH for 5 minutes.
9. Serve and enjoy!

Nutrition Values

(Calories 240| Total Fats 17g | Carbs: 2g| Protein 19g | Dietary Fiber: 0g)

Apple and Almond Porridge

(Prep Time: 2 Mins |Total Time: 5 Mins |Serves: 1)

Ingredients:
- 1 tbsp Almond Butter
- 1 medium Gala Apple, grated
- 2 tbsp Flaxseed
- 3 tbsp ground Almonds
- ½ cup Almond Milk
- Pinch of Cinnamon

Cooking Direction
1. Place all of the ingredients in your Instant Pot.
2. Give it a good stir to combine.
3. Put the lid on and seal.
4. Set the Instant Pot to MANUAL and cook on HIGH for about 3 minutes.
5. Do a quick pressure release.
6. Stir once before serving and enjoy!

Nutrition Values

(Calories 443| Total Fats 18.5g | Carbs: 40g| Protein g | Dietary Fiber: 13.2g)

Tomato Poached Eggs

(Prep Time: 8 Mins |Total Time: 15 Mins |Serves: 1)

Ingredients:
- 1 Tomato, chopped
- 4 Eggs
- ½ Onion, diced
- ¼ tsp Smoked Paprika
- Pinch of Turmeric
- Pinch of Pepper
- 1 ½ cups Water

Cooking Direction
1. Pour the water into the Instant Pot and lower the trivet.
2. Grease 4 ramekins and set aside.
3. In a bowl, beat the eggs with the paprika, pepper, and turmeric.
4. Add the diced onion and tomatoes and stir to combine.
5. Divide the eggs between the ramekins.
6. Place the ramekins on the trivet and put the lid on.
7. Set the Instant Pot to STEAM and cook for 5 minutes.
8. Do a quick pressure release.
9. Serve and enjoy!

Nutrition Values
(Calories 195| Total Fats 14g | Carbs: 6.5g| Protein 10g | Dietary Fiber: 1.5g)

Veggie Quiche

(Prep Time: 8 Mins |Total Time: 25 Mins | Serves: 4)

Ingredients:
- 8 Eggs
- ¼ cup Almond Milk
- 1 Green Onion, sliced
- ½ cup chopped Kale
- 1 Tomato, chopped
- ½ Red Bell Pepper, diced
- 1 Carrot, shredded
- ½ tsp dried Parsley
- Pinch of Pepper
- Pinch of Paprika
- 1 ½ cups Water

Cooking Direction
1. Pour the water into your IP.
2. In a large bowl, whisk together the eggs, almond milk, pepper, and paprika.
3. Add the veggies and stir to combine well.
4. Grease a round pie pan and pour the egg and veggie mixture into it.
5. Lower the trivet into the IP and place the pan on it.
6. Put the lid on and turn clockwise to seal.
7. Set your Instant Pot to MANUAL and cook on HIGH for 20 minutes. Do a natural pressure release.
8. Serve and enjoy!

Nutrition Values
(Calories 170| Total Fats 10g | Carbs: 6.1g | Protein 13.5g | Dietary Fiber: 1.4g)

Carrot and Pecan Muffins

(Prep Time: 25 Mins |Total Time: 40 Mins |Serves: 8)

Ingredients:
- ½ cup chopped Pecans
- 1 tsp Baking Powder
- ¼ cup Coconut Oil
- ½ cup Almond or Coconut Milk
- 3 Eggs
- 1 cup Almond Flour
- 1/3 cup Pure Applesauce
- 1 tsp Apple Pie Spice
- 1 cup shredded Carrots

Cooking Direction
1. Pour the water into your Instant Pot and then lower the trivet.
2. In a mixing bowl, place all of the ingredients except the pecans and the carrots.
3. Beat with an electric mixer until fluffy and smooth.
4. Fold in the pecans and the carrots.
5. Divide the mixture between 8 silicone muffin cups and place the muffin cups on the trivet.

6. Set the Instant Pot to MANUAL and cook on HIGH for 15 minutes.
7. Do a quick pressure release.
8. Serve and enjoy!

Nutrition Values
(Calories 265| Total Fats 25g | Carbs: 6g| Protein 6g | Dietary Fiber: 2g)

Beef Egg Muffins
(Prep Time: 15 Mins |Total Time: 25 Mins |Serves: 2)

Ingredients:
- 4 Eggs
- 1 Green Onions, sliced
- ¼ cup ground Beef
- ¼ cup diced Bell Peppers
- Pinch of Pepper
- ¼ tsp dried Parsley
- ½ tbsp Olive Oil
- 1 ½ cups Water

Cooking Direction
1. Set your Instant Pot to SAUTE and heat the olive oil in it.
2. Add the beef and cook until it becomes brown.
3. Transfer to a bowl.
4. Add the eggs to the bowl and beat along with the pepper.
5. Stir in the remaining ingredients and divide the mixture between 4 silicone muffin cups.
6. Pour the water into the IP and lower the trivet.
7. Place the muffin cups on the trivet and close the lid.
8. Cook on HIGH for 8 minutes.
9. Do a quick pressure release.
10. Serve and enjoy!

Nutrition Values
(Calories 236| Total Fats 16g | Carbs: 2.2g| Protein 20g | Dietary Fiber: 0.6g)

Egg Bake with Carrots
(Prep Time: 10 Mins |Total Time: 20 Mins |Serves: 4)

Ingredients:
- 8 Eggs
- 1 cup shredded Carrots
- 2 cups shredded Sweet Potatoes
- ¼ tsp Turmeric Powder
- ¼ tsp Thyme
- ¼ tsp Parsley
- 2 tsp Olive Oil
- ½ cup Almond Milk

Cooking Direction
1. Set the Instant Pot to SAUTE and heat the olive oil in it.
2. Add the potatoes and carrots and cook for about 2 minutes, stirring occasionally.
3. Meanwhile, beat the eggs and almond milk in a bowl.
4. Stir in the herbs and spices and pour the mixture over the veggies.
5. Close the lid and press CANCEL.
6. Set the IP to MANUAL and cook on HIGH for 7 minutes.
7. Do a quick pressure release.
8. Serve and enjoy!

Nutrition Values
(Calories 220| Total Fats 7g | Carbs: 17.2 | Protein 6g | Dietary Fiber: 2g)

Veggie and Beef Casserole
(Prep Time: 15 Mins |Total Time: 40 Mins |Serves: 4)

Ingredients:
- 1 tbsp Coconut Oil
- 6 Eggs, beaten
- 8 ounces ground Beef
- 1 tsp minced Garlic
- ¾ cup sliced Leek
- 1 Sweet Potato, shredded
- ¾ cup chopped Kale
- 1 ½ cups Water

Cooking Direction

1. Set your Instant Pot to SAUTE and add the coconut oil to it.
2. When melted, add the leeks and cook for 2 minutes.
3. Add the beef and cook until it becomes brown.
4. Stir in the garlic and kale and cook for 1 more minute.
5. Transfer the mixture to a bowl.
6. Add the eggs and potatoes to the bowl and stir well to combine everything.
7. Transfer the mixture to a greased baking dish.
8. Pour the water into your Instant Pot and lower the trivet.
9. Place the prepared dish on the trivet and close the lid.
10. Set the IP to MANUAL and cook on HIGH for 25 minutes.
11. Do a quick pressure release. Serve and enjoy!

Nutrition Values
(Calories 425| Total Fats 30g | Carbs: 13g| Protein 24g | Dietary Fiber: 1.6g)

Sausage & Asparagus Dill

(Prep Time: 10 Mins |Total Time: 50 Mins | Serves: 5)

Ingredients
- Coconut oil, for greasing the dish
- 1 pound breakfast sausage
- ¼ cup coconut milk
- 8 free range eggs, beaten
- ½ cup coconut cream
- 1 tbsp. minced fresh dill
- 6-8 stalks asparagus, chopped
- 1 thinly sliced leek
- ¼ tsp. garlic powder
- Sea salt and pepper

Directions
1. Grease a square baking dish and set aside.
2. Place the sausage in a pan set over medium heat; break them into small pieces.
3. Cook for a few minutes and add asparagus and leeks; continue cooking for about 5 minutes more or until sausage is no longer pink.
4. Remove the pan from heat, discarding excess fat.
5. Whisk together eggs, garlic powder, dill, cream, salt and pepper in a bowl; pour the mixture into the prepared baking dish and add the sausage mixture; mix well.
6. Add water to the instant pot and insert a trivet; place the dish onto the trivet and lock lid.
7. Cook on high for 25 minutes and then let pressure come down on its own.
8. Remove the casserole and cut into equal slices.

Nutrition Values
(Calories 442| Total Fats 18.5g | Carbs: 59.8g| Protein 14.8g | Dietary Fiber: 10.5g)

Breakfast Eggs Cheese

(Prep Time: 10 Mins |Total Time: 40 Mins |Serves: 6)

Ingredients:
- 1/2 cup coconut cream
- 6 eggs
- 1 cup cooked ham
- 1 red onion, chopped
- 1 cup vegan cheddar cheese
- 1 cup chopped kale leaves
- 1 tsp Herbes de Provence
- 1/8 tsp. sea salt
- 1/8 tsp. pepper

Cooking Direction
1. In a bowl, whisk together coconut cream and eggs until well combined; stir in the remaining ingredients and pour the mixture into a heatproof bowl or dish, cover.
2. Add a cup of water in your instant pot and place a trivet over water.
3. Add the bowl and lock lid; cook on high for 20 minutes and then release pressure naturally.
4. Serve hot with a glass of fresh orange juice.

Nutrition Values
(Calories 285| Total Fats 18.3g | Carbs: 14.4g| Protein 16.6g | Dietary Fiber: 5g)

Kale Egg Breakfast Casserole

(Prep Time: 15 Mins |Total Time: 45 Mins |Serves: 6)

Ingredients:

- 2 tablespoons coconut oil
- 1 ⅓ cups sliced leek
- 2 teaspoons minced garlic
- 1 cup chopped kale
- 8 eggs
- ⅔ cups sweet potato, peeled and grated
- 1 ½ cups breakfast sausage,

Cooking Direction

1. Set your instant pot to sauté mode and melt coconut oil;
2. Stir in garlic, leeks, and kale and sauté for about 5 minutes or until tender; transfer the veggies to a plate and clean the pot.
3. Whisk together eggs, beef sausage, sweet potato and the sautéed veggies in a large bowl until well blended; pour the mixture in a heatproof bowl or pan.
4. Add water to the instant pot and insert a trivet; place the bowl onto the trivet and lock lid.
5. Cook on manual for 25 minutes and then let pressure come down on its own.
6. Remove the casserole and cut into equal slices.

Nutrition Values

(Calories 280| Total Fats 19g | Carbs: 7g| Protein 25g | Dietary Fiber: 1g)

Simple Hardboiled Eggs

(Prep Time: 3 Mins |Total Time: 10 Mins | Serves: 6)

Ingredients:

- 12 Eggs
- 1 cup of Water

Cooking Direction

1. Pour the water into the Instant Pot and place the eggs inside.
2. Put the lid on and then turn it clockwise to seal.
3. After the chiming sound, set the Instant Pot to MANUAL.
4. Cook on HIGH for 7 minutes.
5. Release the pressure quickly.
6. Prepare an ice bath and place the eggs inside.
7. Let cool until safe to handle.
8. Peel and serve as desired.
9. Enjoy!

Nutrition Values

(Calories 140| Total Fats 9g | Carbs: 1.8g| Protein 12g | Dietary Fiber: 0g)

Korean Steamed Eggs

(Prep Time: 5 Mins |Total Time: 10 Mins | Serves: 1)

Ingredients:

- 1 large egg
- pinch of sesame seeds
- 1 tsp chopped scallions
- 1/3 cup cold water
- pinch of garlic powder
- pinch of salt
- pinch of pepper

Cooking Direction

1. In a small bowl, whisk together water and eggs until frothy; strain the mixture through a fine mesh into a heat proof bowl.
2. Whisk in the remaining ingredients until well combined; set aside.
3. Add a cup of water to an instant pot and place a steamer basket or trivet in the pot; place the bowl with the mixture over the basket and lock lid.
4. Cook on high for 5 minutes and then natural release pressure.
5. Serve hot with a glass of freshly squeezed orange juice.

Nutrition Values

(Calories 76| Total Fats 5.2g | Carbs: 0.9g| Protein 6.5g | Dietary Fiber: 0.2g)

Easy Breakfast Casserole

(Prep Time: 25 Mins |Total Time: 50 Mins | Serves: 6)

Ingredients:

- 1½ pound breakfast sausage
- 1 large yam or sweet potato, diced
- 2 tbsp. melted coconut oil
- 10 eggs, whisked
- ½ tsp. garlic powder
- 2 cups chopped spinach
- ½ yellow onion, diced
- ½ tsp. sea salt

Cooking Direction

1. Coat a 9x12 baking dish with cooking spray.
2. Toss the diced sweet potatoes in coconut oil and sprinkle with salt. Set aside.
3. Set a sauté pan over medium heat; add yellow onion and sauté for about 4 minutes or until fragrant.
4. Stir in breakfast sausage and cook for about 5 minutes or until the sausages are no longer pink.
5. Transfer the sausage mixture to the baking dish and add spinach and sweet potatoes.
6. Top with eggs and sprinkle with garlic powder and salt. Mix until well combined and pour the mixture in a heatproof bowl or pan.
7. Add water to the instant pot and insert a trivet; place the dish onto the trivet and lock lid.
8. Cook on high for 25 minutes and then let pressure come down on its own.
9. Remove the casserole and cut into equal slices.

Nutrition Values

(Calories 76| Total Fats 5.2g | Carbs: 0.9g| Protein 6.5g | Dietary Fiber: 0.2g)

Tomato Dill Frittata

(Prep Time: 10 Mins |Total Time: 30 Mins | Serves: 4)

Ingredients:

- 8 free-range eggs, whisked
- 2 tbsp. chopped fresh chives
- 2 tbsp. chopped fresh dill
- 4 tomatoes, diced
- 1 tsp. red pepper flakes
- 2 garlic cloves, minced
- Coconut oil, for greasing the pan
- Sea salt
- Black pepper

Cooking Direction

1. Grease a cast iron skillet or saucepan and set aside.
2. In a large bowl, whisk together the eggs; beat in the remaining ingredients until well mixed.
3. Pour the egg mixture into the prepared pan and pour the mixture in a heatproof bowl or pan.
4. Add water to the instant pot and insert a trivet; place the pan onto the trivet and lock lid.
5. Cook on high for 20 minutes and then let pressure come down on its own.
6. Remove the casserole and cut into equal slices.
7. Garnish the frittata with extra chives and dill to serve.

Nutrition Values

(Calories 166| Total Fats 10.3g | Carbs: 7.2g| Protein 12.7g | Dietary Fiber: 1.9g)

Egg & Ham Casserole

(Prep Time: 10 Mins |Total Time: 35 Mins| Serves: 4)

Ingredients:

- 1 cup almond milk
- 10 large eggs
- 2 cups shredded vegan cheddar cheese
- 1 cup chopped ham
- 1/2 onion, diced
- 4 medium red potatoes, chopped
- 1 teaspoon salt
- 1 teaspoon pepper

Cooking Direction

1. Grease an instant pot with nonstick cooking spray and add two cups of water; insert a steamer basket.
2. Whisk almond milk and eggs in a bowl until well blended; beat in cheese, onion, ham, potatoes, salt and pepper until well combined.
3. Transfer the egg mixture into a heatproof bowl and insert into the pot. Lock lid and press manual button; set for 25 minutes.
4. When done, let pressure come down on its own and then serve the quiche with your favorite toppings.

Nutrition Values
(Calories 528| Total Fats 30g | Carbs: 41.1g| Protein 26.9g | Dietary Fiber: 5.8g)

Spicy Gluten-Free Pancakes

(Prep Time: 10 Mins |Total Time: 26 Mins | Serves: 4)

Ingredients:
- 4 tablespoons coconut oil
- 1 cup coconut milk
- ½ cup tapioca flour
- ½ cup almond flour
- 1 teaspoon salt
- ½ teaspoon chili powder
- ¼ teaspoon turmeric powder
- ¼ teaspoon black pepper
- ½ inch ginger, grated
- 1 serrano pepper, minced
- 1 handful cilantro, chopped
- ½ red onion, chopped

Cooking Direction

1. In a bowl, combine coconut milk, tapioca flour, almond flour and spices until well blended; stir in ginger, Serrano pepper, cilantro, and red onion until well combined.
2. Grease the interior of the instant pot with coconut oil; pour in the batter and seal the pot with vent closed; set pressure to low and cook for 30 minutes.
3. Serve the crispy pancakes with freshly squeezed orange juice.

Nutrition Values
(Calories 447| Total Fats 34.6g | Carbs: 34g| Protein 4.6g | Dietary Fiber: 3.3g)

Cauliflower Pudding

(Prep Time:5 Mins |Cook Time:20 Mins |Servings: 4)

Ingredients:
- 1½ cups unsweetened coconut milk or unsweetened almond milk
- 1 cup water
- 1 cup cauliflower rice (pulse florets in food processor until rice-like consistency)
- 2 teaspoons organic ground cinnamon powder
- 1 teaspoon pure vanilla extract
- Pinch of salt

Cooking Direction

1. Add all ingredients to Instant Pot. Stir until combined.
2. Press "Manual" button. Cook on HIGH 20 minutes.
3. When done, naturally release pressure for 10 minutes, then quick release remaining pressure. Remove lid. Serve.

Nutrition Values
(Calories: 213; Fat: 21.6g, Carbohydrates: 6.3g, Protein: 2.7g, Dietary Fiber: 2.5g)

Sausage and Cauliflower Mash

(Prep Time:3 Mins |Cook Time:5 Mins |Servings: 2)

Ingredients:
- 1 large head cauliflower, cut into florets
- 2 Tablespoons of olive oil
- ½ cup unsweetened coconut milk or unsweetened almond milk
- 1 Tablespoon non-dairy butter or ghee, melted
- 1 teaspoon organic mustard powder
- Pinch of sea salt, pepper
- 1 Tablespoon arrowroot powder

- 2 cups ground sausage (mild, spicy – your choice)
- ½ cup vegetable broth
- 1½ cups water

Cooking Direction

1. Add 1 cup water, and trivet to Instant Pot. Place cauliflower on top of trivet.
2. Lock lid, ensure valve is sealed. Press "Manual" button. Cook on HIGH 4 minutes.
3. When done, quick release pressure, remove the lid. Remove cauliflower, and trivet. Discard water. Transfer cauliflower to oven-proof dish, keep warm at 200°F.
4. In a large bowl, combine cauliflower, milk, ghee, mustard powder, salt, pepper. Use a potato masher to mash the cauliflower until broken apart. Set aside.
5. Press "Sauté" on Instant Pot. Heat olive oil. Brown ground sausage.
6. Add vegetable broth, ½ cup water. Stir.
7. Close, seal lid. Press "Manual" button. Cook on HIGH 8 minutes.
8. When done, quick release pressure, remove lid.
9. Press "Sauté" on Instant Pot. Sprinkle arrowroot flour over ingredients. Allow to thicken, stirring occasionally.
10. Transfer cauliflower rice to serving dish. Spoon sausage, sauce over cauliflower. Serve.

Nutrition Values
(Calories: 618 Fat: 47.2g, Carbohydrates: 31.2g, Dietary Fiber: 11.8g, Protein: 17.3g)

Spinach and Mushroom Frittata

(Prep Time:10Mins |Cook Time:7Mins |Servings: 4)

Ingredients:
- 1 cup fresh baby spinach
- 8 large eggs
- 6 bacon slices, diced
- Pinch of salt, pepper
- 1 cup water

Cooking Direction

1. Press "Sauté" on Instant Pot. Add diced bacon. Cook until brown. Set aside. Turn off "Sauté" function.
2. In a large bowl, add eggs, spinach, bacon, salt, pepper. Stir until combined.
3. Grease 4 individual ramekins with nonstick cooking spray. Divide egg mixture evenly between ramekins. Cover with aluminum foil.
4. Add 1 cup water, and trivet to Instant Pot. Place ramekins on top.
5. Lock, seal lid. Press "Manual" button. Cook on HIGH 5 minutes.
6. When done, naturally release pressure 10 minutes, remove lid. Serve.

Nutrition Values
(Calories: 293, Fat: 20.9g, Carbohydrates: 3.2g, Dietary Fiber: 1.3, Protein: 23.3g)

Egg and Asparagus Frittata

(Prep Time:10Mins |Cook Time:23Mins |Servings: 4)

Ingredients:
- 6 large eggs
- ½ cup of unsweetened almond milk or unsweetened coconut milk
- Pinch of salt, pepper
- 2 Tablespoons fresh chives, chopped
- 1 cup fresh asparagus, stemmed, cut into bite-sized pieces

Cooking Direction

1. Grease an eight-inch cake pan with non-stick cooking spray.
2. In a bowl, mix together eggs, milk, salt, pepper, chives, asparagus. Stir.
3. Pour mixture in cake pan. Cover with foil.
4. Add 1 cup water, and trivet to Instant Pot.
5. Place cake pan on trivet. Lock, seal lid. Press "Manual." Cook on HIGH 23 minutes.
6. When done, naturally release pressure 10 minutes, then quick release. Remove lid.
7. Remove pan. Allow to set 5 minutes before slicing. Serve.

Nutrition Values
(Calories: 170, Fat: 13.8g, Carbohydrates: 3.4g, Dietary Fiber: 1.4g, Protein: 9.7g)

Hard Boiled Egg Loaf

(Prep Time:5Mins |Cook Time:10 Mins| Servings: 6)

Ingredients:
- 12 large eggs
- Pinch of salt, pepper

Cooking Direction
1. Grease a baking dish that will fit your Instant Pot with non-stick cooking spray.
2. Crack eggs into baking dish. Season with salt, pepper. Don't stir.
3. Add 1 cup water, and steamer rack to Instant Po. Place baking dish on rack.
4. Close, seal lid. Press "Manual" button. Cook on HIGH 5 minutes.
5. When done, naturally release pressure 5 minutes, then quick release remaining pressure. Remove lid. Allow pan to settle 5 minutes.
6. Transfer egg loaf to a cutting board. Slice. Serve.

Nutrition Values
(Calories: 63, Fat: 4.4g, Carbohydrates: 0.3g, Dietary Fiber: 0g, Protein: 5.5g)

Turkey Sausage Frittata

(Prep Time:5Mins |Cook Time:23Mins| Servings: 4)

Ingredients:
- 1½ cups ground turkey breakfast sausage
- 1 Tablespoon of olive oil
- 12 large eggs, beaten
- 1 cup of unsweetened coconut milk or unsweetened almond milk
- 1 teaspoon of salt
- 1 teaspoon of freshly cracked black pepper

Cooking Direction
1. Press "Sauté" function on Instant Pot. Add olive oil.
2. Add breakfast turkey to Instant Pot. Cook until brown, stirring occasionally. Turn off "Sauté" function and set aside.
3. Grease a spring form pan with nonstick cooking spray. Add cooked turkey.
4. In a bowl, add eggs, milk, salt, pepper. Stir until combined. Pour over turkey.
5. Add 2 cups water, and trivet to Instant Pot.
6. Place spring form pan on top of trivet.
7. Lock the lid, seal valve. Press "Manual" button. Cook on HIGH, 7 minutes.
8. When cooking is done, naturally release pressure. Remove the lid.
9. Remove pan. Allow to settle 5 minutes, then slice.
10. Serve.

Nutrition Values
(Calories: 471, Fat: 31.7g, Carbohydrates: 4.3g, Dietary Fiber: 1.3g, Protein: 42.9g)

Cabbage with Turkey Sausages Breakfast

(Prep Time: 8Mins |Cook Time: 12Mins |Servings: 4)

Ingredients
- 1lb Turkey Sausage sliced
- 2 Tbsp olive oil
- 1 head cabbage sliced
- 1 onion (diced)
- 4 cloves minced garlic
- 3 tsp vine vinegar or to taste

Cooking Direction
1. Place the oil and sliced sausages in your Instant Pot.
2. Press SAUTÉ button on your Instant Pot and sauté sausages about 10-12 minutes.
3. Add sliced cabbage, onion and garlic and sauté for 10 minutes, stirring frequently.
4. Press CANCEL button and transfer the sausages and cabbage mixture to serving plate.
5. Sprinkle with wine vinegar and serve.

Nutrition Values
(Calories 641; Fat: 15g, Carbohydrates 16.4g, Fiber 6g, Protein 14.43g)

Coconut Flake Cereals Porridge

(Prep Time: 3Mins |Cook Time:12Mins |Servings: 4)

Ingredients
- 6 Tbsp organic unsweetened shredded coconut
- 1 1/2 Tbsp raw whole golden flaxseed
- 1 cup unsweetened coconut milk, preferably additive free
- 1/2 tsp vanilla extract

Toppings
- Liquid stevia drops
- Ground cinnamon or cardamom, to taste

Cooking Direction
1. Press SAUTÉ button on your Instant Pot.
2. When the word "hot" appears on the display, pour the milk and cook for 2 minutes, stirring frequently.
3. Add organic unsweetened shredded coconut, raw whole golden flaxseed, and vanilla extract; stir well for 2 - 3 minutes.
4. Lock lid into place and set on the MANUAL setting for 6 -7 minutes.
5. When the timer beeps, press "Cancel" and carefully flip the Quick Release valve to let the pressure out.
6. Serve hot with liquid stevia to taste and sprinkle with ground cinnamon or cardamom, to taste.

Nutrition Values
(Calories 281.93, Fat 29.14g, Carbohydrates 6.76g, Fiber 2.04g, Protein 2.83g)

Ground Pork with Eggs Frittata

(Prep Time:7Mins |Cook Time:13Mins| Servings: 4)

Ingredients
- 2 Tbsp ghee
- 1 onion, finely chopped
- 1 lb ground pork grass-fed
- 6 free-range eggs
- 2 Tbsp fresh cilantro, roughly chopped
- Salt and ground black pepper to taste
- 1 cup water for Instant Pot

Cooking Direction
1. Press SAUTÉ button on your Instant Pot.
2. When the word "hot" appears on the display, heat ghee and sauté the onions about 3 - 4 minutes.
3. Add the ground pork and sauté with a pinch of salt for 2 minutes.
4. Sprinkle fresh cilantro, stir and press the Stop button.
5. Whisk the eggs in a bowl with a pinch of salt and pepper.
6. Pour eggs in your Instant Pot and stir.
7. Lock lid into place and set on the MANUAL setting for 5 minutes.
8. Use Quick Release - turn the valve from sealing to venting to release the pressure.
9. Serve hot.

Nutrition Values
(Calories 253, Fat: 11.o3g, Carbohydrates 0.93g, Fiber 0.17g, Protein 34.95g)

Italian Turkey Sausage Muffins

(Prep Time:5Mins |Cook Time:15Mins |Servings: 4)

Ingredients
- 1 lb Turkey Italian sausage
- 2 cups chopped kale
- 6 pastured eggs
- 1/4 cup Extra Virgin Olive oil
- 2 cloves garlic
- 2 Tbsp Italian seasoning
- 2 Tbsp dried minced onion
- Sea salt and ground black pepper to taste
- 1 cup water for Instant Pot

Cooking Direction
1. Place the kale leaves, eggs, olive oil, garlic, Italian seasoning, onion, salt, and pepper in your blender and pulse/ blend for about 1 minute, or until thoroughly mixed.
2. Transfer to a large bowl and stir in the sausage until well mixed.
3. Fill the muffin tins to just beneath the rim.
4. Pour water into the inner stainless steel pot in the Instant Pot, and place the trivets inside (steam rack or a steamer basket).
5. Place a muffin tins on a trivet.

6. Lock lid into place and set on the MANUAL setting for 10 minutes.
7. When the beep sounds, quick release the pressure by pressing Cancel, and twisting the steam handle to the Venting position.

8. Serve hot or cold.

Nutrition Values
(Calories 349,23, Fat:28.77g, Carbohydrates 5,27g, Fiber 0,72g, Protein 18,61g)

Mustard Eggs and Avocado Mash
(Prep Time: 5Mins |Cook Time: 10Mins| Servings: 4)

Ingredients
- 2 cups water for Instant Pot
- 6 free-range eggs
- 1/2 cup stone ground mustard
- 1 avocado, chopped
- 1 tsp of lemon juice, freshly squeezed
- 1 Tbsp fresh chopped parsley (optional)
- Salt and pepper, to taste

Cooking Direction
1. Pour water into the inner stainless-steel pot in the Instant Pot and place the steamer basket.
2. Lock lid into place and set on the MANUAL setting for 5 minutes.
3. It will take the cooker approximately 5 minutes to build to pressure and then 5 minutes to cook.
4. Use Quick Release - turn the valve from sealing to venting to release the pressure.
5. Place the eggs in cold water and peel. Cut the eggs into small pieces and season with the salt and pepper.
6. Wash, peel and clean avocado.
7. Mash avocado with the fork, and sprinkle with the salt and pepper.
8. Combine the eggs, mustard, mashed avocado, lemon juice and fresh parsley.
9. Refrigerate for one hour and serve.

Nutrition Values
(Calories 161, Fat: 12.05g, Carbohydrates 4.97g, Fiber: 3.24g, Protein 9,35g)

Oysters and Eggs Frittata
(Prep Time:5Mins |Cook Time:15Mins |Servings: 4)

Ingredients
- 1 Tbsp coconut oil (melted)
- 1/2 cup green onion, sliced
- 2 cups mushrooms, sliced
- 10 oysters, well drained
- 1 cup coconut milk (canned)
- 2 Tbsp cooked, crumbled bacon
- 6 eggs from free-range chickens
- 1 cup water for Instant Pot

Cooking Direction
1. Press SAUTÉ button on your Instant Pot.
2. When the word "hot" appears on the display, add the coconut oil and sauté the green onions, mushrooms, oysters and crumbled bacon about 5 minutes.
3. Beat the eggs, coconut milk, and milk, with salt and pepper with a wire whisk until well blended. Pour mixture over oyster mixture.
4. Cancel the SAUTÉ functions.
5. Lock lid into place and set on the MANUAL setting for 8 minutes.
6. Use Quick Release - turn the valve from sealing to venting to release the pressure.
7. Serve hot.

Nutrition Values
(Calories 389.87, Fat: 18.2g, Carbohydrates 18.46g, Fiber:0.45g, Protein 36,28g)

Simple Sour Broccoli
(Prep Time:20Mins |Cook Time:8Mins| Servings: 4)

Ingredients
- 1 head broccoli, cut into florets
- 2 Tbsp garlic-infused olive oil
- 1 tsp garlic minced
- 1 Tbsp lemon juice, fresh squeezed
- Salt and ground black pepper
- 1 cup water for Instant Pot

Cooking Direction

1. Leave the broccoli in the salted water for 15 minutes.
2. Rinse off with water and pat down dry on kitchen paper.
3. Spread the florets on a greased baking pan and drizzle with olive oil and the minced garlic.
4. Pour water into the inner stainless steel pot in the Instant Pot, and place the trivet inside (steam rack or a steamer basket).
5. Place the baking pan on a trivet.
6. Lock lid into place and set on the MANUAL setting for 2 minutes.
7. Use Quick Release - turn the valve from sealing to venting to release the pressure.
8. Season broccoli with the lemon juice and salt and pepper to taste.
9. Serve warm or cold.

Nutrition Values
(Calories 112.4; Fat: 0.45g, Carbohydrates 10,62g, Fiber:1.28g, Protein 4,35g)

Breakfast Simple Pancakes

(Prep Time: 5 Mins |Total Time: 12 Min| Serves: 2)

Ingredients:
- ½ cup of fat-free milk
- ½ cup of all-purpose white flour
- 1 tablespoon canola oil
- 2 large eggs
- 1/8 teaspoon ground nutmeg

Cooking Direction
1. Mix together milk, flour, eggs and nutmeg in a bowl.
2. Put the oil in the Instant Pot and select "Sauté".
3. Put half of the mixture in the Instant Pot and sauté for 2 minutes.
4. Flip over the side and sauté for another 2 minutes.
5. Repeat with the rest of the mixture and dish out.

Nutrition Values
(Calories:135; Total Fat: 6.2g; Carbs: 13.7g; Dietary Fiber: 0.4g; Protein: 5.8g)

Breakfast Quinoa with Berries

(Prep Time: 5 Mins |Total Time: 10 Min| Serves: 3)

Ingredients:
- 1½ cups quinoa, well rinsed
- 2 tablespoons maple syrup
- 1 cup fresh berries
- 2 cups water
- 1 cup milk

Cooking Direction
1. Put all the ingredients in the Instant Pot and lock the lid.
2. Set the Instant Pot to "Manual" for 5 minutes at high pressure.
3. Release the pressure quickly and serve in small bowls.

Nutrition Values
(Calories:97; Total Fat: 6.4g; Carbs: 3.5g; Dietary Fiber: 1.8g; Protein: 7.8g)

Apple Streusel

(Prep Time: 5 Mins |Total Time: 10 Min| Serves: 3)

Ingredients:
- 1 cup fast cooking oats
- 2 apples, peeled, cored and diced
- 2 tablespoons brown sugar
- ¾ cup milk
- 2 tablespoons pecans, chopped

Cooking Direction
1. Mix brown sugar in milk and set aside.
2. Put the oats, apples, pecan and milk mixture in the Instant Pot and close the lid.
3. Set the Instant Pot to "Manual" for 3 minutes at high pressure.
4. Release the pressure quickly and dish out the prepared apple streusel.

Nutrition Values
(Calories:251; Total Fat: 9.4g; Carbs: 40.1g; Dietary Fiber: 5.9g; Protein: 5.4g)

Berries Compote

(Prep Time: 5 Mins |Total Time: 10 Min| Serves: 4)

Ingredients:
- 1½ cups fresh strawberries, hulled and sliced
- 1½ cups fresh blueberries, sliced
- 2 tablespoons fresh lemon juice
- 1 tablespoon corn starch mixed in 1 tablespoon water
- ¾ cup sugar

Cooking Direction
1. Put the strawberries, blueberries, sugar and lemon juice in the Instant Pot and lock the lid.
2. Set the Instant Pot to "Manual" for 3 minutes at high pressure.
3. Release the pressure naturally and stir in corn starch mixture.
4. Transfer compote into an airtight container and refrigerate till serving.

Nutrition Values
(Calories:200; Total Fat: 0.4g; Carbs: 51.9g; Dietary Fiber: 2.4g; Protein: 0.8g)

Salsa Eggs

(Prep Time: 5 Mins |Total Time: 20 Min| Serves: 2)

Ingredients:
- 3 eggs
- 1 cup prepared mild salsa
- 1 cup water
- 3 tablespoons olive oil, as required
- Salt and black pepper, to taste

Cooking Direction
1. Arrange the trivet on the Instant Pot and add water.
2. Grease a large ramekin with olive oil and add salsa.
3. Crack eggs over salsa and cover the ramekin with foil.
4. Place the ramekin on the trivet and lock the lid.
5. Set the Instant Pot to "Manual" for 15 minutes at low pressure.
6. Release the pressure quickly and serve hot.

Nutrition Values
(Calories:279; Total Fat: 27.6g; Carbs: 1.5g; Dietary Fiber: 0.5g; Protein: 8.3g)

Sausage Hash

(Prep Time: 5 Mins |Total Time: 20 Min| Serves: 5)

Ingredients:
- 4 large eggs, beaten
- 8-ounce ground sausage
- 1/3 cup water
- 1 pound bag frozen hash browns
- 1 cup cheddar cheese, grated

Cooking Direction
1. Put the sausage, water and hash browns in the Instant Pot and select "Sauté".
2. Sauté for 3 minutes and add beaten eggs.
3. Set the Instant Pot to "Manual" for 5 minutes at low pressure.
4. Release the pressure quickly and sprinkle with cheddar cheese.

Nutrition Values
(Calories:500; Total Fat: 34.8g; Carbs: 26.1g; Dietary Fiber: 1.8g; Protein: 22.3g)

Barley Porridge

(Prep Time: 5 Mins |Total Time: 20 Min| Serves: 6)

Ingredients:
- 1 cup pearled barley
- ¼ cup agave syrup
- ½ cup whipped cream
- 3 cups coconut milk
- ¼ cup dried dates

Cooking Direction
1. Put all the ingredients except cream in the Instant Pot and close the lid.
2. Set the Instant Pot to "Manual" for 10 minutes at high pressure.

3. Release the pressure naturally and dish out in serving bowls.
4. Top with whipped cream and serve.

Nutrition Values
(Calories:485; Total Fat: 32.1g; Carbs: 49.5g; Dietary Fiber: 8.4g; Protein: 6.5g

Simple Bread

(Prep Time: 5 Mins |Total Time: 30 Min| Serves: 6)

Ingredients:
- 2 cups all-purpose flour
- 2 tablespoons olive oil
- ½ teaspoon bicarbonate baking soda
- 1 teaspoon salt
- 1¼ cup whole milk plain yogurt

Cooking Direction
1. Arrange the trivet in the Instant Pot and add water.
2. Grease a baking dish with olive oil and keep aside.
3. Mix together flour, baking soda and salt in a bowl and stir in yogurt.
4. Knead the dough lightly with hands till dough becomes a little bit sticky.
5. Transfer the dough into prepared baking dish and drizzle with remaining oil.
6. Cover the baking dish with foil and transfer it on the trivet.
7. Set the Instant Pot to "Manual" for 15 minutes at high pressure.
8. Release the pressure naturally for 10 minutes and quickly release rest of the pressure.
9. Dish out and cut into desired slices.

Nutrition Values
(Calories:227; Total Fat: 6.8g; Carbs: 34.3g; Dietary Fiber: 1.1g; Protein: 7g)

Simple Oatmeal

(Prep Time: 5 Mins |Total Time: 20 Min| Serves: 2)

Ingredients:
- ½ cup steel cut oats
- 2 cups water
- 1 tablespoon olive oil
- Pinch of salt
- ¼ cup maple syrup

Cooking Direction
1. Put all the ingredients except maple syrup in the Instant Pot and lock the lid.
2. Set the Instant Pot to "Manual" for 12 minutes at high pressure.
3. Release the pressure naturally and dish out in serving bowls.
4. Top with maple syrup and serve.

Nutrition Values
(Calories:240; Total Fat: 8.4g; Carbs: 40.3g; Dietary Fiber: 2.1g; Protein: 2.7g)

Eggs with Spinach

(Prep Time: 5 Mins |Total Time: 20 Min| Serves: 8)

Ingredients:
- 3 tablespoons olive oil
- 20 cups fresh baby spinach, chopped
- 8 eggs
- ½ cup scallions, chopped
- Salt and black pepper, to taste

Cooking Direction
1. Put the oil and scallions in the Instant Pot and select "Sauté".
2. Sauté for 3 minutes and add baby spinach, salt and black pepper.
3. Sauté for 2 minutes and whisk in eggs.
4. Set the Instant Pot to "Manual" at high pressure for 6 minutes.
5. Release the pressure naturally and dish out.

Nutrition Values
(Calories:127; Total Fat: 9.9g; Carbs: 3.5g; Dietary Fiber: 1.8g; Protein: 7.8g)

Apple Breakfast Quinoa

(Prep Time: 5 Mins |Total Time: 10 Mins |Serves: 2)

Ingredients:

- 1 Apple, seeded and chopped
- 1 cup Quinoa
- 2 tbsp Cinnamon
- ¼ tsp Salt
- ½ tsp Vanilla Extract
- 1 ½ cups Water

Cooking Direction

1. Pour the water into your IP.
2. Add the remaining ingredients and give it a good stir to combine.
3. Close the lid and set your Instant Pot to MANUAL.
4. Cook for 8 minutes on HIGH.
5. Let the pressure drop on its own.
6. Divide the granola between 2 serving bowls.
7. Serve and enjoy!

Nutrition Values

(Calories 100| Total Fats 5.5g | Carbs: 7g | Protein 6g | Dietary Fiber: 12g)

Cheddar Hash Browns

(Prep Time: 5 Mins |Total Time: 10 Mins |Serves: 2)

Ingredients:

- ½ cup Frozen Hash Browns
- 2 Eggs
- ¼ cup grated Cheddar Cheese
- 1 ½ Bacon Slices, chopped
- Pinch of Pepper
- ¼ tsp Salt
- 2 tbsp Milk
- 1 ½ cups Water

Cooking Direction

1. Add the bacon in your IP and cook in until crispy on SAUTE.
2. Add the hash browns and saute for 2 more minutes.
3. Transfer the mixture to a greased baking dish that can fit into the Instant Pot.
4. Pour the water into your IP and lower the trivet.
5. In a bowl, whisk together the eggs, milk, cheese, salt, and pepper.
6. Pour the mixture over the hash browns.
7. Place the baking dish on the trivet and close the lid.
8. Cook for 5 minutes on MANUAL.
9. Release the pressure quickly. Serve and enjoy!

Nutrition Values

(Calories 164| Total Fats 11g | Carbs: 7g | Protein 12g | Dietary Fiber: 1.5g)

Cinnamon Swirl Toast

(Prep Time: 5 Mins |Total Time: 35 Mins |Serves: 2)

Ingredients:

- 2 Eggs
- ½ cup Milk
- 1 ½ cups cubes Cinnamon Swirl Bread
- 1 ½ tbsp Maple Syrup
- 1 tsp Butter
- ½ tsp Vanilla
- Pinch of Salt
- 1 ½ cups Water

Cooking Direction

1. Pour the water into your IP and lower the trivet.
2. Grease a small baking dish with the butter.
3. Whisk the eggs in a bowl.
4. Whisk in the milk, vanilla, maple, and salt.
5. Arrange the bread cubes in the baking dish and pour the egg mixture over.
6. Place the dish on the trivet and close the lid.
7. Set the IP to MANUAL. Cook on HIGH for 15 minutes.
8. Do a quick pressure release.
9. Serve and enjoy!

Nutrition Values

(Calories 183| Total Fats 3g | Carbs: 21g | Protein 8g | Dietary Fiber: 2g)

Banana and Walnut Oatmeal

(Prep Time: 5 Mins |Total Time: 25 Mins | Serves: 2)

Ingredients:

- 1 cup Oatmeal
- 1 Cup chopped Walnuts
- 1 Banana, mashed
- 1 2/3 cup Water
- 2 ½ tbsp Honey
- Pinch of Salt

Cooking Direction

1. Pour the water into your IP.
2. Whisk in the honey and banana.
3. Stir in the rest of the ingredients and close the lid.
4. Set the IP to PORRIDGE and cook for 10 minutes.
5. Do a natural pressure release, about 10 minutes.
6. Serve and enjoy!

Nutrition Values

(Calories 370| Total Fats 12g | Carbs: 50g | Protein 10g | Dietary Fiber: 3,4g)

Arugula Eggs with Hollandaise Sauce

(Prep Time: 5 Mins |Total Time: 12 Mins |Serves: 2)

Ingredients:

- ¼ cup Arugula
- 2 Mozzarella Slices
- 2 Slices of Whole Wheat Bread, chopped
- 1 ounces Hollandaise Sauce
- 2 Large Eggs
- 1 ½ cups Water

Cooking Direction

1. Pour the water into your IP and lower the trivet.
2. Arrange the bread at the bottom of two large (previously greased) ramekins.
3. Chop the arugula and whisk it with the eggs.
4. Divide the egg mixture between the ramekins.
5. Cover the ramekins with aluminum foil and place on the trivet.
6. Close the lid and cook on HIGH for 5 minutes.
7. Do a quick pressure release and discard the foil.
8. Top the eggs with mozzarella and drizzle the sauce over.
9. Serve and enjoy!

Nutrition Values

(Calories 230| Total Fats 14.6g | Carbs: 9g | Protein 15g | Dietary Fiber: 0.1g)

Cranberry Bread Pudding

(Prep Time: 5 Mins |Total Time: 35 Mins |Serves: 2)

Ingredients:

- 1 cups cubed Cinnamon Raisin Bread
- 2/3 cup Milk
- 1 Egg Yolk
- ¼ cup Sugar
- 2/3 tsp Vanilla Extract
- 1/3 cup dried Cranberries
- Pinch of Salt
- 1 ½ cups Warm Water

Cooking Direction

1. Pour the water into your IP and lower the trivet.
2. Whisk together the eggs, sugar, vanilla, salt, and milk, in a bowl.
3. Add the bread in it and let the mixture soak for 15 minutes.
4. Transfer the mixture to a baking dish and cover with aluminum foil.
5. Place the dish on the trivet and close the lid.
6. Cook on HIGH for 12 minutes.
7. Serve and enjoy!

Nutrition Values

(Calories 313| Total Fats 25g | Carbs: 17g | Protein 11g | Dietary Fiber: 21g)

Bacon and Egg Sandwich

(Prep Time: 5 Mins |Total Time: 20 Mins |Serves: 2)

Ingredients:

- 4 Bread Slices
- 2 Eggs
- 2 tbsp grated Cheese
- 1 tsp Olive Oil
- 4 Bacon Slices
- 1 ½ cups Water

Cooking Direction

1. Cook the bacon in the IP on SAUTE until crispy.
2. Crumble it in a bowl.
3. Pour the water into your IP and lower the trivet. Stir in the oil.
4. Divide the bacon between 2 ramekins and crack the eggs over.
5. Sprinkle the cheese on top.
6. Cover the ramekins with foil and place on the trivet.
7. Close the lid and cook on HIGH for 6 minutes.
8. Do a quick pressure release.
9. Assemble the sandwiches and serve.
10. Serve and enjoy!

Nutrition Values

(Calories 370| Total Fats 13g | Carbs: 31g | Protein 20g | Dietary Fiber: 1.5g)

Cheesy Mushroom Oats

(Prep Time: 5 Mins |Total Time: 30 Mins |Serves: 2)

Ingredients:

- 1 tbsp Butter
- 6 ounces sliced Mushrooms
- ¼ Onion, diced
- ½ cup Steel-Cut Oats
- 1 Thyme Sprig
- 1 tsp minced Garlic
- ¼ cup grated Cheddar Cheese
- 7 ounces Chicken Broth
- ½ cups Water

Cooking Direction

1. Melt the butter in the IP on SAUTE.
2. Add the onions and mushrooms and cook for 3-4 minutes.
3. Add the garlic and cook for one more minute.
4. Place the oats inside and cook for an additional minute.
5. Pour the water and broth over and give it a good stir.
6. Place the thyme sprig inside and close the lid.
7. Cook on HIGH for 12 minutes.
8. Do a natural pressure release. Serve and enjoy!

Nutrition Values

(Calories 266| Total Fats 12g | Carbs: 31g | Protein 9g | Dietary Fiber: 3g)

Maple and Vanilla Quinoa Bowl

(Prep Time: 5 Mins |Total Time: 20 Mins |Serves: 2)

Ingredients:

- 1 cup Quinoa, uncooked
- 2 tbsp Maple Syrup
- 1 tsp Vanilla Extract
- 2 tbsp Coconut Flakes
- 1 ½ cups Water

Cooking Direction

1. Dump all of the ingredients in your Instant Pot.
2. Stir well to combine.
3. Close and seal the lid and set the IP to MANUAL.
4. Cook the mixture for 5-8 minutes on HIGH.
5. Let the pressure come down on its own.
6. Serve and enjoy!

Nutrition Values

(Calories 372| Total Fats 2.5g | Carbs: 35.7g | Protein 6g | Dietary Fiber: 3g)

Onion, Tomato, and Sweet Potato Frittata

(Prep Time: 5 Mins |Total Time: 15 Mins |Serves: 2)

Ingredients:

- 3 Large Eggs, beaten
- 1 tbsp Olive Oil
- 1 tbsp Coconut Flour
- ½ Onion, diced
- 1 Tomato, chopped
- 4 ounces Sweet Potato, shredded
- 2 tbsp Milk
- 1 ½ cups Water

Cooking Direction

1. Pour the water into your IP and lower the trivet.
2. Whisk the oil, eggs, and milk in one large bowl.
3. Fold in the flour and veggies.
4. Pour the mixture into a greased baking dish.
5. Place the dish on the trivet and close the lid of the IP.
6. Set the Instant Pot to MANUAL and cook on HIGH for 16 minutes.
7. Do a quick pressure release.
8. Serve and enjoy!

Nutrition Values

(Calories 202| Total Fats 11.6g | Carbs: 14g | Protein 11g | Dietary Fiber: 2g)

Meat-Loaded Quiche

(Prep Time: 5 Mins |Total Time: 40 Mins |Serves: 2)

Ingredients:

- 2 Ham Slices, diced
- ½ cup cooked and crumbled Sausage
- 2 Bacon Slices, cooked and crumbled
- ½ cup grated Cheddar Cheese
- 3 Eggs, beaten
- ¼ cup Milk
- 1 Green Onion, sliced
- Salt and Pepper, to taste
- 1 ½ cups Water

Cooking Direction

1. Pour the water into your IP and lower the trivet.
2. Combine all of the ingredients in a bowl.
3. Pour the mixture into a baking dish.
4. Cover the dish with aluminum foil and place on the trivet.
5. Close the lid and cook on HIGH for 22 minutes.
6. Press CANCEL and wait 10 minutes before releasing the pressure quickly.
7. Serve and enjoy!

Nutrition Values

(Calories 660| Total Fats 40g | Carbs: 8g | Protein 40g | Dietary Fiber: 0.3g)

Honey Oatmeal

(Prep Time: 5 Mins |Total Time: 10 Mins |Serves: 2)

Ingredients:

- ½ cup Steel-Cut Oats
- ½ cup warm Milk
- 3 tbsp Honey
- Pinch of Cinnamon
- Pinch of Salt
- 2 cups Water

Cooking Direction

1. Pour 1 cup of the water into the Instant Pot and lower the trivet.
2. In a heatproof bowl, place the oats and the remaining water.
3. Close the lid and cook on HIGH for 6 minutes.
4. Do a quick pressure release.
5. Stir in the honey, cinnamon, salt, and milk.
6. Serve and enjoy!

Nutrition Values

(Calories 155| Total Fats 2g | Carbs: 28g | Protein 4g| Dietary Fiber: 2.3g)

Tomato, Pepper, and Sausage Breakfast

(Prep Time: 5 Mins |Total Time: 40 Mins |Serves: 2)

Ingredients:

- 2 Green Bell Peppers, chopped
- 4 Italian Sausage Links
- 14 ounces diced Tomatoes
- 1 Garlic Clove, minced
- 1 tsp Italian Seasoning
- 1 ½ cups Water

Cooking Direction

1. Pour the water into the Instant Pot and lower the trivet.
2. Grease a baking dish with some cooking spray and dump all of the ingredients in it.
3. Stir to combine well.
4. Place the dish in the trivet and close the lid.
5. Set the IP to MANUAL and cook on HIGH for 22 minutes.
6. Release the pressure naturally.
7. Serve and enjoy!

Nutrition Values

(Calories 400| Total Fats 30g | Carbs: 9g | Protein 20g| Dietary Fiber: 0.8g)

Orange French Toast

(Prep Time: 5 Mins |Total Time: 35 Mins |Serves: 2)

Ingredients:

- 2/3 cup Milk
- 1 Egg
- ¼ tsp Vanilla
- 2 tbsp Sugar
- 1/3 Challah Loaf, chopped
- 2 tbsp melted Butter
- Pinch of Salt
- Zest of 1 Orange
- 1 cups Water

Cooking Direction

1. Pour the water into the Instant Pot and lower the trivet.
2. Place the bread at the bottom of a baking dish.
3. Whisk together the remaining ingredients and pour the mixture over the chopped bread.
4. Place the dish on the trivet.
5. Close and seal the lid and set the IP to MANUAL.
6. Cook on HIGH for 25 minutes.
7. Release the pressure quickly. Serve and enjoy!

Nutrition Values

(Calories 450| Total Fats 16g | Carbs: 63g | Protein 14g| Dietary Fiber: 2)

Breakfast Burrito

(Prep Time: 5 Mins |Total Time: 20 Mins |Serves: 2)

Ingredients:

- 2 Burrito Wraps
- ¼ Onion, sliced
- 2 tsp diced Jalapeno
- ¼ cup diced Ham
- ¼ tsp Taco Seasoning
- 2 Eggs
- ½ cup cubed Potatoes
- ¼ tsp Chili Powder
- 1 1/2 cups Water

Cooking Direction

1. Pour the water into the Instant Pot and lower the trivet.
2. Beat the eggs along with the chili powder and taco seasonings.
3. Pour the mixture into a greased baking dish.
4. Stir in the remaining ingredients, except the wraps.
5. Place the dish on the trivet and cook for 13 minutes on HIGH.
6. Release the pressure quickly.
7. Divide the filling between the burrito wraps, and wrap them up.
8. Serve and enjoy!

Nutrition Values

(Calories 460| Total Fats 11g | Carbs: 35g | Protein 12g| Dietary Fiber: 4)

Giant Coconut Pancake

(Prep Time: 5 Mins |Total Time: 40 Mins |Serves: 2)

Ingredients:
- ½ cup Coconut Flour
- 2 tbsp Honey
- 1 Egg
- ½ tsp Coconut Extract
- ½ cup ground Almonds
- ¼ tsp Baking Soda
- 1 ½ cups Coconut Milk

Cooking Direction
1. Whisk together the wet ingredients in a bowl.
2. Gently whisk in the remaining ingredients.
3. Coat the IP with some cooking spray and pour the mixture into it.
4. Close the lid and set the Instant Pot to MANUAL.
5. Cook on LOW for 35-40 minutes.
6. Serve and enjoy!

Nutrition Values

(Calories 350| Total Fats 15g | Carbs: 38g | Protein 16g| Dietary Fiber: 18g)

Kale and Sausage Egg Casserole

(Prep Time: 5 Mins |Total Time: 40 Mins |Serves: 2)

Ingredients:
- 1 tbsp Coconut Oil
- ½ Sweet Potato, shredded
- 3 Eggs
- 4 ounces cooked and crumbled Chorizo
- 1/3 cup sliced Leeks
- ½ cup chopped Kale
- ½ tsp minced Garlic
- 1 ½ cups Water

Cooking Direction
1. Melt the coconut oil in the IP on SAUTE.
2. Add the garlic and leeks and cook for 2 minutes.
3. Stir in the kale and saute for another minute.
4. Beat the eggs and pour over the veggies.
5. Stir in the potatoes and chorizo.
6. Transfer the mixture to a baking dish and pour the water into the IP.
7. Lower the trivet and place the dish on it.
8. Close the lid and cook on HIGH for 20 minutes.
9. Do a quick pressure release. Serve and enjoy!

Nutrition Values

(Calories 425| Total Fats 30g | Carbs: 13g | Protein 24g| Dietary Fiber: 1.6g)

Egg and Rice Porridge

(Prep Time: 5 Mins |Total Time: 40 Mins |Serves: 2)

Ingredients:
- ¼ cup Rice
- 2 Eggs
- 1 cup Water
- 1 cup Chicken Broth
- 2 Scallions, chopped
- ½ tbsp Sugar
- 1 tbsp Olive Oil
- 1 tsp Soy Sauce
- ¼ tsp Salt
- ¼ tsp Pepper

Cooking Direction
1. Combine the rice, water, broth, salt, and sugar, in the Instant Pot.
2. Close the lid and set the IP to PORRIDGE.
3. Cook for 30 minutes.
4. Do a quick pressure release and transfer to a bowl.
5. Wipe the IP clean and add the olive oil.
6. Cook the scallions on SAUTE for about a minute.
7. Add the remaining ingredients and cook until the eggs are set.
8. Stir the mixture into the rice. Serve and enjoy!

Nutrition Values

(Calories 214| Total Fats 2g | Carbs: 24g | Protein 10g| Dietary Fiber: 2.3g)

Oat Porridge with Pomegranates

(Prep Time: 5 Mins |Total Time: 5 Mins |Serves: 2)

Ingredients:

- 1 cup Oats
- 2 tbsp Pomegranate Molasses
- ¾ cups Pomegranate Juice
- A pinch of Salt
- 1 1/2 cups Water
- 1 tbsp Honey, optional

Cooking Direction

1. Combine all of the ingredients, except the molasses, in the Instant Pot and close the lid.
2. Set the IP to MANUAL and cook on HIGH for 3 minutes.
3. Release the pressure quickly.
4. Stir in the pomegranate molasses and divide between 2 serving bowls.
5. Serve and enjoy!

Nutrition Values

(Calories 400| Total Fats 6g | Carbs: 50g | Protein 14g| Dietary Fiber: 7)

Black Bean Hash Breakfast

(Prep Time: 5 Mins |Total Time: 15 Mins |Serves: 2)

Ingredients:

- 1 cup grated Sweet Potatoes
- ½ cup chopped Onions
- ½ tsp minces Garlic
- 1/3 cup Veggie Broth
- ½ cup canned Black Beans
- 1 tsp Chili Powder
- 1 tbsp Olive Oil
- 2 tbsp chopped Scallions

Cooking Direction

1. Heat the oil in your Instant Pot on SAUTE.
2. Add the onions and cook for about 3 minutes.
3. Stir in the garlic and cook for another minute.
4. Add the remaining ingredients, give it a good stir, and close the lid.
5. Cook on MANUAL on HIGH for 3 minutes.
6. Release the pressure quickly.
7. Serve and enjoy!

Nutrition Values

(Calories 140| Total Fats 9g | Carbs: 28g | Protein 5g| Dietary Fiber: 2g)

Apricot Oat Breakfast

(Prep Time: 5 Mins |Total Time: 10 Mins |Serves: 2)

Ingredients:

- 1 cup Coconut Milk
- ½ cup Steel-Cut Oats
- 1 Large Apricot, diced
- ½ tsp Vanilla Extract
- 1 tbsp Honey
- 1 1/2 cups Water

Cooking Direction

1. Pour the coconut milk, vanilla, and oats in the Instant Pot.
2. Stir to combine and close the lid.
3. Cook for 3 minutes on HIGH.
4. Do a natural pressure release, about 10 minutes.
5. Serve and enjoy!

Nutrition Values

(Calories 240| Total Fats 4g | Carbs: 22g | Protein 4.5g| Dietary Fiber: 4g)

Dark Chocolate & Cherry Oatmeal

(Prep Time: 5 Mins |Total Time: 15 Mins |Serves: 2)

Ingredients:

- ½ cup Steel-Cut Oats
- ½ cup frozen and pitted Cherries
- 2 tbsp Dark Chocolate Chips
- 1 tbsp Sugar
- A pinch of Salt
- 1 ¾ cups Water

Cooking Direction

1. Pour the water into the Instant Pot.
2. Stir in the oats, cherries, salt, and sugar.
3. Close the lid and set the IP to POULTRY.
4. Cook for 12 minutes.
5. Do a quick pressure release.

6. Stir in the chocolate chips.
7. Serve and enjoy!
Nutrition Values

(Calories 283| Total Fats 6g | Carbs: 54g | Protein 5g| Dietary Fiber: 5.5g)

Lemon Tapioca Bowl

(Prep Time: 5 Mins |Total Time: 15 Mins |Serves: 2)

Ingredients:
- 2 tbsp Lemon Juice
- ½ cups plus 2 tbsp Milk
- ½ tsp Lemon Zest
- 2 tbsp Brown Sugar
- 1/3 cup Tapioca Pearls
- 1 1/2 cups Water

Cooking Direction
1. Pour the water into the Instant Pot and lower the trivet.
2. Whisk together the remaining ingredients in a baking dish.
3. Place the dish on the lowered trivet.
4. Close the lid and set the IP to STEAM.
5. Cook for 10 minutes and then release the pressure quickly.
6. Serve and enjoy!

Nutrition Values
(Calories 290| Total Fats 9g | Carbs: 22g | Protein 8g| Dietary Fiber: 2g)

Cinnamon Breakfast Bread

(Prep Time: 5 Mins |Total Time: / Mins |Serves: 2)

Ingredients:
- 1/3 cup Flour
- ¼ tbsp Yeast
- 1 tbsp Flaxseed Meal
- ½ tsp Cinnamon
- 1 tbsp Sugar
- 1/3 cup Hot Water
- Pinch of Sea Salt
- 1 1/2 cups Water

Cooking Direction
1. Pour the water into the Instant Pot and lower the trivet.
2. Combine the dry ingredients in a large bowl.
3. Gently whisk in the wet ingredients until a sticky dough is made.
4. Transfer the dough to a clean and lightly floured surface and knead with your hands for a couple of minutes.
5. Transfer to a greased loaf pan and place on the lowered trivet.
6. Close the lid and cook for 20 minutes on HIGH.
7. Do a quick pressure release.
8. Serve and enjoy!

Nutrition Values
(Calories 380| Total Fats 5g | Carbs: 41g | Protein 4g| Dietary Fiber: 2.1g)

Ham Muffins

(Prep Time: 5 Mins |Total Time: 20 Min| Serves: 8)

Ingredients:
- 8-ounce cooked ham, crumbled
- 8 eggs
- 1½ cups water
- 1 cup red bell pepper, seeded and chopped
- Salt and black pepper, to taste

Cooking Direction
1. Arrange the trivet in the Instant Pot and add water.
2. Whisk together eggs, ham, red bell pepper, salt and black pepper and pour into 8 muffins moulds.
3. Place the muffins moulds on the trivet and lock the lid.
4. Set the Instant Pot to "Manual" for 8 minutes at high pressure.
5. Release the pressure naturally and dish out.

Nutrition Values
(Calories:114; Total Fat: 6.9g; Carbs: 2.6g; Dietary Fiber: 0.6g; Protein: 10.4g;)

Chapter 3 Soup and Stews

Chicken and Root Veggie Soup

(Prep Time: 5 Mins |Total Time: 50 Mins |Serves: 4)

Ingredients:

- 1 ½ pounds Chicken Drumsticks
- 1 Rutabaga, peeled and
- 2 Carrots, diced
- ½ Onion, diced
- 1 Parsnip, peeled and diced
- 2 Celery Stalks, diced
- 1 Bay Leaf
- Pinch of Black Pepper
- 4 cups Homemade Chicken Broth

Cooking Direction

1. Dump all of the ingredients in your Instant Pot.
2. Stir well to combine and close the lid.
3. When sealed, set the IP to SOUP.
4. Cook on the default setting.
5. When the timer goes off, do a natural pressure release.
6. Transfer the drumsticks to a cutting board and remove the meat from the bones.
7. Place the meat back to the IP and stir to combine.
8. Serve immediately and enjoy!

Nutrition Values

(Calories 410| Total Fats 11g | Carbs: 20g| Protein 54g | Dietary Fiber: 4g)

Pomodoro Soup with Cabbage

(Prep Time: 5 Mins |Total Time: 25 Mins |Serves: 4)

Ingredients:

- 1 ½ cups diced Tomatoes
- 1 tsp minced Garlic
- ½ Onion, diced
- 3 cups Water
- 1 ½ tbsp Coconut Oil
- ½ Cabbage Head, chopped
- ½ cup Tomato Paste
- ½ tsp dried Parsley

Cooking Direction

1. Set your Instant Pot to SAUTE and add the coconut oil to it.
2. When melted, add the onion and cook for 3 minutes.
3. Add the garlic and saute for 30 seconds more.
4. Add the remaining ingredients and stir well to combine.
5. Put the lid on and seal.
6. Set the Instant Pot to MANUAL and cook on HIGH for 5 minutes.
7. Let the pressure drop naturally.
8. Serve and enjoy!

Nutrition Values

(Calories 123| Total Fats 6g | Carbs: 16g| Protein 4g | Dietary Fiber: 5g)

Gingery Butternut Squash Soup with Gala Apples

(Prep Time: 5 Mins |Total Time: 15 Mins |Serves: 4)

Ingredients:

- 1 medium Gala Apple, peeled and cut into cubes
- 1 tbsp Olive Oil
- 1 medium Butternut Squash, peeled and cubed
- 3 ½ cups Homemade Veggie Broth
- 1 tsp grated Ginger

Cooking Direction

1. Set your Instant Pot to SAUTE and add the olive oil to it.
2. When hot and sizzling, add the squash.
3. Cook for about 5 minutes.
4. Add the remaining ingredients and give the mixture a good stir.
5. Put the lid on and then turn it clockwise to seal.
6. Set the Instant Pot to MANUAL.

7. Cook on HIGH pressure for 10 minutes.
8. Do a quick pressure release.
9. Serve and enjoy!

Nutrition Values
(Calories 103| Total Fats 3.5g | Carbs: 18g| Protein 1g | Dietary Fiber: 4g)

Steak Soup with Vegetables
(Prep Time: 5 Mins |Total Time: 30 Mins |Serves: 4)

Ingredients:
- 1 pound Flank Steak, cut into small cubes
- 1 Onion, diced
- 3 Carrots, diced
- 8 ounces Mushrooms, sliced
- 2 cups Homemade Beef Stock
- 1 Bell Pepper, diced
- 1 Celery Stalk, diced
- 1 cup diced Tomatoes
- 1 tsp Garlic Powder
- ½ tsp Thyme
- 2 cups Water
- 1 Bay Leaf

Cooking Direction
1. Set your Instant Pot to SAUTE and add half of the coconut oil to it.
2. When melted, add the beef and cook until it becomes browned. Transfer to a plate.
3. Melt the remaining coconut oil and add the onions, peppers, and celery.
4. Cook for 3 minutes and then add the mushrooms.
5. Cook for another 2 minutes and then add the remaining ingredients.
6. Stir to combine and close the lid.
7. Set your IP to SOUP and cook for 15 minutes.
8. Do a quick pressure release.
9. Serve and enjoy!

Nutrition Values
(Calories 315| Total Fats 7g | Carbs: 18g| Protein 46.5g | Dietary Fiber: 3g)

Vegetarian Chili Potato Stew
(Prep Time: 5 Mins |Total Time: 20 Mins |Serves: 4)

Ingredients:
- 4 cups Homemade Chicken Broth
- 3 Large Russet Potatoes, peeled and cubed
- ½ Red Onion, diced
- 1 tsp minced Garlic
- 2 Jalapeno Peppers, seeded and diced
- ½ tsp Cumin
- ½ tsp Chili Powder
- 1 tbsp Olive Oil

Cooking Direction
1. Set your Instant Pot to SAUTE and add the oil to it.
2. When sizzling, add the onions and cook for 3 minutes.
3. Stir in the garlic and cook for an additional minute.
4. Add the rest of the ingredients and stir well to combine.
5. Put the lid on and seal.
6. Set the IP to MANUAL and cook on HIGH for 7 minutes.
7. Do a natural pressure release.
8. If you want to, you can blend the soup with a hand blender for a creamier texture.
9. Serve and enjoy!

Nutrition Values
(Calories 255| Total Fats 4.5g | Carbs: 50g| Protein 6g | Dietary Fiber: 4g)

Lamb and Sweet Potato Stew
(Prep Time: 5 Mins |Total Time: 40 Mins |Serves: 4)

Ingredients:
- 1 pound Lamb Meat, cut into cubes
- 2 Carrots, sliced
- 2 Sweet Potatoes, peeled and cubed
- 1 Onion, sliced
- 2 ½ cups Homemade Veggie or Beef Broth
- 2 tbsp Arrowroot mixed with 2 tbsp Water
- 1 ½ tbsp Olive Oil
- ½ tsp Thyme

- ¼ tsp Parsley
- ¼ tsp Garlic Powder

Cooking Direction

1. Set your Instant Pot to SAUTE and heat the oil in it.
2. Add the meat and cook it until it becomes brown.
3. Add the onions and cook for a minute or two.
4. Place the rest of the ingredients, except the arrowroot, inside and stir to combine.
5. Close the lid and seal, and set the IP to MANUAL.
6. Cook on HIGH for 12 minutes.
7. Do a natural pressure release and stir in the arrowroot mixture.
8. Close the lid again and cook on MANUAL on HIGH for another minute or so, until thickened.
9. Serve and enjoy!

Nutrition Values

(Calories 322| Total Fats 11g | Carbs: 29g| Protein 25g | Dietary Fiber: 4g)

Curried Zucchini Coconut Soup

(Prep Time: 5 Mins |Total Time: 30 Mins |Serves: 10)

Ingredients:

- 10 cups chopped Zucchini
- 13 ounces Coconut Milk
- 32 ounces Homemade Chicken Broth (or Homemade Veggie Broth for a vegetarian version)
- 1 tbsp Thai Kitchen's Curry Paste
- ½ tsp Garlic Powder

Cooking Direction

1. Place all of the ingredients in your Instant Pot.
2. Stir well to combine and close the lid.
3. Set the Instant Pot to MANUAL and cook for 10 minutes.
4. Quickly release the pressure by turning the handle to 'Venting'.
5. Blend the soup with a hand blender until smooth and creamy.
6. Serve and enjoy!

Nutrition Values

(Calories 110| Total Fats 10g | Carbs: 6g| Protein 3g | Dietary Fiber: 1g)

Rosemary Turkey Chowder

(Prep Time: 5 Mins |Total Time: 30 Mins |Serves: 4)

Ingredients:

- 1 ¼ tsp dried Rosemary
- 2 Celery Stalks, diced
- 1 cup Broccoli Florets
- ¾ pound Turkey Breast, cut into cubes
- 2 tbsp Coconut Oil
- ½ Yellow Onion, diced
- 3 ½ cups Homemade Chicken Broth
- 2/3 pound Sweet Potatoes, cubed
- 1 tsp minced Garlic

Cooking Direction

1. Set the IP to SAUTE and add the coconut oil to it.
2. When melted, add the onions and cook for 3 minutes.
3. Add celery, garlic, and rosemary, and cook for another minute.
4. Add the turkey cubes and cook until they are no longer brown.
5. Dump the rest of the ingredients in the IP and stir to combine.
6. Close the lid and set the Instant Pot to MANUAL.
7. Cook on HIGH for 6 minutes.
8. Do a natural pressure release.
9. Serve immediately and enjoy!

Nutrition Values

(Calories 240| Total Fats 12g | Carbs: 12g| Protein 28g | Dietary Fiber: 2.5g)

Easy Vegetarian Spring Soup

(Prep Time: 5 Mins |Total Time: 25 Mins |Serves: 8)

Ingredients:
- 3 large Carrots, sliced
- 1 Leek, chopped
- 8 cups Homemade Bone Broth
- 2 tsp minced Garlic
- 4 cups chopped Spinach
- 10 Radishes, sliced
- 1 Onion, sliced
- 1 cup Broccoli Florets

Cooking Direction
1. Dump all of the ingredients in your Instant Pot.
2. Give the mixture a good stir to combine the ingredients well.
3. Put the lid on and turn it clockwise to seal.
4. After the chime, press SOUP.
5. Set the cooking time for 10 minutes.
6. Let the pressure drop naturally before opening the lid.
7. Serve immediately.
8. Enjoy!

Nutrition Values

(Calories 240| Total Fats 0.2g | Carbs: 9g| Protein 20g | Dietary Fiber: 2g)

Pork and Mushroom Stew

(Prep Time: 5 Mins |Total Time: 55 Mins |Serves: 6)

Ingredients:
- 2 ½ pounds Pork Cheeks, cut into pieces
- 1 ½ cups Homemade Chicken Broth
- 1 Onion, diced
- 2 tsp minced Garlic
- Juice of 1 Lemon
- 8 ounces Mushrooms, sliced
- 2 tbsp Olive Oil
- 1 Leek, sliced

Cooking Direction
1. Set your Instant Pot t SAUTE and add the oil to it.
2. When hot, add the meat and brown it on all sides.
3. Transfer the meat to a plate and add the onions and leeks.
4. Cook for 3 minutes.
5. Stir in the garlic and cook for an additional minute.
6. Return the meat to the pot and place all of the other ingredients inside.
7. Stir to combine and close the lid.
8. Cook on MEAT/STEW for 45 minutes.
9. Do a quick pressure release and open the lid.
10. Serve immediately and enjoy!

Nutrition Values

(Calories 510| Total Fats 16g | Carbs: 6g| Protein 52g | Dietary Fiber: 1.5g)

Tasty Instant Pot Greek Fish Stew

(Prep Time: 10 Mins |Total Time: 30 Mins |Serves: 5)

Ingredients:
- 5 large white fish fillets
- 1 large red onion, chopped
- 4 cloves of garlic
- 1 leek, sliced
- 1 carrot, chopped
- 3 sticks celery, chopped
- 1 can tomatoes
- 1/2 tsp. saffron threads
- 8 cups fish stock
- 2 tbsp. fresh lemon juice
- 1 tbsp. lemon zest
- handful parsley leaves chopped
- handful mint leaves chopped

Cooking Direction
1. Combine all ingredients in your instant pot and lock lid; cook on high for 20 minutes and then release pressure naturally.
2. Serve with gluten-free bread.

Nutrition Values

(Calories 443| Total Fats 18.4g | Carbs: 9.7g| Protein 58.8g | Dietary Fiber: 1.8g)

Cream of Butternut Squash & Ginger Soup

(Prep Time: 5 Mins |Total Time: 25 Mins |Serves: 4)

Ingredients:

- 1 teaspoon extra-virgin olive oil
- 1 large Onion, roughly chopped
- 1 sprig of Sage
- 4 pound butternut Squash, diced
- ½" piece of fresh ginger, minced
- ¼ teaspoon nutmeg
- salt and pepper
- 4 cups vegetable stock
- ½ cup Toasted salty Pumpkin Seeds, to serve

Cooking Direction

1. In your instant pot, sauté onion with salt, pepper and sage until softened.
2. Remove the onion mixture to a bowl and add squash cubes to the pot; sauté for 10 minutes and then add in the remaining ingredients including onion mixture.
3. Lock lid and cook on high pressure for 15 minutes; release pressure naturally and then discard sage.
4. Using an immersion blender, blend the mixture until smooth and serve garnished with toasted salt pumpkin seeds.

Nutrition Values

(Calories 323| Total Fats 9.6g | Carbs: 59.7g| Protein 9.2g | Dietary Fiber: 10.6g)

Tasty Mushroom Coconut Milk Soup

(Prep Time: 10 Mins |Total Time: 20 Mins | Serves: 4)

Ingredients:

- 1 ½ pounds mushroom, trimmed
- 1 clove garlic, minced
- 2 red onions, chopped
- 4 cups vegetable stock
- 2 cups coconut milk
- 1 tablespoon fresh thyme
- 1/8 teaspoon sea salt
- Thyme sprigs
- 1/8 teaspoon pepper

Cooking Direction

1. Grill the mushrooms, turning frequently, for about 5 minutes or until charred and tender; set aside.
2. In an instant pot, sauté red onion in a splash of water. Stir in vegetable stock and cook for a few minutes.
3. Add the remaining ingredients and lock the lid; cook on high pressure for 3 minutes and then release the pressure naturally.
4. Transfer the mixture to a blender and blend until very smooth.
5. Serve garnished with thyme sprigs.

Nutrition Values

(Calories 338| Total Fats 29.2g | Carbs: 18.1g| Protein 8.8g | Dietary Fiber: 5.8g)

Green Bean and Turkey Soup

(Prep Time: 5 Mins |Total Time: 35 Mins |Serves: 2)

Ingredients:

- 2/3 cup Green Beans
- ½ pounds Turkey Breasts, diced
- 1/3 cup diced Onions
- 1/3 cup diced Carrots
- 1 small Tomato, chopped
- 2 cups Chicken Stock
- 1 tbsp chopped Parsley
- ½ Turnip, chopped
- ¼ tsp Salt

Cooking Direction

1. Place everything except the green beans in the Instant Pot.
2. Close the lid and set the pot to SOUP.
3. Cook for 20 minutes and then release the pressure quickly.
4. Stir in the green beans and cook for additional 30 minutes.
5. Release the pressure quickly. Serve and enjoy!

Nutrition Values

(Calories 140| Total Fats 1.5g | Carbs: 15g | Protein 7g| Dietary Fiber: 3.2g)

Tomato Soup

(Prep Time: 10 Mins |Total Time: 25 Mins |Serves: 4)

Ingredients
- 3 pounds fresh tomatoes, chopped
- 2 teaspoons dried parsley, crushed
- 2 tablespoons homemade tomato sauce
- 4 cups low-sodium vegetable broth
- Freshly ground black pepper, to taste
- ¼ cup fresh basil, chopped
- 1 tablespoon olive oil
- 1 garlic clove, minced
- 2 tablespoons sugar
- 1 medium onion, chopped
- 2 teaspoons dried basil, crushed
- 1 tablespoon balsamic vinegar

Directions

1. Put the oil, garlic and onion in the Instant Pot and select "Sauté".
2. Sauté for 4 minutes and add the tomatoes, herbs, tomato sauce, broth and black pepper.
3. Cook for about 3 minutes and lock the lid.
4. Set the Instant Pot to "Soup" and cook for 10 minutes at high pressure.
5. Release the pressure quickly and stir in the vinegar and sugar.
6. Put the mixture in the immersion blender and puree the soup.
7. Garnish with basil and serve.

Nutrition Values
(Calories: 146; Total Fat: 4.5 g; Carbs: 23.5 g; Sugars: 16.4 g; Protein: 5.4 g)

Corn Soup

(Prep Time: 10 Mins |Total Time: 15 Mins |Serves: 4)

Ingredients
- 2 tablespoons butter
- 2 medium garlic cloves, thinly sliced
- 2 bay leaves
- 2 medium leeks, finely chopped
- 6 corn with cobs, cut in halves
- 4 sprigs Tarragon
- 1 tablespoon chives, minced
- Salt and black pepper, to taste

Cooking Direction

1. Put the butter, garlic and leeks in the Instant Pot and select "Sauté".
2. Sauté for 4 minutes and add the bay leaves, corn with cobs and tarragon sprigs.
3. Set the Instant Pot to "Soup" and cook for 10 minutes at high pressure.
4. Release the pressure quickly and discard corn cobs, bay leaf and tarragon sprigs.
5. Transfer the mixture into the blender and puree the soup.
6. Season the corn soup with salt and pepper and simmer for 3 minutes.

Nutrition Values
(Calories: 323; Total Fat: 11.5g; Carbs: 55.8g; Sugars: 2.38g; Protein: 8.3g)

Bacon Potato Cheesy Soup

(Prep Time: 10 Mins |Total Time: 30 Mins |Serves: 6)

Ingredients
- 8 large potatoes, peeled and cubed
- 1 teaspoon salt
- 2 cups half and half cream
- 1 teaspoon black pepper
- 2 tablespoons dried parsley
- 1 cup cheddar cheese, shredded
- 1 cup frozen corn
- 3 tablespoons butter
- ¼ teaspoon red paprika flakes
- 3 oz. cream cheese, cubed
- 6 slices meatless bacon, crumbled
- ½ cup onions, chopped

Cooking Direction

1. Put the butter and onions in the Instant Pot and select "Sauté".
2. Sauté for 4 minutes and add salt, black pepper, paprika flakes, dried parsley and pepper.

3. Sauté for 4 minutes and half and half cream, cheddar cheese, frozen corn, cream cheese and bacon.
4. Place the trivet in the Instant Pot and put potatoes on it.
5. Set the Instant Pot to "Soup" and cook for 12 minutes at high pressure.
6. Release the pressure quickly and dish out the potatoes.
7. Mash the potatoes and put them back in the pot.

Nutrition Values
(Calories: 669; Total Fat: 28g; Carbs: 88g; Sugars: 7.5g; Protein: 20g)

Corn and Potato Soup

(Prep Time: 10 Mins |Total Time: 27 Mins |Serves: 4)

Ingredients

- 2 cups fresh corn kernels
- 2 large russet potatoes, peeled and chopped
- 2 tablespoons butter
- 2 celery stalks, chopped
- 2 garlic cloves, chopped finely
- 1 teaspoon black pepper, freshly ground
- 6 cups low-sodium vegetable broth
- 3 tablespoons corn-starch
- ¼ cup half-and-half
- 3 carrots, peeled and chopped
- 1 medium onion, chopped
- 2 tablespoons dried parsley, crushed

Cooking Direction

1. Put the butter, carrot, celery, garlic and onions in the Instant Pot and select "Sauté".
2. Sauté for 4 minutes and add corn kernels, potatoes, broth, parsley and black pepper.
3. Set the Instant Pot to "Soup" and cook for 10 minutes at high pressure.
4. Release the pressure quickly and open the lid.
5. Dissolve the cornstarch in half-and-half and add to the Instant Pot.

Select "Sauté" and cook for about 3 minutes.

Nutrition Values
(Calories: 343; Total Fat: 8.7g; Carbs: 59.1g; Sugars: 8.2g; Protein: 10g)

Creamy Broccoli Soup

(Prep Time: 5 Mins |Total Time: 22 Mins |Serves: 3)

Ingredients

- 1 cup broccoli florets, washed and blanched
- 2 garlic cloves, minced
- 2 tablespoons butter
- 1 teaspoon black pepper, freshly ground
- ½ cup full fat milk
- 1 small onion, chopped
- 1 tablespoon celery leaves, chopped
- 1 teaspoon salt
- ½ cup cream
- 1 cup vegetable stock

Cooking Direction

1. Put the butter, celery, garlic and onions in the Instant Pot and select "Sauté".
2. Sauté for 4 minutes and add broccoli florets, vegetable stock, salt and black pepper.
3. Set the Instant Pot to "Soup" and cook for 10 minutes at high pressure.
4. Release the pressure quickly and open the lid.
5. Put the mixture in the blender and add milk and cream.
6. Put back in the Instant Pot and let it simmer for 3 minutes.

Nutrition Values
(Calories: 134; Total Fat: 10.1g; Carbs: 8.9g; Sugars: 4.6g; Protein: 3.4g)

Creamy Mushroom Soup

(Prep Time: 10 Mins |Total Time: 25 Mins |Serves: 4)

Ingredients

- 10 oz. cremini mushrooms, thinly sliced
- 1 tablespoon olive oil
- 3 garlic cloves, minced
- 2 carrots, peeled and diced
- ½ teaspoon dried thyme
- ½ cup half-and-half

- 2 tablespoons fresh parsley leaves, chopped
- 2 tablespoons butter
- 1 onion, diced
- 2 stalks celery, diced
- ¼ cup all-purpose flour
- 1 bay leaf
- 1 sprig rosemary

Cooking Direction

1. Put the olive oil, mushrooms, carrot, butter, celery, garlic, thyme and onions in the Instant Pot and select "Sauté".

2. Sauté for 4 minutes and add in the flour until light brown.
3. Add bay leaf and close the lid.
4. Set the Instant Pot to "Soup" and cook for 10 minutes at high pressure.
5. Release the pressure quickly and add half and half.
6. Season with salt and black pepper and garnish with rosemary and parsley.

Nutrition Values
(Calories: 208; Total Fat: 13.6g; Carbs: 18g; Sugars: 4.8g; Protein: 5.1g)

Pumpkin and Tomato Soup

(Prep Time: 10 Mins | Total Time: 15 Mins | Serves: 4)

Ingredients
- 4 tablespoons pumpkin puree
- 1 cup tomatoes, chopped
- 4 tablespoons butter
- 1 carrot, roughly chopped
- 1 potato, roughly diced
- 3 tablespoons sun dried tomatoes
- 4 cups water
- 1 onion, roughly sliced
- 3 tablespoons tomato paste
- 1 teaspoon pumpkin spice powder
- 2 teaspoons salt
- 2 pinches black pepper

Cooking Direction

1. Put the butter, carrots and onions in the Instant Pot and select "Sauté".
2. Sauté for 4 minutes and add potatoes, tomatoes, tomato paste, sun dried tomatoes, pumpkin puree, water, salt and black pepper.
3. Set the Instant Pot to "Soup" and cook for 15 minutes at high pressure.
4. Release the pressure naturally and add blend the mixture to a smooth consistency.
5. Sprinkle pumpkin spice powder and serve.

Nutrition Values
(Calories: 190; Total Fat: 12.7g; Carbs: 18.5g; Sugars: 5.9g; Protein: 2.8g)

Bacon and Cauliflower Soup

(Prep Time: 10 Mins | Total Time: 30 Mins | Serves: 4)

Ingredients
- 3 cups cauliflower florets
- 12 slices of meatless bacon, crisp fried
- 2 tablespoons butter
- 1 large onion, chopped
- 4 potatoes, chopped
- ½ cup heavy cream
- 1 tablespoon salt
- 1 tablespoon black pepper

Cooking Direction

1. Put the butter and onions in the Instant Pot and select "Sauté".

2. Sauté for 4 minutes and add potatoes, browned bacon and cauliflower florets.
3. Set the Instant Pot to "Soup" and cook for 15 minutes at high pressure.
4. Release the pressure naturally and blend all the ingredients to a smooth paste.
5. Season with salt and black pepper and add heavy cream.

Nutrition Values
(Calories: 344; Total Fat: 16.7g; Carbs: 44.1g; Sugars: 6.6g; Protein: 8.3g;)

Spinach Cream Soup

(Prep Time: 5 Mins |Total Time: 20 Mins |Serves: 3)

Ingredients

- 1 cup spinach puree
- ½ cup fresh cream
- 3 tablespoons butter
- 1 cup white sauce
- 3 garlic cloves, minced
- 1 medium onion, roughly sliced
- 1 tablespoon tomato paste
- 1 tablespoon sun dried tomatoes
- 4 cups water
- 2 teaspoons salt
- 2 pinches black pepper

Cooking Direction

1. Put the butter, garlic, salt, black pepper and onions in the Instant Pot and select "Sauté".
2. Sauté for 4 minutes and add water, spinach puree and tomato paste.
3. Set the Instant Pot to "Soup" and cook for 10 minutes at high pressure.
4. Release the pressure naturally and add fresh cream and white sauce.
5. Blend the contents of the Instant Pot to a smooth consistency and garnish with sun dried tomatoes.

Nutrition Values

(Calories: 305; Total Fat: 23.7g; Carbs: 17.6g; Sugars: 6.7g; Protein: 5.9g)

Cheesy Red Beans Soup

(Prep Time: 8 Mins |Total Time: 23 Mins |Serves: 3)

Ingredients

- 1 cup red beans
- 3 tablespoons butter
- 1 carrot, roughly chopped
- 1 medium onion, roughly sliced
- 3 garlic cloves, minced
- 3 tablespoons tomato paste
- ½ cup Mexican cheese, shredded
- ½ cup half and half
- 4 cups water
- 2 teaspoons salt
- 2 pinches black pepper
- Crunchy tortilla chips, to garnish

Cooking Direction

1. Put the butter, garlic, salt, black pepper, carrots and onions in the Instant Pot and select "Sauté".
2. Sauté for 5 minutes and add red beans, water, tomato paste and salt.
3. Set the Instant Pot to "Soup" and cook for 8 minutes at high pressure.
4. Release the pressure naturally and add Mexican cheese and half and half.
5. Garnish with crispy tortilla chips and serve.

Nutrition Values

(Calories: 418; Total Fat: 18.5g; Carbs: 49g; Sugars: 5.9g; Protein: 17.6g)

Sour Cream Black Beans Soup

(Prep Time: 7 Mins |Total Time: 20 Mins |Serves: 3)

Ingredients

- 1 cup black beans
- 5 garlic cloves, minced
- 3 tablespoons tomato paste
- ¼ cup sour cream
- 4 cups water
- 3 tablespoons butter
- 1 onion, roughly sliced
- 1 potato, roughly diced
- 1 tablespoon sun dried tomatoes
- 2 tablespoons fresh cream
- 2 teaspoons salt
- 2 pinches black pepper
- Crunchy nachos chips, for garnish

Cooking Direction

1. Put the butter, garlic and onions in the Instant Pot and select "Sauté".
2. Sauté for 3 minutes and add black beans, tomato paste, water, sun dried tomatoes, salt and black pepper.

3. Set the Instant Pot to "Soup" and cook for 10 minutes at high pressure.
4. Release the pressure naturally and add sour cream.

5. Blend the contents of the Instant Pot to a smooth consistency and serve with fresh cream and broken nachos chips.

Nutrition Values
(Calories: 339; Total Fat: 13.1g; Carbs: 45g; Sugars: 4.2g; Protein: 13.1g)

Basil Tomato Soup

(Prep Time: 5 Mins |Total Time: 17 Mins |Serves: 2)

Ingredients
- ½ cup tomatoes
- 2 tablespoons tomato paste
- 2 tablespoons sun dried tomatoes
- 2tablespoons butter
- 1tablespoon basil leaves, freshly chopped
- 1 carrot, roughly chopped
- 1 onion, roughly sliced
- 1 potato, roughly diced
- 4 cups water
- 2 teaspoons salt
- ¼ teaspoon black pepper

Cooking Direction

1. Put the butter, onions, carrots, basil leaves, salt and black pepper in the Instant Pot and select "Sauté".
2. Sauté for 4 minutes and add potatoes,tomatoes, sun dried tomatoes, tomato paste and water.
3. Set the Instant Pot to "Soup" and cook for 8 minutes at high pressure.
4. Release the pressure naturally and blend the contents of the Instant Pot to a smooth consistency.

Nutrition Values
(Calories: 239; Total Fat: 12.8g; Carbs: 29.6g; Sugars: 7.6g; Protein: 4.2g)

Feta Cheese and Spinach Soup

(Prep Time: 10 Mins |Total Time: 25 Mins |Serves: 3)

Ingredients
- 1 cup spinach puree
- ½ cup feta cheese, crumbled
- 3tablespoons butter
- 4garlic cloves, minced
- 1 onion, roughly sliced
- 1 tablespoon tomato paste
- 1 tablespoon sun dried tomatoes
- 1 cup white sauce
- ½ cup fresh cream
- 4 cups water
- 2 teaspoons salt
- ¼ teaspoon black pepper

Cooking Direction

1. Put the butter, onions and garlic in the Instant Pot and select "Sauté".
2. Sauté for 4 minutes and add tomato paste, spinach, salt, pepper and water.
3. Set the Instant Pot to "Soup" and cook for 10 minutes at high pressure.
4. Release the pressure naturally and add white sauce and fresh cream.
5. Blend the contents of the Instant Pot to a smooth consistency.
6. Garnish with feta cheese and sun dried tomatoes.

Nutrition Values
(Calories: 360 ; Total Fat: 28.3g; Carbs: 18.3g; Sugars: 9.7g; Protein: 9.2g)

Chestnut Soup

(Prep Time: 10 Mins |Total Time: 25 Mins |Serves: 4)

Ingredients
- ½ pound fresh chestnuts
- 4 tablespoons butter
- 1 sprig sage
- ¼ teaspoon white pepper
- ¼ teaspoon nutmeg
- 1 onion, chopped

- 1 stalk celery, chopped
- 1 potato, chopped
- 2 tablespoons rum
- 2 tablespoons fresh cream

Cooking Direction
1. Puree the fresh chestnuts in a blender.
2. Put the butter, onions, sage, celery and white pepper in the Instant Pot and select "Sauté".
3. Sauté for 4 minutes and add potato, stock and chestnuts.
4. Set the Instant Pot to "Soup" and cook for 15 minutes at high pressure.
5. Release the pressure naturally and add rum, nutmeg and fresh cream.
6. Blend the contents of the Instant Pot to a smooth consistency.

Nutrition Values
(Calories: 290; Total Fat: 13.3g; Carbs: 36.5g; Sugars: 2.5g; Protein: 3g)

Tortilla and White Beans Soup

(Prep Time: 10 Mins |Total Time: 27 Mins |Serves: 4)

Ingredients
- 1 cup white beans
- 4 tablespoons butter
- ¼ teaspoon white pepper
- 1 onion, roughly sliced
- 1 tablespoon sun dried tomatoes
- ¼ cup fresh cream
- 4 cups water
- 2 teaspoons salt
- 1 carrot, roughly chopped
- 4 garlic cloves, minced
- 4 tablespoons tomato paste
- Crunchy tortilla chips, for garnish

Cooking Direction
1. Put the butter, garlic, carrots, onions and white pepper in the Instant Pot and select "Sauté".
2. Sauté for 5 minutes and add white beans, potatoes, sun dried tomatoes, tomato paste, salt and water.
3. Set the Instant Pot to "Soup" and cook for 12 minutes at high pressure.
4. Release the pressure naturally and add sour cream.
5. Blend the contents of the Instant Pot to a smooth consistency and top with crunchy tortilla chips.

Nutrition Values
(Calories: 353; Total Fat: 14.7g; Carbs: 44.2g; Sugars: 5.3g; Protein: 14g)

Vegetable Noodle Soup

(Prep Time: 8 Mins |Total Time: 20 Mins |Serves: 5)

Ingredients
- ½ cup potatoes, diced
- ½ cup peas
- ½ cup carrots
- ½ cup cauliflower
- 6 oz. noodles, cooked and drained
- ½ cup onions
- 3 garlic cloves, minced
- ½ inch ginger, minced
- 1 cup tomatoes, diced
- 10 oz. baby carrots
- 2 teaspoons Worcestershire sauce
- 32 oz. vegetable stock
- 1 tablespoon olive oil
- 1 teaspoon salt
- 1 teaspoon black pepper

Cooking Direction
1. Put the oil, ginger, garlic, carrots, onions and cauliflowers in the Instant Pot and select "Sauté".
2. Sauté for 5 minutes and add potatoes, tomatoes, peas, vegetable stock and Worcestershire sauce.
3. Set the Instant Pot to "Soup" and cook for 12 minutes at high pressure.
4. Release the pressure naturally and add cooked noodles.
5. Season with salt and black pepper and serve immediately.

Nutrition Values
(Calories: 148; Total Fat: 4g; Carbs: 24.8g; Sugars: 7.8g; Protein: 4.6g)

Manchow Soup

(Prep Time: 10 Mins |Total Time: 25 Mins |Serves: 4)

Ingredients

- 3 oz. fried noodles, for garnish
- ½ cup green bell peppers
- ½ cup bean sprouts
- ½ cup mushrooms
- ½ cup broccoli
- ½ cup baby carrots
- 2 green onions, chopped
- 4 garlic cloves, minced
- ½ inch ginger, minced
- 1 teaspoon soy sauce
- 1 teaspoon vinegar
- 2 teaspoons chilli sauce
- 3 cups vegetable stock
- 1 tablespoon oil
- Salt and pepper, to taste
- Roasted crushed peanuts, for garnish

Cooking Direction

1. Put the oil, ginger, garlic, carrots, onions and carrots in the Instant Pot and select "Sauté".
2. Sauté for 4 minutes and add soy sauce, chilli sauce, vinegar and vegetable stock.
3. Set the Instant Pot to "Soup" and cook for 10 minutes at high pressure.
4. Release the pressure naturally and add cooked noodles.
5. Season with salt and black pepper and garnish with fried noodles and crushed roasted peanuts.

Nutrition Values

(Calories: 379; Total Fat: 20.8g; Carbs: 43.6g; Sugars: 2.4g; Protein: 8.7g)

Chinese Noodle Soup

(Prep Time: 10 Mins |Total Time: 30 Mins |Serves: 8)

Ingredients

- 12 oz. noodles, cooked and drained
- 1 cup red bell peppers
- 1 cup mushrooms
- 1 cup broccoli
- 1 cup bok choy
- 4 green onion whites
- 8 garlic cloves, minced
- 1 inch ginger, minced
- 2 teaspoons soy sauce
- 1 teaspoon white chilli vinegar
- 20 oz. baby carrots
- 2 teaspoons chilli sauce
- 8 cups vegetable stock
- 2 tablespoons oil
- Salt and pepper, to taste
- Onion greens, for garnish

Cooking Direction

1. Put the oil, ginger, garlic, baby carrots and onions in the Instant Pot and select "Sauté".
2. Sauté for 4 minutes and add broccoli, bok choy, red bell peppers, mushrooms, soy sauce, chilli vinegar, chilli sauce and vegetable stock.
3. Set the Instant Pot to "Soup" and cook for 15 minutes at high pressure.
4. Release the pressure naturally and add cooked noodles.
5. Season with salt and black pepper and garnish with onion greens.

Nutrition Values

(Calories: 145; Total Fat: 4.7g; Carbs: 22.6g; Sugars: 6.1g; Protein: 4g)

Japanese Udon Noodle Soup

(Prep Time: 10 Mins |Total Time: 27 Mins |Serves: 2)

Ingredients

- 3 oz. Japanese udon noodles, cooked and drained
- ½ cup green bell peppers
- ½ cup celery
- ½ cup mushrooms
- ½ cup bamboo shoots
- 2 garlic cloves, minced
- ½ green chilli, finely chopped
- ½ cup baby carrots
- 1 teaspoon rice vinegar soy sauce

- ½ inch ginger, minced
- 1 green onion white
- 1 teaspoon rice wine vinegar
- 1 teaspoon red chilli sauce
- 1 tablespoon sesame oil
- Bean sprouts and green onions, for garnish
- Salt and pepper, to taste

Cooking Direction

1. Put the oil, ginger, garlic, baby carrots and onions in the Instant Pot and select "Sauté".

2. Sauté for 4 minutes and add bamboo shoots, celery, green bell peppers, mushrooms, soy sauce, rice wine vinegar, chilli sauce.
3. Set the Instant Pot to "Soup" and cook for 13 minutes at high pressure.
4. Release the pressure naturally and add cooked udon noodles.
5. Season with salt and black pepper and garnish with onion greens and bean sprouts.

Nutrition Values

(Calories: 179; Total Fat: 3.9g; Carbs: 30g; Sugars: 2.7g; Protein: 3.6g)

Chestnut Bacon Soup

(Prep Time: 10 Mins |Total Time: 34 Mins |Serves: 4)

Ingredients

- 5 meatless bacon strips, cooked crispy
- 1 bay laurel leaf
- ½ pound fresh chestnuts
- 3 tablespoons butter
- 1 sprig sage
- ¼ teaspoon white pepper
- ¼ teaspoon nutmeg
- 1 onion, chopped
- 1 potato, chopped
- 2 tablespoons fresh cream

Cooking Direction

1. Puree the fresh chestnuts in a blender.

2. Put the butter, onions, sage, celery and white pepper in the Instant Pot and select "Sauté".
3. Sauté for 4 minutes and add potato, bay laurel leaf, stock and chestnuts.
4. Set the Instant Pot to "Soup" and cook for 20 minutes at high pressure.
5. Release the pressure naturally and add nutmeg and fresh cream.
6. Blend the contents of the Instant Pot to a smooth consistency and serve with bacon.

Nutrition Values

(Calories: 435; Total Fat: 25.4g; Carbs: 37.7g; Sugars: 2.4g; Protein: 16.7g)

Pearl Barley Soup

(Prep Time: 8 Mins |Total Time: 26 Mins |Serves: 6)

Ingredients

- 1 cup all-purpose flour
- 2 onions, chopped
- 2 celery stalks, chopped
- 2 carrots, chopped
- 4 tablespoons olive oil
- 2 cups mushroom, sliced
- 28 oz. vegetable stock
- ¾ cup pearl barley
- 2 teaspoons dried oregano
- 1 cup purple wine
- Salt and pepper, to taste

Cooking Direction

1. Put the oil, garlic and onions in the Instant Pot and select "Sauté".
2. Sauté for 3 minutes and add rest of the ingredients.
3. Set the Instant Pot to "Soup" and cook for 15 minutes at high pressure.
4. Release the pressure naturally and serve hot.

Nutrition Values

(Calories: 310; Total Fat: 10.1g; Carbs: 43.8g; Sugars: 4.2g; Protein: 6.6g)

Lemon Rice Soup

(Prep Time: 10 Mins |Total Time: 26 Mins |Serves: 6)

Ingredients

- ¾ cup lengthy grain rice
- 1 cup onions, sliced
- 1 cup carrots, chopped
- 6 cups vegetable broth
- Salt and pepper, to taste
- ¾ cup lemon juice, freshly squeezed
- 3 teaspoons minced garlic
- 1 cup celery, chopped
- 2 tablespoons olive oil
- 2 tablespoons all-purpose flour

Cooking Direction

1. Put the oil, garlic, celery and onions in the Instant Pot and select "Sauté".
2. Sauté for 4 minutes and add rest of the ingredients except all-purpose flour and lemon juice.
3. Set the Instant Pot to "Soup" and cook for 12 minutes at high pressure.
4. Release the pressure naturally and add the whisked lemon juice+ all-purpose flour mixture.
5. Let it simmer till the soup becomes thick and season with salt and pepper.

Nutrition Values

(Calories: 225; Total Fat: 12g; Carbs: 25.5g; Sugars: 4.9g; Protein: 5.1g)

Basil Coriander Lemon Soup

(Prep Time: 10 Mins |Total Time: 27 Mins |Serves: 3)

Ingredients

- ½ cup onions, sliced
- ½ cup carrots, chopped
- 16 oz. can vegetable broth
- 1/3 cup fresh coriander, chopped
- ¼ cup lemon juice, freshly squeezed
- 2 teaspoons garlic, minced
- ½ cup celery, chopped
- 2 tablespoons olive oil
- 1/3 cup fresh basil leaves, chopped
- Salt and pepper, to taste
- 2 tablespoons all-purpose flour

Cooking Direction

1. Put the oil, garlic, celery and onions in the Instant Pot and select "Sauté".
2. Sauté for 4 minutes and add rest of the ingredients except all-purpose flour and lemon juice.
3. Set the Instant Pot to "Soup" and cook for 13 minutes at high pressure.
4. Release the pressure naturally and add the whisked lemon juice and all-purpose flour mixture.
5. Let it simmer till the soup becomes thick and season with salt and pepper.

Nutrition Values

(Calories: 135; Total Fat: 9.6g; Carbs: 11.2g; Sugars: 3.7g; Protein: 1.4g)

Beetroot Soup

(Prep Time: 10 Mins |Total Time: 30 Mins |Serves: 4)

Ingredients

- 2 pounds beetroot, peeled and diced
- 3 teaspoons garlic, minced
- ½ cup onions, sliced
- ½ cup celery, chopped
- ½ cup carrots, chopped
- 3 tablespoons olive oil
- 4 cups vegetable broth
- 3 tablespoons fresh coriander, chopped
- Salt and pepper, to taste
- 3 tablespoons fresh cream

Cooking Direction

1. Put the oil, garlic, celery and onions in the Instant Pot and select "Sauté".
2. Sauté for 4 minutes and add rest of the ingredients except fresh cream.
3. Set the Instant Pot to "Soup" and cook for 16 minutes at high pressure.
4. Release the pressure naturally and add the fresh cream.

5. Season with salt and pepper and garnish with coriander leaves.

Nutrition Values
(Calories: 251; Total Fat: 12.8g; Carbs: 27.6g; Sugars: 20.4g; Protein: 9.2g)

Lentil and Smoked Paprika Soup

(Prep Time: 10 Mins |Total Time: 21 Mins |Serves: 10)

Ingredients
- 2 cups red lentils, rinsed
- 2cups green lentils, rinse
- 1½ pounds potatoes
- 1½ bunches rainbow chard
- 2 onions, chopped finely
- 4 teaspoons cumin
- 2teaspoons salt
- 2 celery stalks
- 6 garlic cloves, minced
- 3 teaspoons smoked paprika
- 4 carrots, sliced
- 10 cups water
- Salt and pepper, to taste

Cooking Direction
1. Put the oil, garlic, celery and onions in the Instant Pot and select "Sauté".
2. Sauté for 4 minutes and add rest of the ingredients except lentils.
3. Set the Instant Pot to "Soup" and cook for 7 minutes at high pressure.
4. Release the pressure naturally and add season with salt and pepper.

Nutrition Values
(Calories: 209; Total Fat: 0.8g; Carbs: 39.6g; Sugars: 3.9g; Protein: 11.9g; Cholesterol: 0mg; Sodium: 501mg)

Squash and Potato Soup

(Prep Time: 5 Mins |Total Time: 35 Mins |Serves: 2)

Ingredients:
- 1 ½ cups Bone Broth
- 1 cups cubed Sweet Potatoes
- 1 cup cubed Butternut Squash
- 1 tbsp Coconut Oil
- ½ Onion, chopped
- 1 Garlic Clove, minced
- ½ tsp Tarragon
- 1 tsp Ginger Powder
- ¼ tsp Turmeric Powder
- ½ tsp Curry Powder
- Salt and Pepper, to taste

Cooking Direction
1. Set your IP to SAUTE and melt the coconut oil in it.
2. Add the onions and cook for 3 minutes.
3. Add the garlic and cook for 30-60 seconds.
4. Add the rest of the ingredients and stir well to combine.
5. Close the lid and cook on MANUAL for 10 minutes.
6. Release the pressure naturally, about 15 minutes.
7. Transfer the soup to a blander or get a hand blender instead.
8. Blend the soup until creamy and smooth.
9. Serve and enjoy!

Nutrition Values
(Calories 252| Total Fats 6g | Carbs: 20g | Protein 7g| Dietary Fiber: 2.5g)

Creamy Potato and Broccoli Soup with Cheddar

(Prep Time: 5 Mins |Total Time: 25 Mins |Serves: 2)

Ingredients:
- ½ cup grated Cheddar Cheese
- ½ cup Half and Half
- 1 pounds Yukon Potatoes, cubed
- ½ Broccoli Head, chopped
- 1 tbsp Butter
- 1 Garlic Clove, minced
- 2 cups Vegetable Broth

Cooking Direction
1. Melt the butter in your Instant Pot on SAUTE.

2. Add garlic and cook for one minute.
3. Add the broth, potatoes, and broccoli, and stir to combine.
4. Close the lid and cook on HIGH for 5 minutes.
5. Do a quick pressure release.
6. Stir in the cheese and cream.
7. Blend with a hand blender immediately.
8. Serve and enjoy!

Nutrition Values

(Calories 515| Total Fats 32g | Carbs: 24g | Protein 22g| Dietary Fiber: 2g)

Plantain and Red Bean Stew

(Prep Time: 5 Mins |Total Time: 70 | Serves: 2)

Ingredients:

- ½ Plantain, chopped
- 1 Carrot, chopped
- ¼ Onion, chopped
- ¼ pounds dry Red Beans
- 1 tbsp Olive Oil
- ½ Tomato, chopped
- Salt and Pepper, to taste
- Water, as needed

Cooking Direction

1. Heat the oil in the Instant Pot on SAUTE.
2. Add the beans and pour water just to cover them.
3. Close the lid and cook for 30 minutes on HIGH.
4. Do a quick pressure release.
5. Stir in the remaining ingredients and cook for 20-25 more minutes on HIGH.
6. Release the pressure naturally.
7. Serve and enjoy!

Nutrition Values

(Calories 150| Total Fats 3g | Carbs: 16g | Protein 4g| Dietary Fiber: 4g)

Worcestershire Chili

(Prep Time: 5 Mins |Total Time: 55 Mins |Serves: 2)

Ingredients:

- ½ pound ground Beef
- 2 Carrots, slice
- ½ tsp Salt
- 1 tbsp Worcestershire Sauce
- ½ Bell Pepper, chopped
- 14 ounces canned diced Tomatoes
- 2 tsp Chili Powder
- ½ tbsp chopped Parsley
- 1/2 Onion, chopped
- ½ tsp Paprika
- ½ tsp Garlic Powder
- 1 tbsp Olive Oil

Cooking Direction

1. Heat the oil in the Instant Pot on SAUTE.
2. Add onions and cook for 3 minutes.
3. Stir in the spices and cook for 30 more seconds.
4. Add the beef and cook until it becomes browned.
5. Stir in the remaining ingredients.
6. Close the lid and set the IP to MEAT/STEW.
7. Cook at the default setting.
8. Do a natural pressure release.
9. Serve and enjoy!

Nutrition Values

(Calories 308| Total Fats 9g | Carbs: 21g | Protein 37g| Dietary Fiber: 3.5g)

Chicken Soup with Carrots and Potatoes

(Prep Time: 5 Mins |Total Time: 30 Mins |Serves: 2)

Ingredients:

- 1 Frozen Chicken Breast
- 1 large Carrot, sliced
- 8 ounces Chicken Stock
- 8 ounces Water
- 2 Potatoes, cubed
- ¼ Onion, diced
- Salt and Pepper, to taste

Cooking Direction

1. Place all of the ingredients in the Instant Pot.

2. Stir to combine and season with some salt and pepper.
3. Close the lid and set the IP to MANUAL.
4. Cook on HIGH for 30 minutes.
5. Press CANCEL and wait for 10 minutes before releasing the pressure quickly.

6. Shred the chicken with two forks and stir to combine.
7. Serve and enjoy!

Nutrition Values
(Calories 100| Total Fats 8g | Carbs: 7g | Protein 15g| Dietary Fiber: 1g)

Leek and Potato Soup

(Prep Time: 5 Mins |Total Time: 45 Mins |Serves: 2)

Ingredients:
- ¾ cup Half and Half
- 2 ½ cups Veggie Broth
- 2 tsp Butter
- 2 Potatoes, diced
- 1 ½ Leeks, sliced
- 1 Bay Leaf
- 1/3 cup dry White Wine
- ½ tsp Salt
- 1 1/2 cups Water

Cooking Direction
1. Melt the butter in your Instant Pot on SAUTE.

2. Add the leeks and cook for 2-3 minutes.
3. Pour the broth, and wine over.
4. Stir in the potatoes, salt, and bay leaf.
5. Close the lid and set the IP to MANUAL.
6. Cook on HIGH for 10 minutes.
7. Do a quick pressure release and stir in the cream.
8. Blend with a hand blender until creamy.
9. Serve and enjoy!

Nutrition Values
(Calories 198| Total Fats 8g| Carbs: 21g | Protein 7g| Dietary Fiber: 1.2g)

Chili and Spicy Chicken Curry

(Prep Time: 5 Mins |Total Time: 35 Mins |Serves: 2)

Ingredients:
- ½ can Beans, drained
- 1 tsp Chili Powder
- 1 tsp Cumin
- ½ can Corn, drained
- ½ pound Chicken Breasts
- ½ can chopped Tomatoes, undrained
- 1 ½ cups Chicken Broth

Cooking Direction
1. Place everything in your Instant Pot and stir well to combine.

2. Close and seal the lid and set the IP to MANUAL.
3. Cook for 20 minutes on HIGH.
4. Do a natural pressure release. This shouldn't take longer than 10 minutes.
5. Shred the chicken inside the IP with 2 forks. Stir to combine.
6. Serve and enjoy!

Nutrition Values
(Calories 604| Total Fats 7g | Carbs: 28g | Protein 32g| Dietary Fiber: 2g)

Rice and Orange Chickpea Stew

(Prep Time: 5 Mins |Total Time: 35 Mins |Serves: 2)

Ingredients:
- 5 ounces Sweet Potatoes, diced
- 1 ½ cups Vegetable Broth
- 10 ounces Chickpeas, canned and drained
- 2 ounces Basmati Rice
- 3 ounces Orange Juice
- ½ tsp Cumin
- 1 tbsp Olive Oil
- ½ Onion, sliced
- Salt and Pepper, to taste

Cooking Direction
1. Set your IP to SAUTE and heat thte oil in it.
2. Add the onions and cook for about 8 minutes.
3. Add the rest of the ingredients and give it a good stir to combine.
4. Set the IP to MANUAL and close the lid.

5. Cook on HIGH for 5 minutes.
6. Do a natural pressure release.
7. Serve and enjoy!

Nutrition Values
(Calories 270| Total Fats 8g | Carbs: 35g | Protein 9g| Dietary Fiber: 5.2g)

Ham and Pea Soup
(Prep Time: 5 Mins |Total Time: 40 Mins |Serves: 2)

Ingredients:
- ½ Onion, diced
- 1/3 pounds Split Peas, dried
- 2 ½ cups Water
- 1 Celery Stalk, diced
- 1/3 pound Ham Chunks
- 1 Carrot, diced
- ½ tsp Thyme

Cooking Direction
1. Place all of the ingredients in your Instant Pot.
2. Stir well to combine.
3. Close the lid and set the IP to MANUAL.
4. Cook for 20 minutes o HIGH. If preferred, cook for an additional 10 minutes.
5. Do a natural pressure release.
6. Serve and enjoy!

Nutrition Values
(Calories 277| Total Fats 4g | Carbs: 39g | Protein 19g| Dietary Fiber: 15g)

Beef Soup with Potatoes
(Prep Time: 5 Mins |Total Time: 25 Mins |Serves: 2)

Ingredients:
- ¼ pounds ground Beef
- 6 ounces Tomato Sauce
- ½ cups Fresh Corn
- 1 1/2 cups Water
- ¼ Onion, chopped
- 1 cup diced Potatoes
- ½ tsp Hot Pepper Sauce
- ¼ tsp Salt

Cooking Direction
1. Coat your IP with some cooking spray and saute the onions on SAUTE for 2-3 minutes.
2. Add the beef and cook until it becomes browned.
3. Add the remaining ingredients and stir to combine.
4. Close the lid and cook for 6 minutes on HIGH.
5. Do a natural pressure naturally.
6. Serve and enjoy!

Nutrition Values
(Calories 240| Total Fats 9g | Carbs: 27g | Protein 14g| Dietary Fiber: 4.2g)

Pumpkin and Corn Chicken Chowder
(Prep Time: 5 Mins |Total Time: 15 Mins |Serves: 2)

Ingredients:
- ¼ cup Half and Half
- ½ Onion, diced
- 1 Chicken Breast, chopped
- 14 ounces Chicken Broth
- ½ tsp minced Garlic
- 8 ounces Pumpkin Puree
- 1 Potato, cubed
- 1 cup Corn, frozen
- 1 tbsp Butter
- Pinch of Nutmeg
- Pinch of Pepper
- Pinch of Red Pepper Flakes
- Pinch of Salt

Cooking Direction
1. Set your IP to SAUTE and melt the butter in it.
2. Add the onions and cook for a few minutes, until it becomes translucent.
3. Add the garlic and cook for 30 more seconds.
4. Stir in the spices, pumpkin puree, and pour the broth over.
5. Bring the mixture to a boil on SAUTE and then stir in the corn, potatoes, and chicken.

6. Close the lid and cook on HIGH for 5 minutes.
7. Do a quick pressure release.
8. Stir in the cream.
9. Serve and enjoy!

Nutrition Values
(Calories 314| Total Fats 21g | Carbs: 16g | Protein 14g| Dietary Fiber: 5.8g)

Lamb Soup
(Prep Time: 5 Mins |Total Time: 40 Mins |Serves: 2)

Ingredients:
- ½ pound Lamb, chopped
- ½ Onion, sliced
- 1 Sweet Potato, cubed
- 1 tbsp Cornstarch
- 1 ½ Carrots, chopped
- 1 1/2 cups Vegetable Broth
- 1 tbsp Olive Oil
- ½ tsp Thyme

Cooking Direction
1. Heat the oil in the Instant Pot on SAUTE.
2. Add the lamb and cook until it is browned on all sides.
3. Add onion and cook for 2 minute.
4. Stir in the remaining ingredients and close the lid.
5. Set the IP to MANUAL.
6. Cook on HIGH for 11 minutes.
7. Release the pressure naturally, for about 10 minutes.
8. Stir in the cornstarch and close the lid.
9. Cook on HIGH for an additional minute or two, until thickened. Serve and enjoy!

Nutrition Values
(Calories 320| Total Fats 11g | Carbs: 28g | Protein 25g| Dietary Fiber: 4g)

Minestrone Soup with Tortellini
(Prep Time: 5 Mins |Total Time: 15 Mins |Serves: 2)

Ingredients:
- 1 Carrot, diced
- ¼ Onion, diced
- 6 ounces Pasta Sauce
- 1 tbsp Olive Oil
- ¼ tsp Sugar
- 5 ounces canned diced Tomatoes
- 4 ounces dried Cheese Tortellini
- 2 cups Veggie Broth
- 1 tsp minced Garlic
- ½ tsp Italian Seasoning
- 1 Celery Stalk, diced
- 1 1/2 cups Water

Cooking Direction
1. Heat the oil in the Instant Pot on SAUTE.
2. Add the onions, celery, and carrots, and cook for 3 minutes.
3. Add the garlic and cook for an additional minute.
4. Add the remaining ingredients and stir well to combine.
5. Seal the lid and cook for 5 minutes on HIGH.
6. Release the pressure quickly.
7. If the tortellini are too al dente for your taste, cook for an additional minute or two.
8. Serve and enjoy!

Nutrition Values
(Calories 250| Total Fats 9g | Carbs: 35g | Protein 7g| Dietary Fiber: 4g)

Pork Shoulder Stew
(Prep Time: 5 Mins |Total Time: 65 Mins |Serves: 2)

Ingredients:
- 1 ½ Carrots, sliced
- 1 tsp Cumin
- 1/3 pound String Beans
- 1 Celeriac, chopped
- ½ can diced Tomatoes
- 5 ounces Coconut Milk
- 1 Garlic Clove, minced
- 2/3 pound Pork Shoulder, chopped
- ¼ Onion, diced
- 1 cup Broth

Cooking Direction
1. Dump all of the ingredients in your Instant Pot.
2. Stir to combine and close the lid.

3. Set the IP to STEW and cook at the default cooking time.
4. Do a natural pressure release.
5. Serve and enjoy!

Vegetable Stew with Tarragon
(Prep Time: 5 Mins |Total Time: 25 Mins |Serves: 2)

Ingredients:
- 2 Tomatoes, chopped
- 1 tbsp Olive Oil
- ½ Onion, diced
- 1 Garlic Clove, minced
- 1 cup cubed Red Potatoes
- 2 Carrots, chopped
- 1 cup cubed Parsnips
- ½ cup chopped Red Bell Peppers
- ½ cup cubed Beets
- 2 cups Veggie Broth
- 2 tsp chopped Tarragon

Cooking Direction

1. Heat the olive oil in your Instant Pot on SAUTE.
2. Add the onions and cook for 3 minutes.
3. Stir in the remaining vegies and then cook for additional 3 minutes.
4. Pour the broth over and stir to combine.
5. Close the lid and cook on HIGH for 7 minutes.
6. Do a natural pressure release. Serve and enjoy!

Fish Stew
(Prep Time: 5 Mins |Total Time: 20 Mins |Serves: 2)

Ingredients:
- 1/3 pound Fish Fillets, chopped
- 2 Potatoes, cubed
- 1 Large carrot, sliced
- ¼ Onion, diced
- 1/3 cup frozen Corn
- 1/3 cup Heavy Cream
- 1 Celery Stalk, diced
- 1 cup Fish Stock
- 1 tbsp Butter
- 1 Bay Leaf
- Salt and Pepper, to taste

Cooking Direction

1. Melt the butter in your IP on SAUTE.
2. Add the onions and cook for about 2-3 minutes.
3. Stir in the remaining ingredients.
4. Seal the lid and cook for 4 minutes on HIGH.
5. Do a natural pressure release.
6. Stir in the heavy cream.
7. Discard the bay leaf before serving and enjoy.

Lentil Soup
(Prep Time: 5 Mins |Total Time: 40 Mins |Serves: 2)

Ingredients:
- ½ cup dry Lentils
- 2 Garlic Cloves, minced
- 1 Carrot, chopped
- ¼ Onion, diced
- 1 Bay Leaf
- 1 tbsp Olive Oil
- 1 Celery Stalk, chopped
- ½ tsp Cumin
- 2 cups Vegetable Broth
- Salt and Pepper, to taste

Cooking Direction

1. Heat the oil in the IP on SAUTE.
2. Add the onions and celery and cook for 3 minutes.
3. Add garlic and saute for 1 more minute.
4. Stir in the rest of the ingredients and close the lid.

5. Set the IP to MANUAL.
6. Cook for 20 minutes on HIGH.
7. Do a natural pressure release.
8. Serve and enjoy!

Nutrition Values

(Calories 260| Total Fats 16g | Carbs: 35g | Protein 13g| Dietary Fiber: 16g)

Turkey Chili

(Prep Time: 5 Mins |Total Time: 60 Mins |Serves: 2)

Ingredients:

- ½ cup grated Cheddar Cheese
- 1 tbsp Olive Oil
- 1 Bell Pepper, chopped
- 2 Garlic Cloves, minced
- ¼ tsp Oregano
- 2 tbsp Hot Sauce
- ½ Onion, diced
- ½ pound Ground Turkey
- ½ can Beans, drained
- ½ can diced Tomatoes, undrained
- ¾ cup Chicken Broth
- Salt and Pepper, to taste

Cooking Direction

1. Heat the oil in the IP on SAUTE.

2. Add onions and pepper and cook for 2-3 minutes.
3. Add garlic and oregano and cook for one more minute.
4. Add the turkey and cook for 4-5 minutes.
5. Stir in the remaining ingredients and close the lid.
6. Cook on BEANS/CHILI at the default cooking time.
7. Do a natural pressure release.
8. Season with some salt and pepper.
9. Top with the cheese.
10. Serve and enjoy!

Nutrition Values

(Calories 700| Total Fats 26g | Carbs: 65g | Protein 65g| Dietary Fiber: 18g)

Navy Bean and Ham Shank Soup

(Prep Time: 5 Mins |Total Time: 30 Mins |Serves: 2)

Ingredients:

- ½ cups dried Beans, soaked overnight and rinsed
- 1/2 pound Ham Shank
- ¼ Onion, died
- 1 Carrot, sliced
- 1 Celery Stalk, diced
- 1 Garlic Clove, minced
- ½ cup Tomato Sauce
- 1 tbsp Olive Oil
- ¼ tsp Salt
- ½ Bell Pepper, chopped
- 1 1/2 cups Water

Cooking Direction

1. Set your Instant Pot to SAUTE and heat the oil in it.
2. Add the onions, carrots, pepper, and celery, and cook for 3 minutes.
3. Stir in the garlic and cook for 1 more minute.
4. Add the rest of the ingredients and stir well to combine.
5. Close the lid and set the IP to MANUAL.
6. Cook on HIGH for 20 minutes.
7. Let the pressure drop naturally.
8. Serve and enjoy!

Nutrition Values

(Calories 640| Total Fats 32g | Carbs: 45g | Protein 35g| Dietary Fiber: 16g)

Leek and Cauliflower Soup

(Prep Time:5Mins |Cook Time:14Mins |Servings: 4)

Ingredients:

- 1/2 large head of cauliflower, chopped into florets
- 1/2 pound leeks, chopped
- 1 Tablespoons olive oil
- 4 cups homemade organic low-sodium chicken or vegetable broth
- 1/2 bay leaf
- 2 garlic cloves, minced

- 1/2 celery stalks, finely chopped
- 1 carrots, chopped
- 1/4 teaspoon fresh nutmeg
- Pinch of salt, pepper
- ⅓ cup fresh cilantro, finely chopped
- ½ cup unsweetened coconut cream

Cooking Direction

1. Press "Sauté" function on Instant Pot and add the oil.
2. Once hot, add garlic, celery, carrots, leeks, and cauliflower. Sauté until leeks wilted.

3. Add nutmeg, salt, pepper, and broth to Instant Pot. Stir.
4. Lock, seal the lid. Press "Manual" button. Cook on HIGH 8 minutes.
5. When done, naturally release pressure. Carefully remove lid. Remove bay leaf.
6. Use an immersion blender to pulse ingredients in your Instant Pot until smooth.
7. Stir in unsweetened coconut cream, fresh cilantro. Season. Serve.

Nutrition Values
(Calories: 151, Fat: 10.63g, Carbohydrates: 13.75g, Dietary Fiber: 1.2g, Protein: 2.69g)

Chicken Kale Soup

(Prep Time:5Mins |Cook Time:15Mins |Servings: 4)

Ingredients:

- 2 pounds boneless, skinless chicken breasts or chicken thighs
- ½ cup olive oil, avocado oil, coconut oil, or ghee
- ¼ cup lemon juice
- 1 teaspoon lemon zest
- 1 yellow onion, finely chopped
- 2 garlic cloves, minced
- 4 cups homemade low-sodium chicken broth
- 1 large bunch of kale, stemmed and roughly chopped
- 2 Tablespoons organic taco seasoning
- 1 teaspoon smoked paprika or regular paprika
- Pinch of salt, pepper
- Fresh green onions, diced

Cooking Direction

1. Press "Sauté" function on Instant Pot. Add 1 tablespoon olive oil.
2. Once hot, add chicken. Sear 2 minutes per side, until brown.
3. In a blender, add chicken broth, onion, garlic, and remaining olive oil. Blend until smooth. Pour in Instant Pot.
4. Stir in lemon juice, lemon zest, kale, taco seasoning, paprika, salt, and pepper.
5. Lock, seal the lid. Press "Manual" button. Cook on HIGH 10 minutes.
6. When done, naturally release pressure 10 minutes, then quick release pressure.
7. Serve in bowls, garnish with fresh green onion.

Nutrition Values
(Calories: 273, Fat: 22.32g, Carbohydrates: 2.4g, Dietary Fiber: 1.1g, Protein: 15.3g)

Chicken Turmeric Soup

(Prep Time:5Mins |Cook Time:15Mins |Servings: 4)

Ingredients:

- 1½ pounds boneless, skinless chicken breasts or chicken thighs
- 2 Tablespoons olive oil, coconut oil, or ghee
- 1 yellow onion, finely chopped
- 2 garlic cloves, minced
- 1 cup cauliflower florets
- 1 cup broccoli florets
- 1 cup carrots, finely chopped
- 1 cup celery stalks, finely chopped
- 4 cups organic homemade low-sodium vegetable or bone or chicken broth

- 1 bay leaf
- 1 teaspoon fresh ginger, grated
- 2 cups swiss chard, stemmed and roughly chopped
- ½ cup unsweetened coconut cream
- 3 teaspoons turmeric powder
- 1 teaspoon cumin powder
- Pinch of cayenne pepper, Pinch of salt, pepper
- Fresh cilantro, lemon wedges

Cooking Direction

1. Press "Sauté" function on Instant Pot. Add olive oil.
2. Once hot, add chicken. Sear 2 minutes per side, until brown. Remove. Set aside.
3. Add onion, ginger, garlic to Instant Pot. Sauté until softened.
4. Add cauliflower, broccoli, carrots, celery. Sauté 1 minute. Return chicken to pot. Add broth, bay leaf, turmeric powder, cumin powder, cayenne pepper, salt, pepper. Stir.

Lock, seal lid. Press "Manual" button. Cook on HIGH 8 minutes.
5. When done, naturally release pressure 5 minutes. Remove the lid. Remove bay leaf.
6. Stir in coconut cream, swiss chard; until chard wilts.
7. Ladle soup in bowls. Garnish with fresh cilantro and lemon wedges. Serve.

Nutrition Values
(Calories: 428, Fat: 42.65g, Carbohydrates: 11.71, Dietary Fiber: 3.4g, Protein: 42.53g)

Thai Broccoli and Beef Soup

(Prep Time:5Mins |Cook Time:15Mins |Servings: 4)

Ingredients:
- 1 pound lean, grass-fed ground beef
- 2 large heads of broccoli, chopped into florets
- 1 cup unsweetened coconut cream
- ⅓ cup fresh cilantro, finely chopped
- 2 Tablespoons organic Thai green curry paste
- 2 Tablespoons olive oil
- 1 medium-sized onion, finely chopped
- 1 2-inch ginger, peeled and minced
- 2 garlic cloves, minced
- 3 Tablespoons low-sodium coconut aminos
- 1 teaspoon organic fish sauce
- 4 cups homemade low-sodium chicken or beef broth
- Pinch of salt, pepper

Cooking Direction
1. Press the "Sauté" function on your Instant Pot and add olive oil.
2. Once hot, add onions. Sauté 2 to 4 minutes.
3. Add ginger, garlic, green curry paste to Instant Pot. Cook 1 minute.
4. Add ground beef. Cook until no longer pink. Stir in coconut aminos, salt, pepper, and fish sauce. Add broth to Instant Pot.
5. Close, seal the lid. Press "Manual" button. Cook on HIGH 8 minutes.
6. When done, naturally release pressure 5 minutes. Carefully remove lid.
7. Stir in broccoli florets. Allow to heat through for a couple minutes.
8. Stir in coconut cream. Season. Serve in bowls.

Nutrition Values
(Calories: 422, Fat: 34.33g, Carbohydrates: 5.6g, Dietary Fiber: 2.9g, Protein: 27.35g)

Roasted Garlic Soup

(Prep Time: 5Mins |Cook Time:35Mins |Servings: 6)

Ingredients:
- 2 bulbs of garlic; around 20 garlic cloves
- 1 large cauliflower head, finely chopped
- ¼ cup ghee or non-dairy butter
- 3 medium shallots or onions, finely chopped
- 6 cups homemade low-sodium vegetable broth
- Pinch of salt, pepper
- 1 cup unsweetened coconut cream

Cooking Direction
1. Press "Sauté" function of Instant Pot. Add the ghee.
2. Once hot, add onions and garlic. Sauté 3 to 5 minutes.
3. Add cauliflower, vegetable broth, salt, and black pepper.
4. Close, seal the lid. Press "Manual" button. Cook on HIGH 30 minutes.
5. When done, quick release pressure and carefully remove lid.
6. Use an immersion blender to puree the soup until smooth.
7. Stir in coconut cream. Season. Serve in bowls.

Nutrition Values
(Calories: 156, Fat: 14.05g Carbohydrates: 8.17g, Dietary Fiber: 2g, Protein: 2.94g)

Turmeric Carrot Soup with Sweet Potatoes

(Prep Time: 5 Mins |Total Time: 35 Mins |Serves: 2)

Ingredients:

- 1 Sweet Potato, chopped
- 2 Carrots, chopped
- 1 tsp Turmeric Powder
- ¼ tsp Paprika
- 1 ½ cups Veggie Broth
- 1 Garlic Clove, minced
- ½ Onion, diced
- 1 tbsp Olive Oil
- Salt and Pepper, to taste

Cooking Direction

1. Heat the oil in the IP on SAUTE.
2. Cook the onion and carrots for 3 minutes.
3. Add the garlic and cook for about a minute.
4. Add the rest of the ingredients and stir to combine. Season with some salt and pepper.
5. Close the lid and cook for 20 minutes on HIGH.
6. Do a quick pressure release.
7. Serve and enjoy!

Nutrition Values

(Calories 99| Total Fats 3g | Carbs: 16g | Protein 4g| Dietary Fiber: 2g)

Brisket and Mushroom Stew

(Prep Time: 5 Mins |Total Time: 30 Mins |Serves: 2)

Ingredients:

- ½ Onion, diced
- 2 Red Potatoes, cubed
- 2 Carrots, chopped
- 5 ounces Golden Mushroom Soup
- 6 ounces Water
- 1 tbsp Canola Oil
- 2/3 pound Beef Brisket, chopped
- 4 ounces Button Mushrooms, sliced
- ½ tsp Parsley

Cooking Direction

1. Heat the oil in the IP on SAUTE.
2. Add the meat and cook until browned on all sides.
3. Add the onion and cook for 2 more minutes.
4. Stir in the rest of the ingredients.
5. Close the lid and set the IP to MANUAL.
6. Cook on HIGH for 15 minutes.
7. Let the pressure drop naturally.
8. Serve and enjoy!

Nutrition Values

(Calories 525| Total Fats 17g | Carbs: 50g | Protein 42g| Dietary Fiber: 6g)

Lobster Bisque Soup

(Prep Time:5Mins |Cook Time:15Mins |Servings: 4)

Ingredients:

- 1 cups frozen or fresh lobster meat
- 1/2 cup homemade low-sodium vegetable or fish broth
- 1/4 cups unsweetened coconut cream
- 1 Tablespoons organic ghee (clarified butter)
- 1 medium yellow or red onion, finely chopped
- 2 garlic cloves, minced
- 1/2 cup dry white wine
- 1/2 cup carrots, finely chopped
- 1/2 cup celery, finely chopped
- 1/2 Tablespoon Worcestershire sauce
- 1/2 teaspoon smoked paprika or regular paprika
- 1/2 Tablespoon fresh parsley, chopped
- 1/2 teaspoon dried thyme
- Pinch of salt, pepper

Cooking Direction

1. Press "Sauté" function on Instant Pot. Add the ghee.
2. Once melted, add onion, celery, carrots, garlic. Cook 5 minutes.
3. Deglaze Instant Pot with the wine. Simmer until reduced by half.
4. Stir in lobster meat, and broth.
5. Close, seal the lid. Press "Steam" function. Cook on HIGH 5 minutes.
6. When done, naturally release pressure. Remove the lid.

7. Stir in coconut cream, Worcestershire sauce, paprika, parsley, thyme, salt, and black pepper. Use an immersion blender to puree soup until smooth.

8. Ladle soup in bowls. Garnish with parsley, fresh ground black pepper. Serve.

Nutrition Values
(Calories: 394, Fat: 29.3g , Carbohydrates: 5.3g, Fiber: 0.67g, Protein: 24.4g)

Chicken Lime Avocado Soup

(Prep Time:8Mins |Cook Time:10Mins |Servings: 4)

Ingredients:
- 2 pounds boneless, skinless chicken breasts or chicken thighs
- 3 fresh celery stalks, finely chopped
- 2 medium-sized carrots, finely chopped
- 2 Tablespoons olive oil, avocado oil, or coconut oil
- 1½ cups fresh green onions, finely chopped
- 2 garlic cloves, minced
- 8 cups homemade low-sodium chicken broth
- 1 teaspoon ground cumin
- Pinch of salt, pepper
- Juice and zest from 2 limes
- ½ cup fresh cilantro, finely chopped
- 4 medium-sized avocados, peeled, cored, finely chopped

Cooking Direction
1. Press "Sauté" function on Instant Pot and add the oil.
2. Once hot, add the chicken. Sear 2 minutes per side until brown.
3. Add garlic, green onions, chicken broth, carrots, celery, lime juice, and lime zest to Instant Pot.
4. Close, seal lid. Press "Manual" button. Cook on HIGH 8 minutes.
5. When cooking is done, naturally release the pressure and carefully remove the lid.
6. Transfer chicken to a cutting board and shred using two forks. Return the shredded chicken to your Instant Pot.
7. Season with cumin, salt, and pepper.
8. Top with fresh cilantro and chopped avocados. Serve.

Nutrition Values
(Calories: 402, Fat: 22.4g, Carbohydrates: 16.3g, Dietary Fiber: 6.83g, Protein: 33.2g)

Spinach Shiitake Mushroom Soup

(Prep Time:9Mins |Cook Time:14Mins |Servings: 4)

Ingredients:
- 1/2 pound fresh green asparagus, trimmed and cut into 1-inch pieces
- 1/2 Tablespoons olive oil or ghee
- 11/2 cup fresh shiitake mushrooms, thinly sliced
- 2 cups fresh baby spinach, roughly chopped
- 1/2 yellow onion, finely chopped
- 2 garlic cloves, minced
- 2 cups homemade low-sodium vegetable or chicken broth
- 1/4 cup unsweetened coconut cream
- 1 bay leaf
- 1/4 teaspoon dried thyme
- ¼ cup of fresh parsley, finely chopped
- 1/4 fresh lemon, juice and zest
- Pinch of salt, pepper

Cooking Direction
1. Press "Sauté" function on Instant Pot and add the oil.
2. Once hot, add onions and garlic. Sauté 1 minute, stirring occasionally.
3. Add asparagus pieces, thinly sliced mushrooms. Sauté 2 to 4 minutes.
4. Stir in vegetable broth, baby spinach, bay leaf, dried thyme, parsley, lemon juice, lemon zest, salt, black pepper.
5. Lock, seal the lid. Press "Manual" button. Cook on HIGH 9 minutes.
6. When done, naturally release pressure. Carefully remove lid. Remove bay leaf.
7. Stir in unsweetened coconut cream. Season. Serve.

Nutrition Values
(Calories: 237, Fat: 8.53g, Carbohydrates: 10.75g, Dietary Fiber: 3.8g, Protein: 8.54g)

Chapter 4 Poultry Recipes

(Prep Time: 8 Mins |Total Time: 25 Mins | Serves: 6)

Ingredients:

- 2 pounds Chicken Thighs
- 1 pound Green Beans
- 1 pound Potatoes, peeled and halved
- Juice of 1 Lemon
- 2 tbsp Olive Oil
- 1 tbsp Ghee
- ½ cup Chicken Stock
- 1 tsp mixed Herbs
- 1 tsp minced Garlic

Cooking Direction

1. Set your Instant Pot to SAUTE and melt the ghee along with the olive oil in it.
2. Add garlic and cook for 1 minute.
3. Add the chicken thighs and cook them on all sides, until they become golden.
4. Stir in the lemon juice and herbs and cook for an additional minute.
5. Add the remaining ingredients and stir well to combine.
6. Close the lid and set the IP to MANUAL.
7. Cook for 15 minutes on HIGH.
8. Release the pressure quickly.
9. Serve and enjoy!

Nutrition Values

(Calories 500| Total Fats 27g | Carbs: 19g| Protein 45g | Dietary Fiber: 3g)

(Prep Time: 5 Mins |Total Time: 25 Mins| Serves: 4)

Ingredients:

- 1 tsp Garlic Powder
- 1 ¾ pounds Chicken Breasts
- ¼ tsp Black Pepper
- 1 cup Homemade Chicken Broth

Cooking Direction

1. Simply dump all of the ingredients in the Instant Pot.
2. Give the mixture a good stir and put the lid on.
3. Turn it clockwise to seal.
4. Set the IP to MANUAL.
5. Cook on HIGH for 20 minutes.
6. Do a quick pressure release and open the lid.
7. Shred the chicken inside the pot with 2 forks.
8. Serve and enjoy!

Nutrition Values

(Calories 430| Total Fats 17g | Carbs: 0g| Protein 45g | Dietary Fiber: 0g)

(Prep Time: 8 Mins |Total Time: 20 Mins |Serves: 4)

Ingredients:

- 1 1/3 pounds Chicken Breasts, cubed
- 1 cup chopped Spinach
- 1/3 cup Basil Leaves
- 1/3 cup Coconut Cream
- 2/3 cup Homemade Chicken Broth
- 1 tsp minced Garlic
- 1 tbsp Olive Oil

Cooking Direction

1. Heat the oil in the Instant Pot on SAUTE.
2. Add the garlic and cook for 1 minute.
3. Add the chicken and cook until it is no longer pink.
4. Stir in the rest of the ingredients.
5. Put the lid on and seal.
6. Set the IP to MANUAL.
7. Cook on HIGH for 8 minutes.
8. Do a quick pressure release.
9. Serve and enjoy!

Nutrition Values

(Calories 320| Total Fats 14g | Carbs: 4g| Protein 35g | Dietary Fiber: 1g)

The Ultimate Mexican Chicken

(Prep Time: 5 Mins |Total Time: 25 Mins| Serves: 6)

Ingredients:

- 2 pounds Chicken Breasts
- Juice of 1 Lime
- 1 Jalapeno, seeded and diced
- ½ tsp Chili Powder
- ½ tsp Cumin
- 1 Green Bell Pepper, diced
- 1 Red Bell Pepper, diced
- 10 ounces Tomatoes, diced
- 1 Red Onion, diced
- 1 tbsp Olive Oil
- Pinch of Black Pepper

Cooking Direction

1. Set the IP to SAUTE and add the olive oil.
2. When sizzling, add the onion and peppers and cook for 3-4 minutes, until soft.
3. Add the rest of the ingredients.
4. Stir to combine and close the lid.
5. Set the Instant Pot to MANUAL.
6. Cook the chicken for 15 minutes on HIGH pressure.
7. Do a quick pressure release and open the lid.
8. Shred the chicken with two forks and stir to combine. This step is optional, you can serve the chicken as it is and garnish with the cooking liquid and veggies on top.
9. Enjoy!

Nutrition Values

(Calories 340| Total Fats 14g | Carbs: 10g| Protein 45g | Dietary Fiber: 2g)

Instant Rotisserie Chicken

(Prep Time: 5 Mins |Total Time: 40 Mins |Serves: 4)

Ingredients:

- 1 Whole Chicken (About 2 ½ - 3 lb)
- 1 ½ tbsp Olive Oil
- 1 cup Homemade Chicken Broth
- 1 tsp Smoked Paprika
- 1 tsp Garlic Powder

Cooking Direction

1. Wash the chicken well and pat dry with some paper towels.
2. In a small bowl, combine the paprika, garlic powder, and oil.
3. Rub this mixture into the chicken.
4. Set your Instant Pot to SAUTE and place the chicken inside.
5. Sear on all sides, until it turns golden.
6. Pour the broth around the chicken and close the lid.
7. Set the IP to MANUAL and cook on HIGH for 25 minutes.
8. Release the pressure quickly.
9. Let sit for 10 minutes before serving.
10. Enjoy!

Nutrition Values

(Calories 585| Total Fats 20g | Carbs: 0.7g| Protein 95g | Dietary Fiber: 0.3g)

Turkey with Leeks and Mushrooms

(Prep Time: 8 Mins |Total Time: 25 Mins| Serves: 6)

Ingredients:

- 2 pounds Turkey Breasts, cut into large pieces
- 2 tbsp Arrowroot
- ½ cup Homemade Chicken Broth
- ½ cup Almond Milk
- 2 Leeks, sliced
- 4 tbsp Ghee
- 1 ¼ pounds Mushrooms, sliced
- ¼ tsp Garlic Powder
- ¼ tsp Black Pepper

Cooking Direction

1. Season the turkey with garlic powder and pepper.
2. Set your IP to SAUTE and add the ghee.
3. When melted, add the turkey pieces and cook until they are no longer pink. Transfer them to a plate.
4. Add the leeks and mushrooms to the IP and cook for 3 minutes.

5. Return the turkey to the pot and pour the broth over.
6. Close the lid and cook for 8 minutes on HIGH.
7. Release the pressure naturally.
8. Whisk together the almond milk and arrowroot and stir into the pot.
9. Cook on SAUTE until thickened.
10. Serve and enjoy!

Nutrition Values

(Calories 555| Total Fats 24g | Carbs: 37g| Protein 50g | Dietary Fiber: 3g)

Chicken with Onion and Green Olives

(Prep Time: 5 Mins |Total Time: 20 Mins | Serves: 4)

Ingredients:
- 4 Chicken Breasts
- 1 can Green Olives, pitted
- ½ cup Red Onion, sliced
- 1 cup Homemade Chicken Broth
- 2 tbsp Ghee
- 2 tbsp Lemon Juice
- Pinch of Pepper

Cooking Direction
1. Set your Instant Pot to SAUTE and add the ghee.
2. When melted, add the chicken and brown on all sides.
3. Add the rest of the ingredients and put the lid on.
4. Set the Instant Pot to MANUAL and cook on HIGH for 10 minutes.
5. Do a quick pressure release.
6. Serve and enjoy!

Nutrition Values

(Calories 500| Total Fats 34g | Carbs: 2g| Protein 44g | Dietary Fiber: 0.5g)

Juicy and Fall-off-Bone Drumsticks

(Prep Time: 5 Mins |Total Time: 45 Mins |Serves: 3)

Ingredients:
- 6 Chicken Drumsticks
- ½ Bell Pepper, diced
- 2 tsp minced Garlic
- 1 tbsp Olive Oil
- 2 cups Water
- ½ Red Onion, diced
- 2 tbsp Tomato Paste
- Pinch of Pepper

Cooking Direction
1. Set your IP to SAUTE and heat the olive oil in it.
2. Add the onions and pepper and cook for 3 minutes.
3. Add the garlic and cook for an additional minute.
4. Place the drumsticks inside.
5. Whisk together the tomato paste and water and pour the mixture over the drumsticks.
6. Put the lid on and seal.
7. Set the IP to MANUAL.
8. Cook on HIGH for 15 minutes.
9. Let the pressure drop on its own.
10. Serve and enjoy!

Nutrition Values

(Calories 450| Total Fats 27g | Carbs: 5.3g| Protein 42g | Dietary Fiber: 1.4g)

Slow-Cooked Turkey

(Prep Time: 15 Mins |Total Time: 4 hours and 15 Mins | Serves: 4)

Ingredients:
- 1 ½ pounds Turkey Breasts
- 1 tbsp Organic Dijon Mustard
- 2 tbsp Olive Oil
- 2 tsp Smoked Paprika
- 1 tsp minced Garlic
- Pinch of Black Pepper
- 1 cup Homemade Chicken Broth

Cooking Direction
1. Set your Instant Pot to SAUTE and add the oil to it.

2. When hot and sizzling, add the turkey and cook until it becomes brown.
3. Whisk together ½ of the broth and the rest of the ingredients and pour over the turkey.
4. Close the lid and set the IP to SLOW COOK.
5. Cook for 2 hours.
6. Do a quick pressure release and pour the remaining broth over.

7. Seal the lid again and cook for another 2 hours.
8. Do a quick pressure release.
9. Serve and enjoy!

Nutrition Values
(Calories 400| Total Fats 30g | Carbs: 2.5g| Protein 40g | Dietary Fiber: 0.5g)

Mediterranean Chicken Wings
(Prep Time: 15 Mins |Total Time: 10 Mins | Serves: 4)

Ingredients:
- 12 Chicken Wings
- 2 tsp Tarragon
- 1 tbsp Oregano
- 6 tbsp Homemade Chicken Broth
- ¼ cup Homemade Chicken Broth
- 2 tbsp Olive Oil
- 1 tbsp Garlic Puree
- 1 tbsp Basil
- Pinch Pepper
- 1 cup of Water

Cooking Direction
1. Pour the water into the Instant Pot and lower the rack.

2. In a bowl, combine the remaining ingredients.
3. Let sit for 15 minutes.
4. Transfer the chicken wings to a baking dish.
5. Place the dish on the rack and close the lid of the IP.
6. Set the Instant Pot to MANUAL and cook for 10 minutes on HIGH.
7. Do a quick pressure release.
8. Serve and enjoy!

Nutrition Values
(Calories 160| Total Fats 13g | Carbs: 0.6g| Protein 11g | Dietary Fiber: 0g)

Juicy Herbed Turkey Breasts
(Prep Time: 10 Mins |Total Time: 20 Mins |Serves: 3)

Ingredients:
- 1 pound Turkey Breasts
- ¼ tsp Oregano
- ¼ tsp Thyme
- 2 tbsp chopped Basil
- 1 tbsp chopped Parsley
- Pinch of Pepper
- ¼ tsp Garlic Powder
- 1 tbsp Olive Oil
- 1 cup Water

Cooking Direction
1. Heat the oil in the IP on SAUTE.

2. Add the turkey and cook until it becomes browned on all sides.
3. Stir in the herbs and spices and pour the water over.
4. Close the lid and set the Instant Pot to MANUAL.
5. Cook on HIGH for 10 minutes.
6. Do a quick pressure release.
7. Serve as desired and enjoy!

Nutrition Values
(Calories 320| Total Fats 15g | Carbs: 0g| Protein 40g | Dietary Fiber: 0g)

Chicken Spaghetti Squash with Shitakes
(Prep Time:8 Mins |Total Time: 40 Mins |Serves: 6)

Ingredients:
- 1 cup sliced Shitake Mushrooms
- 2 pounds Chicken Breasts, chopped
- 1 Spaghetti Squash

- 1 cup Homemade Chicken Broth
- 1 tbsp Arrowroot
- 1 cup Water

- 1 tbsp Coconut Oil

Cooking Direction

1. Pour the water into the IP.
2. Place the spaghetti squash inside the steamer basket and lower it into the IP.
3. Close the lid and set the IP to MANUAL.
4. Cook for 20 minutes on HIGH.
5. Do a quick pressure release and set aside to cool.
6. Discard the cooking liquid and wipe the IP clean.
7. Set the IP to SAUTE and melt the coconut oil inside.
8. Add the chicken and cook until it becomes golden.
9. Add the rest of the ingredients and close the lid.
10. Cook on HIGH for 8 minutes.
11. Meanwhile, scrape out the flesh of the squash with a fork, into spaghetti-like strings.
12. Do a quick pressure release and open the lid.
13. Stir in the spaghetti.
14. Serve and enjoy!

Nutrition Values

(Calories 260| Total Fats 12g | Carbs: 4g| Protein 22g | Dietary Fiber: 0g)

Thai Peanut Chicken

(Prep Time: 5 Mins |Total Time: 33 Mins | Serves: 6)

Ingredients:

- 1 ½ cups toasted peanuts
- 1 ½ lb. chicken breasts
- 2 cloves of garlic, minced
- Salt and pepper to taste
- 2 tbsp. chopped scallions for garnish

Directions

1. Place 1 cup of toasted peanuts in a food processor and pulse until smooth. This will serve as your peanut butter. For the remaining half cup of peanut, chop until fine. Set aside.
2. Press the Sauté button on the Instant Pot and place the chicken breasts and garlic. Keep on stirring for 3 minutes until the meat has turned lightly golden.
3. Season with salt and pepper to taste.
4. Pour the peanut butter that you have prepared earlier. Give a good stir and pour a cup of water.
5. Close the lid and seal off the vent.
6. Press the Manual button and adjust the cooking time to 25 minutes.
7. Do natural pressure release.
8. Garnish with chopped nuts and scallions before serving.

Nutrition Values

(Calories:575; Total Fat: 34.8g; Carbs: 2.5g; Dietary Fiber: 0.2g; Protein:42g)

Thai Goose with Basil

(Prep Time: 10 Mins |Total Time: 40 Mins | Serves: 4)

Ingredients:

- 2 tbsp minced Chilies
- 2 tbsp Coconut Oil
- 2 tsp minced Garlic
- 1 tsp minced Ginger
- 2 cups Goose Cubes
- ¼ cup chopped Basil
- 2 tbsp Coconut Aminos
- 1 ½ cups Water

Cooking Direction

1. Set your Instant Pot to SAUTE and add half of the coconut oil to it.
2. When melted, add the goose and cook until it becomes browned.
3. Transfer the goose to a baking dish.
4. Add the rest of the ingredients, except the water, to the dish and stir to combine.
5. Pour the water into the IP and lower the trivet.
6. Place the baking dish on the trivet and close the lid.
7. Cook on MANUAL for 10 minutes.
8. Do a quick pressure release.
9. Serve and enjoy!

Nutrition Values

(Calories 190| Total Fats 9g | Carbs: 2g| Protein 27g | Dietary Fiber: 1g)

Coconut Kale Chicken

(Prep Time: 3 Mins |Total Time: 30 Mins | Serves: 4)

Ingredients:

- 1 ½ pounds Chicken Breasts, chopped
- ½ cup canned diced Tomatoes
- ¾ cup Coconut Milk
- 1 cup chopped Kale
- 1 Garlic Clove, minced
- ¼ tsp Onion Powder
- ¼ tsp Paprika
- Pinch of Pepper
- 2/3 cup Homemade Chicken Stock
- ½ tsp Oregano
- 1 tbsp Olive Oil

Cooking Direction

1. Heat the oil in the Instant Pot on SAUTE.
2. Add the garlic and cook for 30 seconds.
3. Add chicken, oregano, and spices, and cook until the chicken becomes golden.
4. Pour the stock over and close the lid.
5. Cook on HIGH for 24 minutes.
6. Do a quick pressure release.
7. Open the lid and add the remaining ingredients.
8. Stir to combine and close the lid again.
9. Cook on HIGH for another 4 minutes.
10. Release the pressure quickly and serve drizzled with the sauce.
11. Enjoy!

Nutrition Values

(Calories 455| Total Fats 26g | Carbs: 3g| Protein 55g | Dietary Fiber: 2g)

Instant Pot Garlic Chicken

(Prep Time: 8 Mins | Total Time: 40 Mins | Serves: 4)

Ingredients:

- 3 tbsp. coconut oil
- 5 cloves of garlic, minced
- 4 chicken breasts, halved
- Salt and pepper to taste
- 1 ½ cups water

Directions

1. Press the Sauté button on the Instant Pot and heat the coconut oil. Sauté the garlic until fragrant then stir in the chicken breasts. Season with salt and pepper to taste.
2. Stir for 5 minutes then pour in water.
3. Close the lid and seal off the vent. Press the Manual button and adjust the cooking time to 30 minutes.
4. Do natural pressure release.

Nutrition Values

(Calories:591; Total Fat: 37.5g; Carbs: 1.1g; Dietary Fiber: 0.7g; Protein: 60.8g)

Instant Pot Lemon Olive Chicken

(Prep Time: 10 Mins |Total Time: 30 Mins |Serves: 4)

Ingredients:

- 4 boneless skinless chicken breasts
- ½ cup coconut oil
- 1/4teaspoon black pepper
- 1/2teaspoon cumin
- 1teaspoon sea salt
- 1cup Homemade chicken bone-broth
- 2 tbsp. fresh lemon juice
- 1/2cup red onion, sliced
- 1can pitted green olives
- 1/2 lemon, thinly sliced

Cooking Direction

1. Generously season chicken breasts with cumin, pepper and salt; set your instant pot on sauté mode and melt coconut oil; add chicken and brown both sides.
2. Stir in the remaining ingredients; bring to a gentle simmer and then lock lid.
3. Cook on high for 10 minutes and then use quick release method to release pressure.
4. Serve and enjoy!

Nutrition Values

(Calories 420| Total Fats 38.7g | Carbs: 0.6 g| Protein 42.4g | Dietary Fiber: 0.2g)

Instant Pot Chicken Shawarma

(Prep Time: 10 Mins |Total Time: 25 Mins |Serves: 8)

Ingredients:
- 1 pound chicken thighs
- 1 pound chicken breasts, sliced
- 1/8 teaspoon cinnamon
- 1/4 teaspoon chili powder
- 1 teaspoon ground cumin
- 1/4 teaspoon ground allspice
- 1/4 teaspoon granulated garlic
- 1/2 teaspoon turmeric
- 1 teaspoon paprika
- Pinch of salt
- Pinch of pepper
- 1 cup Homemade chicken broth

Cooking Direction
1. Mix all ingredients in your instant pot and lock lid;
2. Cook on poultry setting for 15 minutes and the release pressure naturally.
3. Serve chicken with sauce over mashed sweet potato drizzled with tahini sauce.

Nutrition Values
(Calories 223| Total Fats 8.7g | Carbs: 0.7 g| Protein 35.5g | Dietary Fiber: 0.2g)

Italian-Inspired Creamy Chicken

(Prep Time:5Mins |Cook Time:15Mins |Servings: 4)

Ingredients:
- 4 boneless, skinless chicken thighs
- 1 teaspoon olive oil
- 1 cup homemade low-sodium chicken broth
- ⅓ cup unsweetened coconut cream or unsweetened almond cream
- 1½ Tablespoons arrowroot powder
- 1 Tablespoon organic basil pesto
- 1 Tablespoon organic Italian seasoning
- 2 Tablespoons organic minced garlic
- 1 Tablespoon organic minced onion
- Pinch of salt, pepper
- Fresh parsley

Cooking Direction
1. Press "Sauté" function on Instant Pot. Add olive oil.
2. Once hot, add onion, garlic. Cook 2 minutes. Add chicken. Cook 2 minutes per side, until golden brown. Season with salt, pepper, Italian seasoning. Stir in broth.
3. Lock, seal the lid. Press "Manual" button. Cook on HIGH 8 minutes.
4. When done, naturally release pressure 5 minutes, then quick release. Remove lid.
5. Press "Sauté" function. Stir in arrowroot powder. Stir to coat ingredients. Whisk in coconut cream, basil pesto. Stir. Allow to simmer until thickens. Season if needed.
6. Serve in bowls. Garnish with fresh parsley.

Nutrition Values
(Calories: 242, Fat: 15g, Carbohydrates: 5.3g, Dietary Fiber: 1.8gg, Protein: 26g)

Instant Pot Pesto Chicken

(Prep Time: 10 Mins | Total Time: 40 Mins | Serves: 4)

Ingredients:
- 2 cups basil leaves
- ¼ cup extra virgin olive oil
- 5 sun-dried tomatoes
- Salt and pepper to taste
- 4 chicken breasts

Directions
1. Put in the food processor the basil leaves, olive oil, and tomatoes. Season with salt and people to taste. Add a cup of water if needed.
2. Place the chicken in the Instant Pot. Pour over the pesto sauce.
3. Close the lid and seal off the vent. Press the Manual button and adjust the cooking time to 30 minutes.
4. Do natural pressure release.

Nutrition Values
(Calories:556; Total Fat: 32.7g; Carbs: 1.1g; Dietary Fiber: 0.7g; Protein:60.8g)

Lemon Chicken

(Prep Time:4 Mins |Cook Time: 15Mins |Servings: 3)

Ingredients:

- 3 boneless, skinless chicken thighs or chicken breasts
- 1/2 small yellow onion, finely chopped
- 2 garlic cloves, minced
- 1 Tablespoons organic Italian seasoning
- 1/4 teaspoon organic smoked or regular paprika
- Zest and juice from 1 lemon
- 1/4 lemon, thinly sliced
- ½ cup homemade low-sodium chicken broth
- 1/4 Tablespoon fresh parsley, finely chopped
- 1 Tablespoons olive oil
- 1/2 Tablespoons ghee (clarified butter)
- 1/2 teaspoon organic garlic powder
- Pinch of salt, pepper

Cooking Direction

1. In a bowl, combine salt, pepper, garlic powder, paprika, Italian seasoning. Coat chicken on all sides with mixture.
2. Press "Sauté" function on Instant Pot. Add the olive oil.
3. Once hot, cook garlic, onions 2 minutes, stirring occasionally. Add chicken. Sear on all sides. Stir in ghee, lemon juice, lemon zest.
4. Place lemon slices on top of chicken.
5. Lock, seal lid. Press "Manual" button. Cook on HIGH 8 minutes.
6. When done, naturally release pressure 5 minutes, then quick release. Remove lid.
7. Serve on a platter. Garnish with fresh parsley, fresh lemon slices. Serve.

Nutrition Values
(Calories: 380, Fat: 22.1g, Carbohydrates: 1.8g, Dietary Fiber: 0.5g, Protein: 42.5g)

Garlic Drumsticks

(Prep Time:7Mins |Cook Time:18Mins |Servings: 3)

Ingredients:

- 3 skin-on fresh chicken drumsticks
- 1/2 teaspoon olive oil
- ¼ cup homemade low-sodium chicken broth
- ½ cup low-sodium coconut aminos
- 1 garlic cloves, minced
- ½ onion, finely chopped
- 1/2 1-inch fresh ginger, peeled and minced
- 1 Tablespoons cider vinegar
- 1 Tablespoons stevia
- Pinch of salt, pepper

Cooking Direction

1. Season drumsticks with salt, pepper.
2. Press "Sauté" function on Instant Pot. Add the olive oil.
3. Once hot, add onion, garlic. Cook 2 minutes. Add drumsticks to pot. Sear.
4. Pour in chicken broth, coconut aminos, ginger, cider vinegar, stevia. Stir.
5. Lock, seal the lid. Press "Manual" button. Cook on HIGH 9 minutes.
6. When done, naturally release pressure 5 minutes, then quick release. Remove lid.
7. Transfer drumsticks to parchment-lined baking pan. Broil in oven, 2 mins per side.
8. Press "Sauté" function on Instant Pot. Allow liquid to simmer until reduced by half.
9. Transfer drumsticks to a platter. Pour sauce over top. Garnish with fresh parsley. Serve.

Nutrition Values
(Calories: 501, Fat: 19.3g , Carbohydrates: 4.3g, Dietary Fiber: 0.4g, Protein: 46g)

Italian Drumsticks

(Prep Time:6Mins |Cook Time:23Mins |Servings: 2)

Ingredients:

- 4 skin-on chicken drumsticks
- 1 Tablespoons olive oil
- 1/2 medium-sized red or yellow onion, finely chopped
- 1/2 teaspoon chili powder
- 1/2 teaspoon smoked paprika or regular paprika
- 4 garlic cloves, minced

- 1/2 Tablespoon Italian seasoning
- 1 Tablespoons balsamic vinegar
- 1 Tablespoons dried thyme
- Pinch of salt, pepper

Marinara Sauce:
- 1 medium beet, finely chopped
- 1 pound fresh orange carrots, finely chopped
- ⅔ cup homemade low-sodium chicken broth
- 2 Tablespoons lemon juice

Cooking Direction
1. Season drumsticks with salt and pepper.
2. In a blender or food processor, add beets, carrots, chicken broth, lemon juice. Pulse until smooth.
3. Press "Sauté" function on Instant Pot. Add the olive oil.
4. Once hot, add onions. Sauté 3 minutes. Add garlic. Sauté 1 minute. Turn off Sauté.
5. Place drumsticks in Instant Pot. Pour in marinara sauce, chili powder, paprika, Italian seasoning, balsamic vinegar, thyme.
6. Close, seal lid. Press "Manual" button. Cook on HIGH 15 minutes.
7. When done, naturally release pressure 5 minutes, then quick release pressure. Remove lid.
8. Transfer to platter. Garnish with fresh basil. Serve.

Nutrition Values
(Calories: 300, Fat: 16.85g , Carbohydrates: 6.89g, Dietary Fiber: 1.8g, Protein: 28.5g)

Chicken Paprikash

(Prep Time:5Mins |Cook Time: 20Mins |Servings: 4)

Ingredients:
- 2 pounds bone-in, skinless, chicken breasts or chicken thighs
- 1 large yellow onion, finely chopped
- 2 garlic cloves, minced
- 3 Tablespoons olive oil or coconut oil
- 1 bay leaf
- 1½ cups homemade low-sodium chicken broth
- 1 cup unsweetened coconut cream
- 3 Tablespoons paprika
- 5 Tablespoons arrowroot powder
- Juice and zest from 1 fresh lemon
- Pinch of salt, pepper

Cooking Direction
1. Season chicken with salt and pepper.
2. Press "Sauté" function. Add olive oil.
3. Once hot, add onion and garlic. Sauté 3 minutes.
4. Add chicken. Sear on all sides until brown.
5. Stir in chicken broth, paprika, salt, black pepper, lemon zest, lemon juice, and bay leaf to Instant Pot.
6. Close, seal lid. Press "Manual" button. Cook on HIGH 7 minutes.
7. When done, naturally release pressure 10 minutes, then quick release remaining pressure. Remove lid. Remove bay leaf.
8. Press "Sauté" function. Stir in arrowroot powder to coat ingredients. Add coconut cream. Allow to simmer until sauce thickens. Season.
9. Transfer to platter. Garnish with fresh parsley. Serve.

Nutrition Values
(Calories: 720, Fat: 43.31g , Carbohydrates: 14.2g, Dietary Fiber: 1.7g, Protein: 67g)

Pork and Cabbage Bowl

(Prep Time:3Mins |Cook Time:15Mins |Servings: 3)

Ingredients:
- 1 pounds ground pork
- 1 Tablespoons olive oil
- 1 shallots, peeled, finely chopped
- 1/ cup homemade low-sodium chicken broth
- 1 cups cauliflower florets, finely chopped
- 3 cups fresh green cabbage, finely shredded
- 1 garlic cloves, minced
- Pinch of salt, pepper

Cooking Direction
1. Press "Sauté" function on Instant Pot. Add the olive oil.
2. Once hot, add ground pork, finely chopped shallots, and minced garlic. Cook until pork

is browned, stirring occasionally. Turn off "Sauté" function.
3. Add cauliflower, cabbage, salt, and black pepper to Instant Pot.
4. Close, seal the lid. Press "Manual" button. Cook on HIGH 3 minutes.

5. When done, quick release pressure. Remove the lid.
6. Transfer to platter. Serve.

Nutrition Values
(Calories: 163 , Fat: 4g, Carbohydrates: 8.6g, Dietary Fiber: 3.85g, Protein: 21g)

Pulled Pork Soup
(Prep Time:10Mins |Cook Time:50Mins |Servings: 3)

Ingredients:
- 1/2 pound organic boneless whole pork shoulder
- 1/2 Tablespoons olive oil
- 1/2 pounds organic cauliflower florets
- 2 cups homemade low-sodium chicken or pork broth
- 2 garlic cloves, minced
- 1/2 large red onion, diced
- 1/4 cup unsweetened coconut cream
- Pinch of salt, pepper

Cooking Direction
1. Press "Sauté" function. Add 1 tablespoon olive oil.
2. Once hot, add pork shoulder. Sear on all sides.

3. Add remaining tablespoon olive oil. Once hot, add onion, and garlic cloves. Cook 5 minutes. Add broth, salt, pepper, cauliflower. Stir.
4. Lock, the lid. Press "Manual" button. Cook on HIGH 45 minutes.
5. When done, naturally release pressure 10 minutes, then quick release remaining pressure. Remove the lid.
6. Transfer pork shoulder to cutting board. Shred using two forks.
7. Using an immersion blender, pulse cauliflower mixture in Instant Pot until smooth. Stir in pulled pork, and coconut cream. Season as needed.
8. Ladle in bowls. Serve.

Nutrition Values
(Calories: 409, Fat: 24.6g, Carbohydrates: 14.8g, Dietary Fiber: 5g, Protein: 34g)

Pork Chops with Red Cabbage
(Prep Time:10Mins |Cook Time: 12Mins |Servings: 4)

Ingredients:
- 4 pork chops
- 1 small head of red cabbage, cored, shredded
- 1 Tablespoon olive oil
- 2 cups homemade low-sodium chicken broth
- 3 Tablespoons arrowroot powder
- 1 teaspoon garlic powder
- 1 teaspoon onion powder
- 1 Tablespoon freshly chopped parsley
- 2 teaspoons dried thyme
- Pinch of salt, pepper
- 1 teaspoon fennel seeds

Cooking Direction
1. In a bowl, combine garlic powder, onion powder, parsley, dried thyme, salt, black pepper, and fennel seeds. Season pork with spices.
2. Press "Sauté" function on Instant Pot. Add the olive oil.

3. Once hot, add pork chops. Sear on both sides. Remove and set aside.
4. Add shredded cabbage, and chicken stock to Instant Pot. Stir.
5. Place pork chops on top of cabbage.
6. Close, seal the lid. Press "Manual" button. Cook on HIGH 8 minutes.
7. When done, quick release pressure. Remove the lid.
8. Transfer cabbage and pork chops to a serving platter.
9. Press "Sauté" function on Instant Pot. Stir in arrowroot powder. Simmer until thickened, stirring occasionally. Pour sauce over cabbage and pork. Serve.

Nutrition Values
(Calories: 369, Fat: 23.6g, Carbohydrates: 19.2g, Dietary Fiber: 5.7g, Protein: 20.9g)

Swedish-Inspired Pork Roast

(Prep Time:10Mins |Cook Time: 1 hour and 30 Mins |Servings: 4)

Ingredients:

- 1 pounds boneless pork loin roast
- 1/2 Tablespoon olive oil
- 1/2 cups homemade low-sodium beef broth
- 1/2 large yellow onion, peeled, grated
- 2 garlic cloves, crushed
- 1/4 Tablespoons of swerve or Erythritol sweetener
- 1/4 Tablespoons sea salt
- 1/4 Tablespoon fresh parsley, finely chopped
- 1/4 teaspoon organic ground cumin powder
- 1/4 teaspoon organic ground cardamom powder
- 1/4 teaspoon fresh ground nutmeg
- 1/4 teaspoon freshly cracked black pepper.

Cooking Direction

1. Season pork loin roast with swerve, salt, cumin powder, cardamom powder, pepper.
2. Press "Sauté" function on Instant Pot. Add the olive oil.
3. Once hot, add onion, garlic. Cook 4 minutes.
4. Add pork roast. Sear on all sides. Stir in beef broth.
5. Lock, seal the lid. Press "Manual" button. Cook on HIGH 85 minutes.
6. When done, naturally release pressure. Remove the lid.
7. Transfer roast to serving platter. Allow to rest 10 minutes before slicing. Ladle liquid over slices. Serve.

Nutrition Values
(Calories: 287, Fat: 6.7g, Carbohydrates: 5.5g, Dietary Fiber: 0.3g, Protein: 48.7g)

Smoky Paprika Chicken

(Prep Time: 8 Mins |Total Time: 33 Mins | Serves: 8)

Ingredients:

- 1 tbsp. olive oil
- 2 lb. chicken breasts
- 2 tbsp. smoked paprika
- Salt and pepper to taste
- ¼ cup water

Directions

1. Press the Sauté button on the Instant Pot and heat the olive oil. Stir in the chicken breasts and smoked paprika for 3 minutes until lightly golden.
2. Season with salt and pepper to taste and pour in the water.
3. Close the lid and seal off the vent.
4. Press the Manual button and adjust the cooking time to 25 minutes.
5. Do natural pressure release.
6. Garnish with cilantro or scallions if desired.

Nutrition Values
(Calories:217; Total Fat: 12.4g; Carbs: 1.5g; Dietary Fiber: 0.7g; Protein: 34g)

Barbecue Chicken Sliders

(Prep Time:10Mins |Cook Time:15 Mins |Servings: 4)

Chicken Sliders:

- 4 boneless, skinless chicken breasts
- Lettuce leaves – your choice, for buns

Barbecue Sauce:

- 6 garlic cloves, minced
- 1 large yellow onion, finely chopped
- ½ cup coconut butter or ghee (clarified butter)
- 2 Tablespoons organic chili powder
- 1 Tablespoon organic cayenne pepper
- 3 cups fresh cherries, pitted and halved
- 1 apple, peeled, cored, finely chopped
- ¼ cup Swerve sweetener
- ⅓ cup Worcestershire sauce
- ¼ cup apple cider vinegar
- 3 Tablespoons organic brown mustard

Cooking Direction

1. Combine barbecue sauce ingredients in blender. Pulse until smooth.
2. Press "Sauté" function on Instant Pot. Add olive oil. Cook onion, garlic 3 minutes.
3. Add chicken breasts. Cover with barbecue sauce.

4. Close, seal lid. Press "Manual" button. Cook on HIGH 15 minutes.
5. When done, quick release or naturally release pressure. Carefully remove lid.
6. Transfer chicken to a cutting board, and shred using two forks.

7. Return shredded chicken to Instant Pot. Stir to coat.
8. Scoop chicken on lettuce leaves. Serve.

Nutrition Values
(Calories: 820, Fat: 50.54g, Carbohydrates: 27.54g, Dietary Fiber: 4.3g, Protein: 63.32g)

Chilli Lime Chicken

(Prep Time: 10 Mins |Total Time: 45 Mins | Serves: 5)

Ingredients:
- 1 lb. chicken breasts, skin and bones removed
- Juice from 1 ½ limes, freshly squeezed
- 1 tbsp. chilli power
- 1 tsp. cumin
- 6 cloves garlic, minced

Directions
1. Place all ingredients in the Instant Pot and give a good stir. Pour a cup of water and season with salt and pepper to taste.
2. Close the lid and seal off the vent.
3. Press the Manual button and adjust the cooking time to 35 minutes.

4. Do natural pressure release.
5. Once the lid is open, take out the chicken breasts and shred using two forks.
6. Place the shredded meat back into the Instant Pot and press the Sauté button. Allow to simmer for about 5 minutes until the sauce thicken.

Nutrition Values
(Calories:166; Total Fat: 8.5g; Carbs: 1.5g; Dietary Fiber: 0.3g; Sugars: 0g; Protein: 19.3g; Cholesterol: 58mg; Sodium: 87mg)

Faux-Tisserie Whole Chicken

(Prep Time:15Mins |Cook Time:35Mins |Servings: 4)

Ingredients:
- 1 x 2-pound whole chicken
- 2 Tablespoons olive oil
- 3 garlic cloves, minced
- 1/4 lemon, quartered
- 1/4 cup of homemade low-sodium chicken broth
- 1 Tablespoons fresh marjoram, finely chopped
- 1 Tablespoons fresh thyme, finely chopped
- 1/2 Tablespoon dried basil
- 1/2 Tablespoon chili powder
- 1/2Tablespoon onion powder
- 1/2 teaspoon organic ground cumin
- Pinch of salt, pepper

Cooking Direction
1. Drizzle light layer of oil over the chicken.
2. In a bowl, combine marjoram, thyme, basil, chili powder, onion powder, ground cumin, salt, and black pepper. Set aside.

3. Stuff garlic and lemon inside the chicken. Secure the chicken legs with string.
4. Press "Sauté" function. Once hot, place chicken in Instant Pot. Sear on all sides.
5. Sprinkle seasoning over chicken skin.
6. Pour chicken broth in Instant Pot. Set trivet in pot. Place chicken on top.
7. Close, seal the lid. Press "Manual" button. Cook on HIGH 25 minutes.
8. When done, naturally release pressure 15 minutes, then quick release pressure. Remove the lid. Transfer chicken to platter. Allow to rest 10 minutes, then remove lemon and garlic. Slice. Serve with side salad.

Nutrition Values
(Calories: 483, Fat: 33.2g, Carbohydrates: 4.3g, Dietary Fiber: 0.9g, Protein: 34g)

Garlic and Smoked Paprika Drumsticks

(Prep Time: 11Mins |Cook Time:24Mins |Servings: 4)

Ingredients:

- 4 fresh chicken drumsticks or chicken legs
- Olive oil
- 1/2 Tablespoons smoked paprika
- 1/4 Tablespoons garlic powder
- Pinch of salt, pepper
- 1/2 cup of water

Cooking Direction

1. In a bowl, combine smoked paprika, garlic powder, salt, pepper. Stir.
2. Drizzle light layer of oil over chicken. Season drumsticks or legs with the spices.
3. Add 1 cup of water to Instant Pot. Place trivet in as well.
4. Place drumsticks on top of the trivet.
5. Lock, seal the lid. Press "Manual" button. Cook on HIGH 16 minutes.
6. When done, naturally release pressure 5 minutes, then quick release pressure. Remove the lid. Transfer chicken to parchment-lined baking tray.
7. Place baking tray under broiler, 2 minutes per side, until skin golden and crispy.
8. Transfer to platter. Serve.

Nutrition Values

(Calories: 473, Fat: 32g, Carbohydrates: 3.2g, Dietary Fiber: 0.3g, Protein: 33.4g)

Chicken Chili

(Prep Time: 15Mins |Cook Time 15Mins |Servings: 4)

Ingredients:

- 2 pounds ground chicken
- 3 Tablespoons olive oil
- 1 medium yellow onion, finely chopped
- 4 garlic cloves, minced
- 3 fresh celery stalks, finely chopped
- 2 Tablespoons organic chili powder
- 2 Tablespoons taco seasoning
- 1 Tablespoon organic ground cumin
- ½ teaspoon organic ground cinnamon
- Pinch of salt, pepper
- 2 cups homemade low-sodium chicken broth
- 1 cup vegetable broth
- Juice from 1 fresh lime
- 1 small can organic tomato puree
- For serving: fresh cilantro, avocado slices

Cooking Direction

1. Press "Sauté" function. Add olive oil.
2. Once hot, add onion, celery. Cook 3 minutes. Add garlic. Cook another 2 minutes.
3. Add ground chicken to pot. Cook until no longer pink.
4. Stir in chili powder, taco seasoning, cumin, cinnamon, salt, pepper.
5. Stir in vegetable broth, lime juice.
6. Close, seal the lid. Press "Manual" button. Cook on HIGH 12 minutes.
7. When done, naturally release pressure 10 minutes, then quick release pressure. Remove the lid.
8. Ladle in bowls. Garnish with fresh cilantro and avocado slices. Serve.

Nutrition Values

(Calories: 395, Fat: 12.2g, Carbohydrates: 22.4g, Dietary Fiber: 3.3g, Protein: 47.2g)

Lemony Chicken with Currants

(Prep Time: 5 Mins |Total Time: 20 Mins | Serves: 2)

Ingredients:

- 1 Lemon, sliced
- 3 tbsp Currants
- 2/3 pound Chicken Fillets
- 1 tbsp Canola Oil
- 1 Garlic Clove, minced
- 1/3 cup chopped Scallions
- 1/3 cup Green Olives
- 1 ¼ cup Water
- Salt and Pepper, to taste

Cooking Direction

1. Heat the oil in the IP on SAUTE.
2. Add the onions, scallions, and garlic, and saute for 3 minutes.

3. Place the chicken inside and arrange the olives and currants over.
4. Top with the lemon slices.
5. Season with some salt and pepper and pour the water over.
6. Cook for 15 minutes on POULTRY.

7. Do a quick pressure release.
8. Serve and enjoy!

Nutrition Values

(Calories 300| Total Fats 16g | Carbs: 7g | Protein 33g| Dietary Fiber: 1g)

Chicken Casserole with Rice and Artichokes

(Prep Time: 8 Mins |Total Time: 25 Mins | Serves: 2)

Ingredients:

- ¼ tsp Garlic Powder
- ¼ Onion, diced
- 1 cup diced canned Tomatoes
- 1 tbsp Olive Oil
- ½ pound Chicken Breast, cubed
- ¼ cup dry White Wine
- 1 cup Chicken Broth
- 1/3 cup Rice
- 4 ounces Artichokes Hearts, chopped

Cooking Direction

1. Heat the olive oil in the IP on SAUTE and add the onions.

2. Cook for 2 minutes and then add the chicken and garlic powder.
3. Cook until golden on all sides.
4. Add the remaining ingredients and stir well to combine.
5. Close the lid and cook for 10 minutes on HIGH.
6. Release the pressure naturally.
7. Serve and enjoy!

Nutrition Values

(Calories 550| Total Fats 19g | Carbs: 34g | Protein 30g| Dietary Fiber: 3g)

Sweet Onion and Pear Chicken

(Prep Time: 5 Mins |Total Time: 25Mins| Serves: 2)

Ingredients:

- 1 tbsp Butter
- ½ pound Boneless Chicken Thighs, chopped
- 1 Large Pear, sliced
- 1 tbsp Balsamic Vinegar
- ½ cup diced Sweet Onions
- 1 ¼ cup Chicken Stock
- Salt and Pepper, to taste

Cooking Direction

1. Melt the butter in the Instant Pot on SAUTE.
2. Add the onions and cook for 5 minutes.

3. Add the chicken and cook until browned on all sides.
4. Dump the rest of the ingredients and stir to combine.
5. Close the lid and cook on HIGH for 15 minutes.
6. Do a quick pressure release.
7. Serve and enjoy!

Nutrition Values

(Calories 290| Total Fats 7g | Carbs: 13.5g | Protein 40g| Dietary Fiber: 2g)

Orange and Cranberry Turkey Wings

(Prep Time: 5 Mins |Total Time: 40 Mins | Serves: 2)

Ingredients:

- ½ pound Turkey Wings
- ½ Butter Stick
- 1 ¼ cup Veggie Stock
- 1 Onion, sliced
- ¼ cup Orange Juice
- 1 cup Cranberries
- Salt and Pepper, to taste

Cooking Direction

1. Melt the butter in your IP and brown the wings on all sides. Transfer to a plate.
2. Add the onions and saute for a few minutes.
3. Add the cranberries and orange juice and cook for 5 more minutes.
4. Return the wings to the pot and pour the water over.

5. Season with some salt and pepper and close the lid.
6. Cook for 15 minutes on POULTRY.
7. Do a quick pressure release and set to SAUTE.

8. Cook for 5 more minutes, until the sauce thickens.
9. Serve and enjoy!

Nutrition Values
(Calories 460| Total Fats 28g | Carbs: 14g | Protein 34g| Dietary Fiber: 1.2g)

Chicken and Fried Rice

(Prep Time: 5 Mins |Total Time: 25 Mins | Serves: 2)

Ingredients:
- 1 tbsp Butter
- 2/3 cup chopped Chicken
- 2 tsp Apple Cider Vinegar
- 2 tbsp chopped Green Onions
- 1 Carrot, chopped
- ½ cup Rice
- Salt and Pepper, to taste
- 1 ¾ cup Chicken Broth

Cooking Direction
1. Place all of the ingredients in your Instant Pot.

2. Stir the ingredients well to combine.
3. Close the lid and cook on RICE for 20 minutes.
4. Do a quick pressure release.
5. Fluff the rice with a fork and stir to combine everything.
6. Serve and enjoy!

Nutrition Values
(Calories 430| Total Fats 10g | Carbs: 55g | Protein 20g| Dietary Fiber: 9g)

Bean and Tomato Chicken

(Prep Time: 8 Mins |Total Time: 20 Mins | Serves: 2)

Ingredients:
- 1 tbsp Oil
- ½ pound Chicken Breast, chopped
- 5 ounces canned Beans
- 5 ounces canned diced Tomatoes
- 2/3 cup Vegetable Stock
- ¼ cup Sour Cream
- Salt and Pepper, to taste

Cooking Direction
1. Heat the oil in the Instant Pot on SAUTE.

2. Add the chicken and cook until golden.
3. Stir in the remaining ingredients.
4. Close the lid and set the IP to SAUTE.
5. Cook for 10 minutes.
6. Do a quick pressure release.
7. Serve and enjoy!

Nutrition Values
(Calories 350| Total Fats 8g | Carbs: 22g | Protein 5g| Dietary Fiber: 5g)

Instant Pot Emergency Broccoli Chicken

(Prep Time:5 Mins | Total Time: 45 Mins | Serves: 5)

Ingredients:
- 1 tbsp. coconut oil
- 3 cloves of garlic, minced
- 1 ½ lb. chicken breasts, cut into strips
- ¼ cup coconut aminos
- 1 head broccoli, cut into florets

Directions
1. Press the Sauté button on the Instant Pot and heat the oil. Sauté the garlic until fragrant. Stir in the chicken breasts and seas with coconut aminos.

2. Close the lid and seal off the vent. Press the Manual button and adjust the cooking time to 30 minutes.
3. Do natural pressure release.
4. Once the lid is open, press the Sauté button and stir in the broccoli. Allow to simmer for 10 minutes.

Nutrition Values
(Calories:263; Total Fat: 15.4g; Carbs: 1.8g; Dietary Fiber: 1.4g; Protein: 28.6g)

Turkey Risotto with Veggies

(Prep Time: 7 Mins |Total Time: 25 Mins | Serves: 2)

Ingredients:

- ¾ cup cooked and shredded Turkey
- 1 tbsp Butter
- 1/3 cup chopped Zucchini
- 1/3 cup chopped Rutabaga
- 1/3 cup chopped Carrots
- ½ cup chopped Swiss Chard
- 1 tsp Soy Sauce
- 2/3 cup Arborio Rice
- 2 ¼ cup Broth

Cooking Direction

1. Place all of the ingredients in the Instant Pot.
2. Stir to combine and set the IP to RICE.
3. Cook for 18 minutes.
4. Do a quick pressure release.
5. Fluff with a fork and stir again to combine.
6. Serve and enjoy!

Nutrition Values

(Calories 580| Total Fats 20g | Carbs: 51g | Protein 44g| Dietary Fiber: 17g)

Turkey Sausage Pilaf

(Prep Time: 3 Mins |Total Time: 25 Mins | Serves: 2)

Ingredients:

- 1 Turkey Sausage, sliced
- 2/3 cup Rice
- 1 cup Spinach
- 1 Carrot, chopped
- 1 Shallot, chopped
- 1 tsp minced Garlic
- 1 tbsp Olive Oil
- 1 Bell Pepper, diced
- 2 ¼ cups Vegetable Broth
- Salt and Pepper, to taste

Cooking Direction

1. Heat the oil in the Instant Pot on SAUTE.
2. Add the shallots, peppers, and garlic, and cook for 3 minutes.
3. Add rice and cook for 30 seconds.
4. Stir in the rest of the ingredients.
5. Set the IP to BEAN/CHILI and cook for 12 minutes.
6. Do a natural pressure release.
7. Fluff with a fork before serving. Enjoy!

Nutrition Values

(Calories 350| Total Fats 56g | Carbs: 55g | Protein 17g| Dietary Fiber: 15.8g)

Grapefruit and Cashew Chicken Fillets

(Prep Time: 5 Mins |Total Time: 30 Mins | Serves: 2)

Ingredients:

- 1/2 pound Chicken Fillets
- 1 tsp Cornstarch
- ¼ cup chopped Cashews
- ½ cup Grapefruit Juice
- 1 tbsp Olive Oil
- 2/3 cup Water
- Salt and Pepper, to taste

Cooking Direction

1. Heat the oil in the Instant Pot on SAUTE.
2. Add chicken and cook until no longer pink.
3. Stir in the rest of the ingredients except the cornstarch.
4. Close the lid and cook on POULTRY for 10 minutes.
5. Do a quick pressure release.
6. Whisk in the cornstarch and cook on SAUTE until the mixture thickens.
7. Serve and enjoy!

Nutrition Values

(Calories 347| Total Fats 16g | Carbs: 14g | Protein 38g| Dietary Fiber: 3g)

Buffalo Chicken with Potatoes

(Prep Time: 5 Mins |Total Time: 35 Mins | Serves: 2)

Ingredients:

- ½ Onion, diced
- 8 ounces Potatoes, diced
- 2 tbsp Buffalo Sauce
- ¼ tsp Garlic Powder
- 1 ½ tbsp Butter
- ½ pound Chicken Breast, chopped
- 2/3 cup Chicken Broth
- ¼ tsp Salt
- Pinch of Pepper

Cooking Direction

1. Melt the butter in your Instant Pot on SAUTE.
2. Add the onions and saute for 3 minutes.
3. Stir in the rest of the ingredients and close the lid.
4. Set the IP to POULTRY.
5. Cook for 15-18 minutes.
6. Do a quick pressure release.
7. Serve and enjoy!

Nutrition Values

(Calories 290| Total Fats 12g | Carbs: 25g | Protein 20g| Dietary Fiber: 1g)

Chicken Curry

(Prep Time: 5 Mins |Total Time: 25 Mins |Serves: 6)

Ingredients:

- 1 ½ lb. boneless chicken breasts
- 2 tbsp. curry powder
- 2 cups chopped tomatoes
- 2 cups coconut milk, freshly squeezed
- 1 thumb-size ginger

Directions

1. Press the Sauté button on the Instant Pot and stir in the chicken for 3 minutes until lightly golden.
2. Stir in the curry powder and continue cooking for 2 more minutes.
3. Add the rest of the ingredients.
4. Close the lid and seal off the vent.
5. Press the Poultry button and cook under the present cooking time (15 minutes).
6. Do natural pressure release.

Nutrition Values

(Calories:336; Total Fat: 22.4g; Carbs: 7.4g; Dietary Fiber: 4.2g; Protein: 28.1g)

Creamy Paprika Goose

(Prep Time: 6 Mins |Total Time: 30 Mins | Serves: 2)

Ingredients:

- ½ Onion, diced
- 2/3 pound Goose Breasts, chopped
- 1 Bell Pepper, diced
- 1 ½ tsp Paprika
- ½ cup Coconut Cream
- 1 tbsp Butter
- 1 Garlic Clove, minced
- 8 ounces Tomato Sauce

Cooking Direction

1. Set your Instant Pot to SAUTE and melt the butter in it.
2. Add the onions and pepper and cook for 3-4 minutes.
3. Add the garlic and cook for 30-60 seconds.
4. Place the goose inside and cook until it is no longer pink.
5. Pour the tomato sauce over and stir in the paprika.
6. Close the lid and cook on POULTRY for 12 minutes.
7. Do a natural pressure release.
8. Stir in the coconut cream.
9. Serve and enjoy!

Nutrition Values

(Calories 496| Total Fats 25g | Carbs: 18g | Protein 48g| Dietary Fiber: 2g)

Turkey Patties

(Prep Time: 10 Mins | Total Time: 30 Mins | Serves: 2)

Ingredients:

- ½ pound Ground Turkey
- ¼ cup Breadcrumbs
- 2 Egg
- 1 ½ cups Chicken Broth
- 1 tbsp Olive Oil
- ¼ tsp Garlic Powder
- ½ tsp dried Parsley
- Salt and Pepper, to taste

Cooking Direction

1. Pour the water into the Instant Pot and lower the trivet.
2. In a bowl, combine the turkey, parsley, egg, spices, and breadcrumbs,
3. Make 2 smaller patties out of the mixture.
4. Arrange on a greased baking dish and place on the trivet.
5. Cook for 5 minutes on HIGH.
6. Do a quick pressure release and discard the cooking liquid.
7. Wipe the pot clean and heat the oil in it on SAUTE.
8. Add the patties and cook until crispy and golden.
9. Serve and enjoy!

Nutrition Values

(Calories 255| Total Fats 15g | Carbs: 8.5g | Protein 25g| Dietary Fiber: 1g)

Chicken Cajun Pasta

(Prep Time: 5 Mins |Total Time: 25 Mins |Serves: 2)

Ingredients:

- 8 ounces Bowtie Pasta
- 1 ½ tbsp Cajun Seasoning
- 6 ounces Coconut Cream
- 6 ounces diced Chicken Breasts
- ¼ cup diced Bell Peppers
- ¼ cup diced Red Onions
- 1 ½ tbsp Butter
- 4 ounces Chicken Broth

Cooking Direction

1. Melt the butter in the IP on SAUTE.
2. Add onions and peppers and cook for 3 minutes.
3. Add the chicken and cook for 3 more minutes.
4. Stir in the remaining ingredients.
5. Close the lid and cook on HIGH for 8 minutes.
6. Do a quick pressure release.
7. Serve and enjoy!

Nutrition Values

(Calories 670| Total Fats 25g | Carbs: 75g | Protein 30g| Dietary Fiber: 1.5g)

Duck a l'Orange

(Prep Time: 5 Mins |Total Time: 50 Mins |Serves: 2)

Ingredients:

- 1 Duck Breast, cut in half
- 1 tbsp Fish Sauce
- 1 Duck Leg, cut in half
- 1 tbsp minced Ginger
- 4 Spring Onions, chopped
- 1 Red Chili, chopped
- 1 tsp chopped Lemongrass
- 1 Whole Star Anise
- 1 ½ cups Orange Juice

Cooking Direction

1. Grease the IP with some cooking spray.
2. Add the duck (skin-side down) and cook until it becomes crispy. Transfer the duck to a plate.
3. Add the ginger and cook for 30 seconds.
4. Add the remaining ingredients and return the duck to the pot.
5. Close the lid and cook for 30 minutes on HIGH.
6. Do a natural pressure release.
7. Serve and enjoy!

Nutrition Values

(Calories 442| Total Fats 22g | Carbs: 9g | Protein 50g| Dietary Fiber: 1g)

Easy Asian Chicken

(Prep Time: 5 Mins |Total Time: 25 Mins |Serves: 5)

Ingredients:
- 1 ½ lb. boneless chicken breasts
- 1 tbsp ginger slices
- 3 tbsp coconut aminos
- ¼ cup organic chicken broth
- 3 cloves of garlic, minced

Directions
1. Place all ingredients in the Instant Pot. Give a good stir.
2. Close the lid and make sure that the vent is sealed.
3. Press the Poultry button and adjust the cooking time to 15 minutes.
4. Do natural pressure release.
5. Once the lid is open, press the Sauté button and allow to simmer until the sauce has reduced. Garnish with chopped scallions and drizzle with sesame oil if desired.

Nutrition Values

(Calories:169; Total Fat: 3.6g; Carbs: 1.2g; Dietary Fiber: 0.6g; Protein: 30.9g)

Pina Colada Chicken

(Prep Time: 5 Mins |Total Time: 35 Mins |Serves: 2)

Ingredients:
- 1 tbsp Coconut Aminos
- ¼ cup Coconut Cream
- ¼ cup chopped Green Onion
- Pinch of Cinnamon
- ½ cup Pineapple Chunks
- 2/3 pounds Chicken Thighs, boneless
- ½ cup Water

Cooking Direction
1. Place the chicken, pineapple, coconut aminos, and cinnamon in the IP.
2. Add the coconut cream and stir to combine.
3. Pour the water over and close the lid.
4. Cook on POULTRY for 15 minutes.
5. Do a quick pressure release.
6. Serve topped with green onions.
7. Enjoy!

Nutrition Values

(Calories 530| Total Fats 2g | Carbs: 11g | Protein 65g| Dietary Fiber: 1.5g)

Instant Pot Cashew Chicken

(Prep Time: 5 Mins |Total Time: 25 Mins |Serves: 9)

Ingredients:
- 2 lb. chicken breasts, sliced thinly
- Salt and pepper
- 1 head broccoli, cut into florets
- 1 cup red bell pepper, cut into cubes
- 1 cup cashew nuts, toasted

Directions
1. Press the Sauté button on the Instant Pot and stir in the chicken breasts for at least 5 minutes. Season with salt and pepper to taste. Pour ½ cup of water for additional moisture.
2. Close the lid and seal off the vent.
3. Press the Poultry button and adjust the cooking time to 10 minutes.
4. Do quick pressure release.
5. Once the lid is open, press the Sauté button and stir in the broccoli and red bell pepper. Allow to simmer for 5 minutes.
6. Toss the cashew nuts last.
7. Serve warm.

Nutrition Values

(Calories:261; Total Fat: 16.2g; Carbs: 5.3g; Dietary Fiber: 1.3g; Protein: 23.7g)

Ground Chicken and Porcini Risotto

(Prep Time: 5 Mins |Total Time: 15 Mins |Serves: 2)

Ingredients:
- 1 cup sliced Porcini Mushrooms
- 1 cup ground Chicken
- 1 cup Basmati Rice
- 1 Shallot, chopped
- 2 cups Chicken Stock
- 1 tbsp Olive Oil

- ¼ cup chopped Celery
- Pinch of Paprika
- Salt and Pepper, to taste

Cooking Direction

1. Heat the oil in the Instant Pot on SAUTE.
2. Add the shallots and celery and cook for 2 minutes.
3. Add the mushrooms and cook for 3 minutes more.

4. Add chicken and cook until it becomes golden.
5. Stir in the remaining ingredients.
6. Close the lid and set the instant pot to RICE.
7. Cook for 8 minutes.
8. Do a natural pressure release.
9. Serve and enjoy!

Nutrition Values

(Calories 610| Total Fats 11g | Carbs: 88g | Protein 32g| Dietary Fiber: 14g)

Chicken Cacciatore

(Prep Time: 5 Mins |Total Time: 30 Mins |Serves: 6)

Ingredients:

- 6 chicken drumsticks, bone-in
- 1 bay leaf
- 2 cups tomato puree (pureed from 3 cups chopped tomatoes)
- ½ cup black olives, pitted
- Salt and pepper to taste

Directions

1. Place all ingredients in the Instant Pot. Pour a cup of water to add more moisture.

2. Close the lid and seal off the vent. Press the Manual button and adjust the cooking time to 25 minutes.
3. Do natural pressure release.
4. Garnish with parsley or cilantro on top if desired.

Nutrition Values

(Calories:256; Total Fat: 13.2g; Carbs: 9.5g; Dietary Fiber: 6.2g; Protein: 25.3g)

Peach Chicken Bake

(Prep Time: 5 Mins |Total Time: 25 Mins |Serves: 2)

Ingredients:

- ½ chopped canned Peaches in Syrup
- ½ pound Chicken Fillets
- 1 tbsp Oyster Sauce
- 1 tsp Sugar
- ½ tsp Onion Powder
- ¼ tsp Cayenne Pepper
- ½ cup Water

Cooking Direction

1. Grease the Instant Pot with cooking spray.
2. Add the chicken and cook until golden.

3. Sprinkle with cayenne, onion powder, and sugar.
4. Add the oyster sauce, and peaches and stir to combine well.
5. Pour the water over and close the lid.
6. Select MEAT/STEW and cook for 10 minutes.
7. Do a quick pressure release.
8. Serve and enjoy!

Nutrition Values

(Calories 480| Total Fats 16g | Carbs: 15g | Protein 32g| Dietary Fiber: 1g)

Sweet and Sour Chicken with Mangos

(Prep Time: 5 Mins |Total Time: 35 Mins |Serves: 2)

Ingredients:

- 4 smallish Chicken Thighs
- 1 Garlic Clove, minced
- 1 tsp minced Ginger
- 1 Mango, chopped
- 2 tbsp Lime Juice
- 1 tsp Fish Sauce
- 2 tbsp Coconut Aminos

- 2 tbsp chopped Cilantro
- 1 tbsp Honey
- 1 tbsp Apple Cider Vinegar
- 1 tbsp Olive Oil
- 2/3 cup Chicken Broth

Cooking Direction

1. Heat the oil in the IP on SAUTE and cook the chicken thighs until golden on both sides. Transfer to a plate.
2. Add the onions, garlic, ginger, and mango, and cook for 2 minutes.
3. Stir in the remaining ingredients and return the chicken to the pot.
4. Close the lid and set the IP to POULTRY.
5. Cook for 12 minutes.
6. Do a quick pressure release.
7. If desired, cook for a few more minutes on SAUTE for a thicker sauce.
8. Serve and enjoy!

Nutrition Values
(Calories 380| Total Fats 13g | Carbs: 26g | Protein 27g| Dietary Fiber: 4g)

Whole Roasted Chicken with Lemon and Rosemary
(Prep Time: 5 Mins |Total Time: 3 H| Serves: 12)

Ingredients:
- 1 whole chicken
- 6 cloves of garlic, minced
- 1 lemon, sliced
- 1 sprig rosemary
- Salt and pepper to taste

Directions
1. Place the whole chicken in a big bowl and rub all the spices onto the surface and insides of the chicken. Allow to marinate in the fridge for at least 2 hours.
2. Place the chicken in the Instant Pot and pour a cup of water.
3. Close the lid and seal off the vent. Press the Manual button and adjust the cooking time to 60 minutes.
4. Do natural pressure release.

Nutrition Values
(Calories:248; Total Fat: 17.2g; Carbs: 0.9g; Dietary Fiber: 0g; Protein: 21.3g;)

Turkey Casserole
(Prep Time: 5 Mins |Total Time: Mins |Serves: 2)

Ingredients:
- 2 Turkey Breasts
- 1 Celery Stalk, chopped
- 1 can Cream of Mushroom Soup
- ½ cup Chicken Broth
- ½ bag of Pepperidge Stuffing Cubes
- ½ Onion, chopped

Cooking Direction
1. Place everything inside your Instant Pot.
2. Stir well to combine and close the lid.
3. Set the Instant Pot to MANUAL and cook on HIGH for 25 minutes.
4. Let the pressure drop naturally.
5. Serve and enjoy!

Nutrition Values
(Calories 650| Total Fats 20g | Carbs: 60g | Protein 45g | Dietary Fiber: 2g)

Apple and Raisin Goose
(Prep Time: 5 Mins |Total Time: 25 Mins |Serves: 2)

Ingredients:
- ½ Shallot, chopped
- ½ tsp Dill
- 2/3 pound Goose Breasts, chopped
- 1 Apple, sliced
- 1 tbsp Butter
- ¼ cup Rasisins
- 2/3 cup Chicken Broth

Cooking Direction
1. Melt the butter in the IP on SAUTE.
2. Add the goose and cook until it is no longer pink.
3. Add the rest of the ingredients to the Instant Pot.
4. Stir well to incorporate them well.
5. Close the lid and set the IP to MANUAL.
6. Cook for 15 minutes on HIGH.
7. Do a quick pressure release.
8. Serve and enjoy!

Nutrition Values
(Calories 260| Total Fats 10g | Carbs: 14g | Protein 30g| Dietary Fiber: 2,1g)

Easy Chicken Vindaloo

(Prep Time: 5 Mins |Total Time: 35 Mins |Serves: 5)

Ingredients:
- 1 lb. chicken thighs, skin and bones not removed
- 2 tbsp. garam masala
- 6 whole red dried chillies
- 1 onion, sliced
- 5 cloves of garlic, crushed

Directions
1. Press the Sauté button and stir in the chicken thighs and Add the garam masala and the rest of the ingredients. Continue cooking for 5 minutes while stirring constantly. Season with salt and pepper to taste.
2. Pour in enough water to submerge half of the chicken.
3. Close the lid and seal off the vent.
4. Press the Poultry button and adjust the cooking time to 25 minutes.
5. Do natural pressure release.
6. Garnish with cilantro if desired.

Nutrition Values
(Calories:206; Total Fat: 15.1g; Carbs: 1.4g; Dietary Fiber: 0.5g; Sugars: 0g; Protein: 15.2g; Cholesterol: 88mg; Sodium: 74mg)

Chicken Verde Brown Rice Casserole

(Prep Time: 5 Mins |Total Time: 35 Mins |Serves: 2)

Ingredients:
- 1/3 cup Salsa Verde
- 2/3 pound Chicken Breasts
- ½ Onion, sliced
- ½ cup Brown Rice
- 2/3 cup Chicken Broth

Cooking Direction
1. Combine everything in your Instant Pot.
2. Close and seal the lid and set it to MANUAL.
3. Cook on HIGH for 8 minutes.
4. Do a natural pressure release,
5. Transfer the chicken to a cutting board and shred with two forks.
6. Return to the pot and give it a good stir.
7. Serve and enjoy!

Nutrition Values
(Calories 420| Total Fats 5g | Carbs: 45g | Protein 45g| Dietary Fiber: 7.4g)

Alfredo Chicken Fettucine

(Prep Time: 5 Mins |Total Time: 10Mins |Serves: 2)

Ingredients:
- ¾ cup cooked and shredded Chicken Meat
- 8 ounces Alfredo Sauce
- 7 ounces Fettucine
- 2 cups Water
- ¼ tsp Garlic Powder
- ¼ tsp Salt
- Pinch of Pepper

Cooking Direction
1. Place everything in the Instant Pot.
2. Give it a good stir to combine.
3. Set the IP to MANUAL.
4. Cook on HIGH for 4 minutes.
5. Do a quick pressure release.
6. Serve topped with some shredded cheese, if desired.
7. Enjoy!

Nutrition Values
(Calories 490| Total Fats 16g | Carbs: 60g | Protein 27g| Dietary Fiber: 3.5g)

Chicken Spaghetti with Spinach in a Mushroom Sauce

(Prep Time: 5 Mins |Total Time: 20 Mins |Serves: 2)

Ingredients:
- 2 cups Broth
- 2 ounces shredded Mozzarella Cheese
- 1 Chicken Breast, chopped
- 1 can Creamy Mushroom Soup
- 1 Garlic Clove, minced
- 2 cups Baby Spinach

- 8 ounces Spaghetti

Directions
1. Set your Instant Pot to SAUTE.
2. Combine the chicken and broth inside.
3. Bring the mixture to a boil.
4. Stir in the remaining ingredients, close the lid, and set the Instant Pot to MANUAL.
5. Cook on HIGH for 4 minutes.
6. Do a quick pressure release.
7. Serve and enjoy!

Nutrition Values
(Calories 520| Total Fats 12g | Carbs: 60g | Protein 27g| Dietary Fiber: 3g)

Apricot Glazed Halved Turkey

(Prep Time: 5 Mins |Total Time: 60 Mins |Serves: 2)

Ingredients:
- ½ Small Turkey
- 2 ounces Apricot Jam
- 1 Carrot, diced
- ¼ Onion, diced
- 1 ¼ cup Chicken Stock
- ¼ tsp Cumin
- ¼ tsp Coriander
- ¼ tsp Salt

Cooking Direction
1. In a small bowl, combine the apricot jam and all of the spices.
2. Rub the glaze over the turkey.
3. Place the turkey inside the Instant Pot.
4. Add the carrot and onion.
5. Pour the broth around (not over) the turkey.
6. Close the lid and set the IP to POULTRY.
7. Cook for 25 minutes.
8. Do a natural pressure release.
9. Serve and enjoy!

Nutrition Values
(Calories 880| Total Fats 20g | Carbs: 80g | Protein 100 g| Dietary Fiber: 5g)

Slow Cooker Rotisserie Chicken

(Prep Time: 5 Mins |Total Time: 12H 10Mins |Serves: 12)

Ingredients:
- 1 whole chicken
- Salt and pepper to taste
- 1 tsp. thyme
- 1 tsp. paprika
- 1 tbsp. garlic powder

Directions
1. Rub and massage the entire chicken with the spices. Place in the fridge for at least 2 hours and allow to marinate.
2. Place aluminium foil at the base of the inner pot. Gently place the chicken inside the pot.
3. Close the lid and do not seal the vent.
4. Press the Slow Cook button and allow to cook for 10 hours.

Nutrition Values
(Calories:249; Total Fat: 17.2g; Carbs: 1.4g; Dietary Fiber: 0.7g; Protein: 21.3g)

Slow Cooked Chicken Drumstick

(Prep Time: 5 Mins |Total Time: 8H 5Mins |Serves: 12)

Ingredients:
- 12 chicken drumsticks
- 1 ½ tbsp. paprika
- ¼ tsp. dried thyme
- ½ tsp. onion powder
- Salt and pepper to taste

Directions
1. Place all ingredients in the Instant Pot. Give a good stir to coat the entire chicken with the spices.
2. Close the lid and do not seal the Vent.
3. Press the Slow Cooker button and adjust the cooking time to 8 hours.

Nutrition Values
(Calories:218; Total Fat: 12.1g; Carbs: 2.5g; Dietary Fiber: 1.2g; Protein: 23.8g)

Fennel Shredded Chicken

(Prep Time: 5 Mins |Total Time: 40 Mins |Serves: 8)

Ingredients:
- 2 lb. chicken thighs, bone in and skin removed
- ¼ cup fennel bulb
- 4 cloves of garlic, minced
- 3 tbsp. lemon juice, freshly squeezed
- 1 tsp. cinnamon

Directions
1. Place all ingredients in the Instant Pot. Season with salt and pepper to taste and add ½ cup of water for moisture.
2. Close the lid and seal off the vent.
3. Press the Manual button and adjust the cooking time to 30 minutes.
4. Do natural pressure release.
5. Take the chicken out from the pot and shred using forks. Place the meat back into the pot and press the Sauté button. Simmer for at least 5 minutes until the sauce has reduced.

Nutrition Values
(**Calories**257; Total Fat: 18.8g; Carbs: 1.9g; Dietary Fiber: 1.3g; Protein: 187g）

Chicken and Mushrooms

(Prep Time: 5 Mins |Total Time: 23 Mins |Serves: 6)

Ingredients:
- 6 boneless chicken breasts, halved
- 1 onion, chopped
- 4 cloves of garlic, minced
- ½ cup coconut milk
- 1 cup mushrooms, sliced

Directions
1. Press the Sauté button on the Instant Pot and stir in the chicken breasts. Stir in the onions and garlic for at least 3 minutes until lightly golden.
2. Stir in the remaining ingredients and season with salt and pepper to taste. Add half a cup of water to add more moisture.
3. Close the lid and seal off the vent.
4. Press the Poultry button and cook on pre-set cooking time.
5. Do natural pressure release.

Nutrition Values
(Calories:383; Total Fat: 11.9g; Carbs: 3.5g; Dietary Fiber: 1.6g; Protein: 62.2g)

Chinese Steamed Chicken

(Prep Time: 5 Mins |Total Time: 20 Mins |Serves: 6)

Ingredients:
- 1 ½ lb. chicken parts (any)
- ¼ cup coconut aminos
- 3 tbsp. sesame oil
- 1 tbsp. five-spice powder
- 1 tsp. grated ginger

Directions
1. Place all ingredients in the Instant Pot and give a good stir. Season with salt and pepper and add water for more moisture.
2. Close the lid and seal off the vent.
3. Press the Poultry button and cook using the pre-set cooking time.
4. Do natural pressure.

Nutrition Values
(Calories:236; Total Fat: 11.3g; Carbs: 1.3g; Dietary Fiber: 0.6g; Protein: 31.3g)

Chicken Stew with Chayote and Spinach

(Prep Time: 5 Mins |Total Time: 28 Mins |Serves: 6)

Ingredients:
- 1 lb. chicken meat (any part)
- 3 cloves of garlic, minced
- 1 thumb-size ginger, sliced
- 1 cup chopped tomatoes
- 2 cups spinach leaves

Directions

1. Press the Sauté button on the Instant Pot and stir in the chicken meat and garlic. Stir for 3 minutes until the garlic becomes fragrant.
2. Stir in the ginger and tomatoes. Season with salt and pepper to taste.
3. Pour in water to submerge the chicken.
4. Close the lid and seal off the vent.
5. Press the Manual button and adjust the cooking time to 15 minutes.
6. Do natural pressure release.
7. Once the lid is open, press the Sauté button and stir in the spinach leaves. Allow to simmer for 5 minutes.

Nutrition Values
(Calories:128; Total Fat: 6.2g; Carbs: 1.9g; Dietary Fiber: 0.5g; Protein: 15.6g)

Slow Cooked Spiced Whole Chicken

(Prep Time: 5 Mins |Total Time: 1H 5 Mins |Serves: 12)

Ingredients:
- 1 whole chicken
- 1 tsp. ground chillies
- 2 sprigs of thyme
- 1 onion, cut into wedges
- Salt and pepper to taste

Directions
1. Place all ingredients in the Instant Pot and massage the chicken to coat with the spices.
2. Pour a cup of water.
3. Close the lid and seal off the vent.
4. Press the Manual button and adjust the cooking time to 60 minutes.
5. Do natural pressure release.

Nutrition Values
(Calories:249; Total Fat: 17.9g; Carbs: 1.2g; Dietary Fiber: 0.5g; Protein: 21.7g)

Instant Pot Crispy Chicken

(Prep Time: 5 Mins |Total Time: 25 Mins |Serves: 8)

Ingredients:
- 2 lb. chicken wings
- 1 cup water
- Salt and pepper to taste
- 1 tbsp. paprika
- 1 tsp. rosemary leaves

Directions
1. Place all ingredients in the Instant Pot. Stir to combine everything. Give a good stir.
2. Close the lid and seal off the vent.
3. Press the Manual button and adjust the cooking time to 10 minutes.
4. Do natural pressure release.
5. Take the chicken out of the Instant Pot and place them in a baking sheet lined with foil.
6. Place in the oven and cook for 10 minutes at 400 degrees Fahrenheit.

Nutrition Values
(Calories:148; Total Fat: 4.1g; Carbs: 1.1g; Dietary Fiber: 0.4g; Protein: 25.2g)

Basil and Tomatoes Chicken Soup

(Prep Time: 5 Mins |Total Time: 25 Mins |Serves: 4)

Ingredients:
- 8 plum tomatoes, chopped
- ¼ cup fresh basil leaves
- 4 skinless chicken breasts, halved
- Salt and pepper to taste
- 5 cups water

Directions
1. Place all ingredients in the Instant Pot. Give a good stir to mix everything.
2. Close the lid and make sure that the vent is sealed.
3. Press the Manual button and adjust the cooking time to 20 minutes.
4. Do natural pressure release.

Nutrition Values
(Calories:431; Total Fat: 7.2g; Carbs: 22.4g; Dietary Fiber:15.3g; Protein: 61.7g)

Chicken and Cauliflower Rice

(Prep Time: 5 Mins |Total Time: 25 Mins |Serves: 4)

Ingredients:
- 1 cauliflower head
- 1 tablespoon coconut oil
- 2 cups left-over chicken, shredded
- Salt and pepper to taste
- 1 scallion, chopped

Directions
1. Place a trivet or a steamer basket in the Instant Pot and pour a cup of water.
2. Place the cauliflower head on the trivet and close the lid. Seal off the vent.
3. Press the Steam button and adjust the cooking time to 10 minutes.
4. Do quick pressure release.
5. Once the lid is open, take the cauliflower out and place in a food processor. Pulse until the texture is a bit grainy or similar to rice grains.
6. Drain the Instant Pot and take the trivet out.
7. Press the Sauté button and heat the oil, sauté the chicken meat and season with salt and pepper to taste.
8. Stir in the cauliflower rice and add the scallions. Continue stirring for 3 minutes.
9. Garnish with parsley if desired.

Nutrition Values
(Calories:581; Total Fat: 16.5g; Carbs: 4.2g; Dietary Fiber: 2.4g; Protein: 98.5g)

Mexican Shredded Chicken

(Prep Time: 5 Mins |Total Time: 45 Mins |Serves: 12)

Ingredients:
- 3 lb. chicken breasts
- 1 tbsp. chilli powder
- ¼ tsp. cumin powder
- ½ tsp. paprika
- ½ tsp. dried oregano

Directions
1. Place all ingredients in the Instant Pot and give a good stir.
2. Season with salt and pepper and pour a cup of water.
3. Close the lid and seal off the vent.
4. Press the Manual button and adjust the cooking time to 35 minutes.
5. Do natural pressure release
6. Once the lid is open, take the chicken breasts out and shred using forks.
7. Place the shredded chicken back into the pot and press the Sauté button. Allow to simmer for 5 minutes.
8. Garnish with cilantro and lime wedges before serving.

Nutrition Values
(Calories:196; Total Fat: 10.5g; Carbs: 0.1g; Dietary Fiber: 0g; Protein: 23.6g)

Eggplant and Chicken Sauté

(Prep Time: 5 Mins |Total Time: 18 Mins |Serves: 6)

Ingredients:
- 1 tbsp. coconut oil
- 1 lb. ground chicken
- 1 tsp. red pepper flakes
- Salt and pepper to taste
- 3 eggplants, sliced

Directions
1. Press the Sauté button in the Instant Pot and heat the coconut oil.
2. Stir in the ground chicken for 3 minutes until lightly golden.
3. Add the remaining ingredients.
4. Close the lid and make sure that the vent is sealed.
5. Press the Manual button and adjust the cooking time to 5 minutes.
6. Do natural pressure release.
7. Once the lid is open, press the Sauté button and allow to simmer for another 5 minutes or until the sauce has reduced.

Nutrition Values
(Calories:202; Total Fat: 8.9g; Carbs: 17.5g; Dietary Fiber: 9.3g; Protein: 16.7g)

Chapter 5 Red Meat Recipes

Easy Caribbean Beef

(Prep Time: 5 Mins |Total Time: 60 Mins |Serves: 4)

Ingredients:
- 2 pounds Beef Roast
- 1 tsp Thyme
- 1 tsp grated Ginger
- 1 tsp Garlic Powder
- 6-8 Whole Cloves
- ¼ tsp Pepper
- 1 cup Water

Cooking Direction
1. Combine all of the herbs and spices and rub the mixture into the beef.
2. Stick the cloves into the meat and then place the meat inside the IP.
3. Pour the water around (not over!) the meat.
4. Put the lid on.
5. Seal and set the IP to MANUAL.
6. Cook on HIGH for 45 minutes.
7. Release the pressure quickly.
8. Shred with two forks and serve as desired.
9. Enjoy!

Nutrition Values

(Calories 700| Total Fats 12g | Carbs: 1.3g| Protein 55g | Dietary Fiber: 0.2g)

Marjoram Leg of Lamb

(Prep Time: 5 Mins |Total Time: 80 Mins |Serves: 4)

Ingredients:
- 6 pounds Leg of Lamb
- 1 Bay Leaf
- ½ tsp Sage
- 2 tsp Marjoram
- 2 Garlic Cloves, minced
- 2 tbsp Arrowroot
- 1 ½ tbsp Olive Oil
- 1 ½ cups Homemade Chicken Broth

Cooking Direction
1. Set your Instant Pot to SAUTE and heat the oil in it.
2. Combine the garlic and herbs and rub into the meat.
3. Add the lamb in the Instant Pot and sear until brown on all sides.
4. Pour the chicken broth over the meat and place the bay leaf inside.
5. Close the lid, seal, and set the IP to MEAT/STEW.
6. Cook for 60 minutes and then release the pressure quickly.
7. Open the lid and whisk in the arrowroot.
8. Set the IP to SAUTE and cook until thickened.
9. Serve and enjoy!

Nutrition Values

(Calories 620| Total Fats 26g | Carbs: 3g| Protein 55g | Dietary Fiber: 0g)

Tomato Brisket

(Prep Time: 5 Mins |Total Time: 6 hours and 20 Mins |Serves: 6)

Ingredients:
- 1 cup Beef Stock
- 3 pounds Beef Brisket
- 28 ounces canned diced Tomatoes
- 4 Garlic Cloves, minced
- 1 Onion, chopped
- 2 tbsp Olive Oil

Cooking Direction
1. Heat half of the oil in the IP on SAUTE.
2. Add the beef and sear it on all sides until it becomes brown.
3. Transfer to a plate.
4. Add the remaining oil.
5. When hot, add the onions and cook for 3 minutes.
6. Add the garlic and cook for 1 more minute.

7. Add the tomatoes and broth.
8. Return the meat to the IP and close the lid.
9. Set the IP to SLOW COOK and cook for 6 hours on LOW.
10. Do a quick pressure release.
11. Serve and enjoy!

Nutrition Values

(Calories 505| Total Fats 19g | Carbs: 10g| Protein 70g | Dietary Fiber: 2g)

Dijon Meatloaf

(Prep Time: 5 Mins |Total Time: 45 Mins |Serves: 4)

Ingredients:

- 1 pound Ground Beef
- 2 tbsp organic Dijon Mustard
- 1 Egg
- 1 small Onion, diced
- ½ cup Almond Flour
- ½ tsp Garlic Powder
- ½ tsp Thyme
- ¼ cup Tomato Sauce
- 1 cup Water

Cooking Direction

1. Pour the water into the IP and lower the trivet.
2. In a large bowl, place the remaining ingredients.
3. Mix with your hand until incorporated.
4. Grease a loaf pan and press the meatloaf mixture in it.
5. Place the loaf pan on the trivet and close the lid.
6. Seal the pot and choose MANUAL.
7. Cook for 35 minutes.
8. Do a quick pressure release.
9. Serve and enjoy!

Nutrition Values

(Calories 410| Total Fats 10g | Carbs: 38g| Protein 41g | Dietary Fiber: 3g)

Pork Chops with Brussel Sprouts

(Prep Time: 5 Mins |Total Time: 35 Mins |Serves: 4)

Ingredients:

- 1 pound Pork Chops
- 1 cup sliced Carrots
- 1 tbsp Arrowroot
- 1 cup Homemade Chicken Stock
- 2 cups Brussel Sprouts
- ½ tsp Thyme
- 2 Garlic Cloves, minced
- 1 cup sliced Onions
- 1 tbsp Ghee
- Pinch of Pepper

Cooking Direction

1. Set your Instant Pot to SAUTE and add the ghee.
2. When melted, add the pork chops and cook until they become browned. Transfer to a plate.
3. Add the onions and cook for 3 minutes.
4. Add the garlic and cook for another minute.
5. Pour the broth over and return the chops to the pot.
6. Close the lid and set the IP to MANUAL.
7. Cook for 15 minutes on HIGH.
8. Do a quick pressure release and open the lid.
9. Stir in the carrots and Brussel sprouts and close the lid again.
10. Cook on HIGH for 3 minutes.
11. Do a quick pressure release and transfer the pork and veggies to a plate.
12. Whisk the arrowroot into the pot and cook on SAUTE until thickened.
13. Drizzle the sauce over the pork and veggies.
14. Serve and enjoy!

Nutrition Values

(Calories 440| Total Fats 32g | Carbs: 12g| Protein 28g | Dietary Fiber: 2g)

Shredded Chipotle Pork

(Prep Time: 5 Mins |Total Time: 40 Mins |Serves: 4)

Ingredients:
- 1 ½ pounds Pork Shoulder
- 2 Chipotle Peppers, diced
- ½ tsp Cumin
- ½ tsp Garlic Powder
- ½ tsp Paprika
- ¼ tsp Pepper
- 1 cup Homemade Beef Broth
- 1 Onion, sliced

Cooking Direction
1. Season the pork well with the spices and place it in the Instant Pot.
2. Arrange the onion slices and peppers on top and pour the broth over.
3. Close the lid and set the IP to MEAT/STEW.
4. Cook for 55 minutes.
5. Let the float valve drop on its own and then open the lid.
6. Let the pork sit for 10 minutes before serving.
7. Enjoy!

Nutrition Values
(Calories 580| Total Fats 40g | Carbs: 2g| Protein 49g | Dietary Fiber: 1g)

Flavorful Braised Chuck

(Prep Time: 5 Mins |Total Time: 80 Mins |Serves: 4)

Ingredients:
- 1 cup Homemade Beef Broth
- 2 Rosemary Sprigs
- 1 Thyme Sprig
- 1 Onion, sliced
- 2 pounds Chuck Roast
- 2 tsp minced Garlic
- 2 tbsp Ghee
- Pinch of Cumin
- Pinch of Black Pepper

Cooking Direction
1. Set your Instant Pot to SAUTE and melt the coconut oil in it.
2. Add the onions and saute for 3 minutes.
3. Stir in the garlic and cook for another minute.
4. Add the beef and sear it on all sides, until is lightly browned.
5. Pour the broth over and add the herbs.
6. Close the lid and set the IP to MANUAL.
7. Cook on HIGH for 50-6 minutes, depending on your desired doneness.
8. Do a natural pressure release.
9. Serve and enjoy!

Nutrition Values
(Calories 660| Total Fats 50g | Carbs: 3g| Protein 47g | Dietary Fiber: 0.5g)

Balsamic Beef Roast

(Prep Time: 5 Mins |Total Time: 65 Mins |Serves: 6)

Ingredients:
- 1 cup Homemade Beef Broth
- 1 tbsp Olive Oil
- 4 tbsp Balsamic Vinegar
- 3 pounds Beef Roast
- 1 tbsp Coconut Oil, melted
- ½ tsp Thyme
- ½ tsp Garlic Powder
- ¼ tsp Onion Powder
- Pinch of Pepper

Cooking Direction
1. Heat the olive oil in your Instant Pot on SAUTE.
2. Add the beef and sear on all sides until it becomes browned.
3. Whisk together the remaining ingredients and pour the mixture over the beef.
4. Close the lid and set the IP to MANUAL.
5. Cook on HIGH for 40 minutes.
6. Do a natural pressure release.
7. Serve and enjoy!

Nutrition Values
(Calories 530| Total Fats 23g | Carbs: 0.5g| Protein 75g | Dietary Fiber: 0g)

Lamb with Tomatoes and Zucchini

(Prep Time: 5 Mins |Total Time: 3 hours and 40 Mins |Serves: 4)

Ingredients:

- 1 pound Lamb, cut into cubes
- 1 tbsp Ghee
- 2 Large Tomatoes, diced
- 1 Zucchini, diced
- ½ Yellow Onion, diced
- 2 Carrots, sliced
- ½ cup Coconut Milk
- 1 tsp minced Garlic
- ½ tsp ground Ginger

Cooking Direction

1. In a bowl, combine the coconut milk, lamb, ginger, and garlic.
2. Cover and let sit in the fridge for 3 hours.
3. Dump the lamb along with the coconut milk into the IP.
4. Add the tomatoes, carrots, onion, and ghee, and close the lid.
5. Set the IP to MANUAL and cook on HIGH for 20 minutes.
6. Open the lid with a quick pressure release and stir in the zucchini.
7. Set the IP to SAUTE and cook for 5 minutes.
8. Serve and enjoy!

Nutrition Values

(Calories 340| Total Fats 22g | Carbs: 12.5g| Protein 24g | Dietary Fiber: 3g)

Basil Beef with Yams

(Prep Time: 5 Mins |Total Time: 45 Mins |Serves: 6)

Ingredients:

- 2 Yams, peeled and chopped
- 1 ½ cups Homemade Bone Broth
- 3 Garlic Cloves, minced
- 2 ½ pounds Beef, cut into cubes
- 1 Bell Pepper, chopped
- 1 Onion, diced
- ½ tbsp dried Basil
- 3 tbsp Tomato Paste
- 1 tbsp Olive Oil

Cooking Direction

1. Heat the olive oil in the Instant Pot on SAUTE.
2. Add the onions and peppers and cook for 3 minutes.
3. Add the garlic and cook for one more.
4. Place the beef inside and cook it until it becomes browned.
5. Stir in the remaining ingredients and close the lid.
6. Set the IP to MANUAL and cook on HIGH for 30 minutes.
7. Do a quick pressure release.
8. Serve and enjoy!

Nutrition Values

(Calories 390| Total Fats 28g | Carbs: 2g| Protein 43g | Dietary Fiber: 1g)

Coconut Oil Pork Chops

(Prep Time: 5 Mins |Total Time: 25 Mins |Serves: 6)

Ingredients:

- 6 Pork Chops
- 1 cup Homemade Bone Broth
- 8 tbsp Coconut Oil
- 1 tbsp Olive Oil
- 1 tsp Whole30 Compliant Seasoning by choice

Cooking Direction

1. Season the pork chops with the seasoning.
2. Set the IP to SAUTE and heat the oil in it.
3. Add the pork chops and cook on both sides until they become browned.
4. Place the coconut oil on top and pour the broth over.
5. Close the lid and set the IP to MANUAL.
6. Cook for 12 minutes on HIGH.
7. Do a quick pressure release.
8. Serve and enjoy!

Nutrition Values

(Calories 430| Total Fats 38g | Carbs: 0g| Protein 22g | Dietary Fiber: 0g)

Cinnamon and Orange Pork Shoulder

(Prep Time: 5 Mins |Total Time: 70 Mins |Serves: 10)

Ingredients:

- 5 pounds Pork Shoulder
- 2 Bay Leaves
- 2 cups Fresh Orange Juice
- 2 Cinnamon Sticks
- 2 tbsp Olive Oil
- 1 Onion, chopped
- 1 Jalapeno Pepper, seeded and diced
- 2 tsp minced Garlic
- 1 tbsp Cumin
- 2 tsp Oregano
- ½ tsp Thyme
- ¼ tsp Garlic Powder
- ¼ tsp Pepper

Cooking Direction

1. Combine half of the oil and spices in a small bowl.
2. Rub the mixture into the meat.
3. Heat the remaining oil in the Instant Pot on SAUTE.
4. Add the meat and sear on all sides. Transfer to a plate.
5. Deglaze the pot with the orange juice and stir the remaining ingredients inside.
6. Add the pork shoulder and close the lid.
7. Set the Instant Pot on MANUAL.
8. Cook on HIGH for 40 minutes.
9. Let the pressure drop on its own.
10. Open the lid and transfer the meat to a cutting board.
11. Shred or slice and serve drizzled with the juices.
12. Enjoy!

Nutrition Values

(Calories 750| Total Fats 55g | Carbs: 14g| Protein 55g | Dietary Fiber: 3g)

Beef Ribs with Button Mushrooms

(Prep Time: 5 Mins |Total Time: 40 Mins |Serves: 4)

Ingredients:

- 2 pounds Beef Ribs
- 1 Onion, chopped
- 2 cups quartered Button Mushrooms
- 1 cup sliced Carrots
- 1 tsp minced Garlic
- 2 tbsp Olive Oil
- ¼ cup Tomato Sauce
- 2 ½ cups Homemade Bone Broth
- ¼ tsp Cumin
- ¼ tsp Pepper

Cooking Direction

1. Add the oil to the IP and set it to SAUTE.
2. When hot and sizzling, and the ribs and cook until they are browned.
3. Add the remaining ingredients and stir well to combine.
4. Close the lid and set the IP to MANUAL.
5. Cook on HIGH for 20 minutes.
6. Do a quick pressure release.
7. Serve and enjoy!

Nutrition Values

(Calories 525| Total Fats 29g | Carbs: 8g| Protein 533g | Dietary Fiber: 2.5g)

Chili Braised Lamb Chops

(Prep Time: 5 Mins |Total Time: 30 Mins |Serves: 4)

Ingredients:

- 1 Onion, diced
- 1 tsp minced Garlic
- 1 tsp Olive Oil
- 4 Lamb Chops
- 2 tbsp Chili Powder
- 14 ounces canned diced Tomatoes
- 2 tbsp Chili Powder
- ½ cup Homemade Beef Broth

Cooking Direction

1. Set the Instant Pot to SAUTE and add the oil.
2. When hot, add the onions and cook for 3 minutes.
3. Stir in the chili powder and garlic and cook for an additional minute.
4. Place the lamb chops inside and brown them on all sides.
5. Add the tomatoes and broth and stir to combine.

6. Close the lid and set the IP to MANUAL.
7. Cook on HIGH for 15 minutes.
8. Do a quick pressure release.
9. Serve and enjoy!

Nutrition Values

(Calories 442| Total Fats 23g | Carbs: 1g| Protein 45g | Dietary Fiber: 0.5g)

Pork with Rutabaga and Apples

(Prep Time: 5 Mins |Total Time: 3 hours and 40 Mins |Serves: 4)

Ingredients:

- 1 pound Pork Loin, cubed
- 1 tbsp Olive Oil
- 1 Onion, diced
- 1 ½ cup Homemade Beef Broth
- 2 Rutabagas, peeled and cubed
- 2 Apples, peeled and cubed
- 1 Celery Stalk, diced
- ½ tsp Cumin
- 1 tbsp dried Parsley
- ¼ tsp Thyme
- ½ cup sliced Leeks

Cooking Direction

1. Heat half of the oil in the IP on SAUTE.
2. Add the beef and cook until browned. Transfer to a plate.
3. Heat the remaining oil and add the onions, leeks, and celery.
4. Cook for 2-3 minutes.
5. Return the beef to the pot and stir in the herbs, spices, and broth.
6. Seal the IP and choose MANUAL.
7. Cook on HIGH for 10 minutes.
8. Do a quick pressure release and open the lid.
9. Stir in the apples and seal again.
10. Cook for another 5 minutes.
11. Do a quick pressure release and serve.
12. Enjoy!

Nutrition Values

(Calories 420| Total Fats 24g | Carbs: 2g| Protein 44g | Dietary Fiber: 1g)

Instant Pot Italian Beef

(Prep Time: 10 Mins |Total Time: 1H 40 Mins |Serves: 8)

Ingredients:

- 3 pound grass-fed chuck roast
- 6 cloves garlic
- 1 tsp marjoram
- 1 tsp basil
- 1 tsp oregano
- 1/2 tsp ground ginger
- 1 tsp onion powder
- 2 tsp garlic powder
- 1 tsp salt
- 1/4 cup apple cider vinegar
- 1 cup Homemade beef broth

Cooking Direction

1. Cut slits in the roast with a sharp knife and then stuff with garlic cloves.
2. In a bowl, whisk together marjoram, basil, oregano, ground ginger, onion powder, garlic powder and salt until well blended; rub the seasoning all over the roast and place it in your instant pot.
3. Add vinegar and broth and lock lid; cook on high for 90 minutes.
4. Release pressure naturally and then shred meat with a fork.
5. Serve along with cooking juices.

Nutrition Values

(Calories 174| Total Fats 9.2g | Carbs: 1.9g| Protein 21g | Dietary Fiber: 0.3g)

Instant Pot Beef and Sweet Potato Stew

(Prep Time: 10 Mins |Total Time: 35 Mins |Serves: 10)

Ingredients:

- 2 pounds ground beef
- 3 cups Homemade beef stock
- 2 sweet potatoes, peeled and diced
- 1 clove garlic, minced
- 1 onion, diced
- 1 (14-oz) can petite minced tomatoes
- 2 (14-oz) cans tomato sauce
- 3-4 tbsp. chili powder

- ¼ tsp. oregano
- 2 tsp. salt
- ½ tsp. black pepper
- Cilantro, optional, for garnish

Cooking Direction

1. Brown the beef in a pan over medium heat; drain excess fat and then transfer it to an instant pot.

2. Stir in the remaining ingredients and lock lid; cook on high for 25 minutes and then release pressure naturally.

3. Garnish with cilantro and serve warm.

Nutrition Values

(Calories 240| Total Fats 6.4g | Carbs: 15.1g| Protein 30.3g | Dietary Fiber: 3.5g)

Healthy Instant Pot Ground Beef Jalapeno Stew

(Prep Time: 25 Mins |Total Time: 4H 25 Mins |Serves: 6)

Ingredients:

- 1-1.5 pounds ground beef
- 1 red bell pepper, chopped
- 1 green bell pepper, chopped
- 2 jalapeños, finely diced
- 1 acorn squash, peeled and diced
- 2 zucchini, sliced
- 4 small carrots, sliced
- 3 green onions, thinly sliced
- 1 (28 ounce) can whole peeled tomatoes
- 4 tbsp. chili powder
- 1 (6 ounce) can tomato paste
- 1 (14 ounce) can tomato sauce

Cooking Direction

1. Brown ground beef in a pan over medium heat.

2. In an instant pot, combine the browned beef, bell peppers, Jalapeños, zucchinis, carrots, onions, and squash.

3. Add whole tomatoes and stir with a spatula to mix well.

4. Stir in chili powder along with the remaining ingredients and lock lid; cook on high for 25 minutes.

5. Serve over green salad.

Nutrition Values

(Calories 265| Total Fats 6.1 g | Carbs: 28.4g| Protein 27.9g | Dietary Fiber: 7.4g)

Beef Meatballs with Mushroom Sauce

(Prep Time:5 Mins |Cook Time:16 Mins |Servings: 4)

Ingredients:

- 2 pounds lean grass-fed ground beef
- 1 yellow onion, finely chopped
- 1 medium carrot, grated
- 2 large eggs
- 2 Tablespoons arrowroot powder
- 2 Tablespoons mustard
- 1 Tablespoon dried oregano
- ¼ cup fresh parsley, chopped
- 1 Tablespoon smoked or regular paprika
- Pinch of salt, pepper
- 2 cups homemade low-sodium beef broth
- 2 cups mushrooms
- ½ cup unsweetened coconut cream
- 2 Tablespoons olive oil

Cooking Direction

1. In a large bowl, add ground beef, onion, grated carrots, egg, arrowroot powder mustard, dried oregano, paprika, salt, and black pepper. Stir until combined.

2. Form ground beef mixture into meatballs. Set aside.

3. Press "Sauté" function on Instant Pot. Add the olive oil.

4. Once hot, place single layer of meatballs in pot. Cook until brown on all sides.

5. Pour beef broth, and mushrooms.

6. Close, seal the lid. Press "Manual" button. Cook on HIGH 16 minutes.

7. When done, naturally release pressure 10 minutes. Remove the lid.

8. Transfer meatballs to serving platter.

9. Use an immersion blender to pulse mushrooms until smooth. Stir in coconut cream, and parsley. Ladle mushroom sauce over meatballs. Serve.

Nutrition Values

(Calories: 514, Fat: 32.07g, Carbohydrates: 8.06g, Dietary Fiber: 1.4g, Protein: 46.88g)

Instant Pot Italian Pulled Pork Ragu

(Prep Time: 10 Mins |Total Time: 60 Mins |Serves: 5)

Ingredients:

- 1 pound pork tenderloin
- 1 teaspoon kosher salt
- black pepper, to taste
- 1 tsp olive oil
- 5 cloves garlic, minced
- 4 cups crushed tomatoes
- 1 cup roasted red peppers
- 2 sprigs fresh thyme
- 2 bay leaves
- 1 tbsp. chopped fresh parsley, divided

Cooking Direction

1. Season your pork with salt and pepper.
2. Set your instant pot on sauté mode and add oil; sauté garlic for about 2 minutes until tender and then add pork; brown for about 2 minutes per side and then stir in the remaining ingredients.
3. Lock lid and cook on high for 45 minutes.
4. Release the pressure naturally and serve.

Nutrition Values

(Calories 186| Total Fats 3g | Carbs: 13 g| Protein 22g | Dietary Fiber: 0g)

Jamaican Jerk Pork Roast – Low Carb & Whole 30

(Prep Time: 10 Mins |Total Time: 60 Mins |Serves: 10)

Ingredients:

- 4 pound pork shoulder
- 1 Tbsp. olive oil
- 1/4 cup Jamaican Jerk spice blend
- 1/2 cup Homemade beef broth

Cooking Direction

1. Rub your roast with oil and dust with spice blend; set an instant pot on sauté mode and brown roast on both sides; stir in broth and lock lid.
2. Cook on high for 45 minutes and then release pressure naturally.
3. Shred and serve.

Nutrition Values

(Calories 544| Total Fats 40.3g | Carbs: 0.1g| Protein 42.5g | Dietary Fiber: 0g)

Easy Taco Meat

(Prep Time: 3 Mins |Cook Time:14 Mins |Servings: 3)

Ingredients:

- 2 pounds organic, lean, grass-fed ground beef
- 4 Tablespoons olive oil or coconut oil
- 2 medium organic red onions, finely chopped
- 6 garlic cloves, minced
- 1 Tablespoon chili powder
- 1 Tablespoon dried oregano
- 1 Tablespoon dried basil
- ⅓ cup fresh cilantro, finely chopped
- 1 teaspoon regular paprika or smoked paprika
- 1 teaspoon cumin
- Pinch of salt, pepper

Cooking Direction

1. Press "Sauté" function on Instant Pot. Add the oil.
2. Once hot, add onion. Cook 3 minutes. Add garlic. Cook 2 minutes. Add ground beef. Cook until brown, stirring occasionally.
3. Add remaining ingredients, except cilantro. Stir well.
4. Lock, seal the lid. Press "Manual" button. Cook on HIGH 9 minutes.
5. When done, naturally release pressure. Remove the lid.
6. Press "Sauté" function. Simmer until most of liquid is reduced.
7. Transfer to bowl. Garnish with fresh cilantro. Serve.

Nutrition Values

(Calories 442, Fat: 34.2g, Carbohydrates: 6.3g, Dietary Fiber: 1.84g, Protein: 29.1g)

Beef Burgundy with Mushrooms

(Prep Time:10 Mins |Cook Time:42 Mins |Servings: 3)

Ingredients:

- 2 pounds organic beef chuck roast, cut into bite-sized pieces
- 3 Tablespoons almond flour
- 3 Tablespoons olive oil, avocado oil, or coconut oil
- 4 garlic cloves, minced
- 1 yellow onion, finely chopped
- 1 cup of red wine
- ½ cup homemade low-sodium beef broth
- 1 teaspoon fresh thyme
- 4 carrots, peeled, cut into bite-sized pieces
- 1 ½ cups mushrooms, sliced
- 2 bay leaves
- Pinch of salt, pepper

Cooking Direction

1. Season beef pieces with salt, pepper. Lightly coat with almond flour.
2. Press "Sauté" function on Instant Pot. Add the olive oil.
3. Once hot, add onions. Cook 3 minutes. Add garlic. Cook 2 minutes. Add beef pieces. Sear on all sides. Remove and set aside.
4. Deglaze Instant Pot with red wine. Scrape up any brown bits along bottom. Simmer, reduce wine by half.
5. Return beef to Instant Pot. Stir in broth, thyme, carrots, mushroom, bay leaves.
6. Lock, seal the lid. Press "Manual" button. Cook on HIGH 40 minutes.
7. When done, naturally release pressure 10 minutes, then quick release remaining pressure. Remove the lid. Remove bay leaves.
8. Season. Transfer to platter. Serve.

Nutrition Values

(Calories 288, Fat: 15.89g, Carbohydrates: 5.07g, Dietary Fiber: 1.5g, Protein: 35g)

Fajita Steak Bowl

(Prep Time:5Mins |Cook Time: 12Mins |Servings: 3)

Ingredients:

- 2½ pounds organic fajita steak, cut into bite-sized pieces
- 4 avocados, peeled, nut removed, diced
- 2 Tablespoons olive oil
- 4 garlic cloves, minced
- 1 teaspoon chili powder
- 1 Tablespoon fresh lime juice
- 1 cup organic low-sodium beef broth
- Pinch of salt, pepper

Cooking Direction

1. Press "Sauté" function on Instant Pot. Add the olive oil.
2. Once hot, add garlic and sauté 2 minutes.
3. Add steak pieces. Cook until almost brown.
4. Add remaining ingredients. Stir well.
5. Lock, seal the lid. Press "Manual" button. Cook on HIGH 10 minutes.
6. When done, quick release pressure. Remove the lid.
7. Press "Sauté" function. Simmer until most of liquid evaporates.
8. Transfer steak pieces to a bowl with diced avocado. Serve.

Nutrition Values

(Calories: 603, Fat: 40.3g, Carbohydrates: 13.5g, Dietary Fiber: 9.1g, Protein: 48.8g)

Garlic and Rosemary Rib Eye Roast

(Prep Time:20Mins |Cook Time:40Mins |Servings: 3)

Ingredients:

- 2 pound boneless organic rib eye beef roast, cut into large pieces
- 2 medium onions, sliced
- 4 garlic cloves, minced
- 2 Tablespoons olive oil
- 2 Tablespoons ghee, melted
- 2 cups mushrooms, sliced
- ¼ cup fresh rosemary
- ¼ cup fresh parsley, finely chopped
- Pinch of salt, pepper

- 1 cups homemade beef broth or water

Cooking Direction

1. Season beef chunks with salt and pepper.
2. In a bowl, combine parsley, rosemary, garlic, and melted ghee. Mix well.
3. Press "Sauté" function on Instant Pot. Add 2 tablespoons of olive oil.
4. Add beef pieces. Sear on all sides. Transfer beef pieces to a cutting board, brush with garlic and herb mixture.
5. Add remaining 2 tablespoons olive oil with sliced onions. Cook until lightly browned, stirring occasionally. Turn off "Sauté" function on Instant Pot.
6. Add mushrooms and beef broth to Instant Pot. Return beef roast pieces to pot.
7. Lock, seal the lid. Press "Manual" button. Cook on HIGH 40 minutes.
8. When done, naturally release pressure. Remove the lid.
9. Remove beef from Instant Pot. Transfer to platter.
10. Use an immersion blender to puree sauce. Pour over beef chunks. Serve.

Nutrition Values

(Calories 445, Fat: 22g, Carbohydrates: 11g,

Dietary Fiber: 2g, Protein: 52g)

Wine and Coffee Beef Stew

(Prep Time: 5Mins |Cook Time:25 Mins |Servings: 4)

Ingredients:

- 2½ pounds organic grass-fed beef chuck stew meat, cut into bite-sized chunks
- 3 Tablespoons olive oil, coconut oil, avocado oil, or ghee
- 2 Tablespoons organic capers
- 2 garlic cloves, minced
- 3 cups of homemade freshly brewed coffee
- 1 cup of homemade organic low-sodium beef bone broth
- 2 cups of fresh organic mushrooms, sliced
- ⅔ cups organic red cooking wine
- 1 medium onion, finely chopped
- 2 Tablespoons arrowroot powder
- Pinch of salt, pepper

Cooking Direction

1. Press "Saute" function on Instant Pot. Add the oil.
2. Once hot, working in batches if necessary, add stewing beef, sear on all sides. Remove and set aside.
3. Add garlic, onion, and mushrooms to Instant Pot. Cook until lightly softened, stirring occasionally. Turn off "Sauté" function on your Instant Pot.
4. Return browned stew meat. Stir in capers, brewed coffee, beef broth, red cooking wine, salt, and pepper.
5. Lock, seal the lid. Press "Manual" button. Cook on HIGH 25 minutes.
6. When done, allow full natural release. Remove the lid.
7. Press "Sauté" function on Instant Pot. Sprinkle the arrowroot powder and allow to simmer until the liquid is reduced and thickens. Transfer beef back to Instant Pot. Stir to coat. Transfer to platter. Serve.

Nutrition Values

(Calories 242, Fat: 13 g, Carbohydrates: 1.35g,

Dietary Fiber: 0.3g, Protein: 30g)

Meatloaf with Pumpkin Barbecue Sauce

(Prep Time:13Mins |Cook Time:20 Mins |Servings: 4)

Meatloaf Ingredients:

- 2½ pounds of organic grass-fed lean ground beef
- 1 cup organic pureed pumpkins
- ½ red onion, finely chopped
- 2 eggs
- 3 garlic cloves, minced
- 1 Tablespoon smoked paprika
- Pinch of salt, pepper
- 1 teaspoon organic cinnamon powder
- 1 teaspoon chili powder

Pumpkin Barbecue Glaze Ingredients:

- 1 cup organic pureed pumpkins
- 2 Tablespoons Worcestershire sauce
- 2 Tablespoons organic lectin-free mustard

- 2 Tablespoons apple cider vinegar
- ½ cup molasses
- 1 Tablespoon parsley, oregano, or thyme, ½ teaspoon of salt
- 2 teaspoons organic ground cinnamon powder

Cooking Direction
1. In a bowl, add and mix all the pumpkin barbecue glaze ingredients until well combined. Set aside.
2. In another large bowl, add meatloaf ingredients. Stir until well combined.
3. Form beef mixture into a loaf, and place on a sheet of aluminum foil. Pour pumpkin sauce over meatloaf. Fold aluminum foil over meatloaf.
4. Add 1 cup of water, and trivet to Instant Pot. Place meatloaf on top of trivet.
5. Lock, seal the lid. Press "Manual" button. Cook on HIGH 20 minutes.
6. When done, quick release pressure. Remove the lid.
7. Remove meatloaf from foil. Allow to rest 5 minutes before slicing. Serve.

Nutrition Values
(Calories 489, Fat: 26.61g, Carbohydrates: 20.33g, Dietary Fiber: 1.9g, Protein: 45.95g)

Sloppy Joes

(Prep Time:10Mins |Cook Time:4 Mins |Servings: 4)

Ingredients:
- 2½ pounds organic grass-fed lean ground beef
- 1 large onion, finely chopped
- 2 Tablespoons olive oil
- ¼ cup Worcestershire sauce
- ¼ cup low-sodium coconut aminos
- 1 teaspoon chili powder, 1 teaspoon paprika, Pinch of salt, pepper
- ¼ cup red wine vinegar
- Sauce ingredients: 1 x 8-ounce can of beets
- 1 cup organic pumpkin puree, 1 Tablespoon balsamic vinegar
- 2 Tablespoons fresh lime juice, 1 cup carrots, diced
- 4 garlic cloves, minced, 1 cup chicken broth or water
- ⅓ cup dried basil, ⅓ cup dried parsley

Cooking Direction
1. Add sloppy joe sauce ingredients to blender/food processor. Blend until smooth.
2. Press "Sauté" function on Instant Pot. Add the olive oil.
3. Once hot, add onions. Cook 4 minutes.
4. Add ground beef to Instant Pot. Cook until no longer pink, stirring occasionally.
5. Stir in Worcestershire sauce, coconut aminos, chili powder, paprika, red wine vinegar, salt, and black pepper.
6. Lock, seal the lid. Press "Manual" button. Cook on HIGH 3 minutes.
7. When done, naturally release pressure 15 minutes, then quick release remaining pressure. Remove the lid.
8. Press "Sauté" function. Simmer until liquid reduces. Transfer to platter. Serve.

Nutrition Values
(Calories: 437, Fat: 25.03g, Carbohydrates: 11.23g, Dietary Fiber: 2.8g, Protein: 45.15g)

Pork Ribs with Sauerkraut

(Prep Time: 5 Mins |Total Time: 40 Mins |Serves: 2)

Ingredients:
- ½ pound Pork Ribs
- 5 ounces Kielbasa, sliced
- 1 tsp Brown Sugar
- 1 tbsp Olive Oil
- 10 ounces Sauerkraut
- ¼ tsp Pepper
- 1/3 cup Water

Cooking Direction
1. Heat the oil in the IP and add the pork ribs.
2. Cook until browned on both sides.
3. Add the remaining ingredients and stir well to combine.
4. Close the lid and set the IP to MANUAL.
5. Cook for 15 minutes on HIGH.
6. Do a natural pressure release.
7. Serve and enjoy!

Nutrition Values
(Calories 400| Total Fats 27g | Carbs: 9g | Protein 28g| Dietary Fiber: 0g)

Mongolian Beef

(Prep Time: 5 Mins |Total Time: 25 Mins |Serves: 2)

Ingredients:

- 2/3 pound Flank Steak
- 1 Carrot, shredded
- ½ tsp minced Garlic
- 1/3 cup Soy Sauce
- ½ tsp minced Ginger
- ¼ cup Brown Sugar
- 1 tbsp Olive Oil
- 5 tbsp Water
- 2 tbsp Cornstarch

Cooking Direction

1. Slice the beef into strips.
2. In the IP, combine the soy sauce, ginger, sugar, garlic, oil, and half of the water.
3. Stir in the flank slices and carrot.
4. Close the lid and set to IP to MANUAL.
5. Cook on HIGH for 7 minutes.
6. Release the pressure naturally.
7. Whisk together the remaining water and cornstarch and stir into the sauce.
8. Cook on SAUTE until thickened.
9. Serve and enjoy!

Nutrition Values

(Calories 480| Total Fats 17g | Carbs: 29g | Protein 51g| Dietary Fiber: 1g)

Instant Beef and Noodles

(Prep Time: 5 Mins |Total Time: 60 Mins |Serves: 2)

Ingredients:

- ½ pound Boneless Chuck
- 1 tbsp Oil
- 8 ounces Noodles
- 1 Garlic Clove, minced
- ¼ Onion, chopped
- 1 cup Water

Cooking Direction

1. Cut the beef into cubes.
2. Heat the oil in the IP and add the onion and garlic.
3. Cook for 2 minutes.
4. Add beef and cook until browned on all sides.
5. Pour the water over and cook on MANUAL for 25 minutes.
6. Do a quick pressure release.
7. Add the noodles and cook for 4 more minutes.
8. Release the pressure quickly.
9. Serve and enjoy!

Nutrition Values

(Calories 620| Total Fats 27g | Carbs: 26g | Protein 54g| Dietary Fiber: 1g)

Beef Taco Pie with Cheese

(Prep Time: 5 Mins |Total Time: 20 Mins |Serves: 2)

Ingredients:

- ½ pound Ground Beef
- 6 ounces Mexican Cheese Blend
- ½ packet Taco Seasoning
- 3 Tortillas
- 1/4 cup Refried Beans
- 1 cup Water

Cooking Direction

1. Pour the water into the IP ad lower the trivet.
2. In a greased baking dish, place one tortilla.
3. Combine the remaining ingredients in a bowl.
4. Place ½ of the mixture on top of the tortilla.
5. Place another tortilla on top and arrange the remaining filling.
6. Top with the third tortilla.
7. Place the dish in the IP and close the lid.
8. Cook on MNAUAL for 12 minutes.
9. Do a quick pressure release.
10. Serve and enjoy!

Nutrition Values

(Calories 360| Total Fats 19g | Carbs: 29g | Protein 25g| Dietary Fiber: 6g)

Beef Brisket with Veggies

(Prep Time: 5 Mins |Total Time: 70 Mins |Serves: 2)

Ingredients:

- 2/3 pound Beef Brisket
- 3 Red Potatoes, chopped
- 2 tbsp Olive Oil
- 1 cup chopped Carrots
- 1 Garlic Clove, minced
- ½ Onion, chopped
- 1 Celery Stalk, chopped
- 1 Bay Leaf
- 1 ½ tbsp Worcestershire Sauce
- 1 cup Beef Broth

Cooking Direction

1. Heat half of the oil in the IP and add the beef.
2. Sear on all sides and then transfer to a plate.
3. Heat the remaining oil and add the onions and celery.
4. Cook for 2 minutes and then add the garlic.
5. Cook for another minute.
6. Stir in the veggies and pour the broth over.
7. Top with the beef, add the bay leaf and drizzle the Worcestershire sauce over.
8. Close the lid and cook for 45 minutes on MANUAL.
9. Serve and enjoy!

Nutrition Values

(Calories 400| Total Fats 18g | Carbs: 10g | Protein 28g| Dietary Fiber: 1g)

BBQ Baby Back Ribs

(Prep Time: 5 Mins |Total Time: 55 Mins |Serves: 2)

Ingredients:

- 1 ½ pounds Baby Back Ribs
- 1 cup Beer
- 6 ounces Barbecue Sauce
- 2 tsp Olive Oil
- ¼ tsp Onion Powder
- ¼ tsp Pepper
- ¼ tsp Garlic Salt
- ¼ tsp Paprika

Cooking Direction

1. Cut the baby ribs into pieces.
2. Combine the spices in a small bowl and rub into the meat.
3. Heat the oil in the IP on SAUTE and brown the meat on all sides.
4. Pour the beer over and close the lid.
5. Cook on HIGH for 25 minutes.
6. Do a quick pressure release.
7. Discard the liquid and brush the ribs with BBQ sauce.
8. Cook on SAUTE until sticky. Serve and enjoy!

Nutrition Values

(Calories 230| Total Fats 7g | Carbs: 36g | Protein 8g| Dietary Fiber: 0.5g)

Pork Roast with Cinnamon and Cranberries

(Prep Time: 5 Mins |Total Time: 75 Mins |Serves: 2)

Ingredients:

- 1 tbsp Apple Cider Vinegar
- 2/3 pound Pork Roast
- 6 ounces Fresh Cranberries
- 1 tbsp chopped Herbs
- 10 ounces Beef Broth
- 1 tbsp Honey
- 1 tbsp Butter
- ¼ tsp Garlic Powder
- ¼ tsp Cinnamon

Cooking Direction

1. Melt the butter in the Instant Pot on SAUTE.
2. Add the pork and sear on all sides.
3. Add the rest of the ingredients and stir well to combine.
4. Close the lid and set the IP to MANUAL.
5. Cook for 55 minutes on HIGH.
6. Do a natural pressure release. Serve and enjoy!

Nutrition Values

(Calories 680| Total Fats 38g | Carbs: 30g | Protein 45g| Dietary Fiber: 1.5g)

Rosemary-Flavored Lamb with Carrots

(Prep Time: 5 Mins |Total Time: 35 Mins |Serves: 2)

Ingredients:
- ¾ pound Boneless Lamb, chopped
- 1 tbsp Flour
- ½ cup sliced Carrots
- 2 Rosemary Spigs
- 1 tbsp Olive Oil
- 1 ½ cup Beef Stock
- 1 ½ tsp minced Garlic
- Salt and Pepper, to taste

Cooking Direction
1. Season the lamb with some salt and pepper.
2. Heat the oil in the IP on SAUTE.
3. Add the lamb and sear on all sides.
4. Whisk together the flour and stock and pour over the lamb.
5. Add the remaining ingredients and close the lid.
6. Cook on HIGH for 20 minutes.
7. Do a quick pressure release.
8. Serve and enjoy!

Nutrition Values
(Calories 290| Total Fats 2g | Carbs: 14.3g | Protein 40g| Dietary Fiber: 3g)

Honey and Mustard Pork Chops

(Prep Time: 5 Mins |Total Time: 20 Mins |Serves: 2)

Ingredients:
- 1 pound Pork Chops
- ½ tbsp Maple Syrup
- 2 tbsp Honey
- 1 ½ tbsp Dijon Mustard
- ½ tsp grated Ginger
- ¼ tsp Cinnamon
- Pinch of Pepper
- ¼ tsp Salt
- 2/3 cup Beef Broth

Cooking Direction
1. Grease the IP with cooking spray and place the pork chops inside.
2. Cook until browned on all sides.
3. In a bowl, whisk together the remaining ingredients.
4. Pour the mixture over the pork.
5. Closet the lid and cook on HIGH for 15 minutes.
6. Do a quick pressure release.
7. Serve and enjoy!

Nutrition Values
(Calories 800| Total Fats 55g | Carbs: 20g | Protein 50g| Dietary Fiber: 1g)

Round Steak with Veggies

(Prep Time: 5 Mins |Total Time: 40 Mins |Serves: 2)

Ingredients:
- ½ pound Round Steak, cubed
- 1 tbsp Butter
- 1 Carrot, sliced
- 2 Bell Peppers, chopped
- ½ cup of Mushroom Slices
- 2 Potatoes, cubed
- ½ tsp Garlic Salt
- 1 ½ cup Beef Broth
- 1 tbsp Flour
- ¼ tsp Onion Powder

Cooking Direction
1. Toss the steak cubes with flour.
2. Melt the butter in the IP on SAUTE.
3. Add the steak and cook until browned on all sides.
4. Stir in the remaining ingredients and close the lid.
5. Cook on MEAT/STEW for about half an hour.
6. Serve and enjoy!

Nutrition Values
(Calories 306| Total Fats 9g | Carbs: 21g | Protein 35g| Dietary Fiber: 1g)

Beef Bourguignon

(Prep Time: 5 Mins |Total Time: 75 Mins |Serves: 2)

Ingredients:

- ½ cup Red Wine
- 1 cup Beef Broth
- 1 Sweet Potato, cubed
- 1 Garlic Clove, minced
- ½ Onion, chopped
- ½ pound Beef, cubed
- 1 tbsp Olive Oil
- 2 Carrots, chopped
- 1 tbsp Maple Syrup
- ¼ pound Bacon Tips

Cooking Direction

1. Heat the oil in the IP and add the onion.
2. Cook for 3 minutes.
3. Add the garlic and saute for 1 minute.
4. Add the beef and cook until it becomes browned on all sides.
5. Stir in the bacon and cook for an additional minute.
6. Add the rest of the ingredients and stir the mixture well to combine.
7. Close the lid and set the IP to MANUAL.
8. Cook on HIGH for 30 minutes.
9. Do a natural pressure release.
10. Serve and enjoy!

Nutrition Values

(Calories 700| Total Fats 34g | Carbs: 30g | Protein 57g| Dietary Fiber: 2g)

Pepperoncini Pot Roast

(Prep Time: 5 Mins |Total Time: 55 Mins |Serves: 2)

Ingredients:

- 2/3 pound Beef Roast
- 2 tbsp Butter
- 1 packet Gravy Mix
- ½ cup Pepperoncini Juice
- 2 Pepperoncini, chopped
- ½ cup Beef Broth

Cooking Direction

1. Whisk together the butter, juice, broth, and gravy mix, in the IP.
2. Stir in the pepperoncini.
3. Place the beef inside and close the lid.
4. Set the Instant Pot to MANUAL.
5. Cook on HIGH for 40 minutes.
6. Do a natural pressure release.
7. Serve and enjoy!

Nutrition Values

(Calories 750| Total Fats 32g | Carbs: 12g | Protein 80g| Dietary Fiber: 1g)

Feta Lamb Meatballs

(Prep Time: 5 Mins |Total Time: 25 Mins |Serves: 2)

Ingredients:

- 1 small Egg
- ¼ cup crumbled Feta Cheese
- ¼ tsp Oregano
- ¼ Onion, diced
- ½ pound ground Lamb
- ¼ cup Breadcrumbs
- 2 tbsp Olive Oil
- ½ tbsp chopped Mint
- ½ Bell Pepper, chopped
- 14 ounces canned diced Tomatoes
- 1 cup Water
- 1 tsp minced Garlic

Cooking Direction

1. In a bowl, combine the meat, feta, breadcrumbs, mint, half of the garlic, and egg.
2. Make meatballs out of the mixture.
3. Heat half of the oil in the IP on SAUTE and add the meatballs.
4. Cook for a few minutes, until browned. Transfer to a plate.
5. Heat the remaining oil and saute the onions, peppers and remaining garlic for 3 minutes.
6. Add the tomatoes and place the meatballs inside.
7. Close the lid and cook on HIGH for 8 minutes.
8. Do a quick pressure release.
9. Serve and enjoy!

Nutrition Values

(Calories 380| Total Fats 17g | Carbs: 17 | Protein 39g| Dietary Fiber: 1g)

Corned Beef with Cabbage

(Prep Time: 5 Mins |Total Time: 60 Mins |Serves: 2)

Ingredients:
- 2/3 pound Corned Beef
- 2 Carrots, sliced
- 1 Celery Stalk, chopped
- 2 cups Water
- ½ Onion, chopped
- ½ tbsp favorite Seasoning
- 2/3 pound Red Cabbage, chopped
- ½ pound Potatoes, chopped

Cooking Direction
1. Combine the beef, water, and seasoning, in the IP.
2. Close the lid and cook on HIGH for 40 minutes.
3. Do a quick pressure release.
4. Stir in the remaining ingredients and close the lid.
5. Cook for 6 more minutes on HIGH.
6. Do a quick pressure release.
7. Serve and enjoy!

Nutrition Values

(Calories 465| Total Fats 30g | Carbs: 18g | Protein 35g| Dietary Fiber: 3g)

Herbed Lamb with Tomatoes

(Prep Time: 5 Mins |Total Time: 50 Mins |Serves: 2)

Ingredients:
- 2 Lamb Shanks
- 1 tsp minced Garlic
- 1 Large Carrot, sliced
- 1 cup chopped Tomatoes
- 1 tbsp chopped Oregano
- 1 Thyme Sprig
- 1 Rosemary Sprig
- 1 tbsp chopped Basil
- 2 tbsp Olive Oil
- ½ Red Onion, sliced
- 1 ½ cups Beef Stock

Cooking Direction
1. Heat the oil in the IP on SAUTE.
2. Add the onion and cook for 3 minutes.
3. Add the garlic and cook for one more.
4. Add the lamb shanks and cook them until browned on both sides.
5. Add the carrots and herbs, and pour the broth over.
6. Close the lid and choose the MANUAL cooking mode.
7. Cook for 20 minutes on HIGH.
8. Do a quick pressure release.
9. Add the tomatoes and close the lid again.
10. Cook on HIGH for 5-6 minutes more.
11. Release the pressure quickly and serve the lamb topped with the sauce.
12. Enjoy!

Nutrition Values

(Calories 700| Total Fats 38g | Carbs: 17g | Protein 65| Dietary Fiber: 1g)

Creamy Pork Sausage

(Prep Time: 5 Mins |Total Time: 15 Mins |Serves: 2)

Ingredients:
- ½ pound Pork Sausage
- 1 ½ tsp minced Garlic
- 1 cup Milk
- 1 tbsp Butter
- 2 tbsp Flour

Cooking Direction
1. Melt the butter in the IP on SAUTE and cook the garlic in it for about a minute.
2. Add the pork sausage and cook while breaking it with a wooden spoon, until it turns brown.
3. Whisk together the milk and flour and pout over.
4. Close the lid and select MANUAL.
5. Cook on HIGH for 6 minutes.
6. Do a quick pressure release.
7. Serve and enjoy!

Nutrition Values

(Calories 500| Total Fats 30g | Carbs: 17g | Protein 26g| Dietary Fiber: 1g)

Grape Jelly Meatballs

(Prep Time: 5 Mins |Total Time: 35 Mins |Serves: 2)

Ingredients:

- ½ pound ground Beef
- 2 tbsp Cornstarch
- ¼ cup Grape Jelly
- ½ tsp Garlic Salt
- ½ tsp Paprika
- ½ cup mild Salsa
- 1 Egg

Cooking Direction

1. In a bowl, combine the beef, cornstarch, salt, and egg.
2. Make meatballs out of the mixture.
3. Whisk the rest of the ingredients in the IP and drop the meatballs inside.
4. Close the lid and hit MANUAL.
5. Cook the meatballs on LOW for 30 minutes.
6. Do a quick pressure release.
7. Serve and enjoy!

Nutrition Values

(Calories 580| Total Fats 19g | Carbs: 26g | Protein 50g| Dietary Fiber: 1g)

Leg of Lamb with Potatoes

(Prep Time: 5 Mins |Total Time: 30 Mins |Serves: 2)

Ingredients:

- 2 pounds Leg of Lamb
- 1 Bay Leaf
- ½ tsp Marjoram
- ½ tsp Sage
- 1 pound Potatoes, chopped
- ½ tsp Thyme
- 1 ½ tbsp Cornstarch
- 2 cups Beef Broth
- 2 tbsp Water
- 1 tsp minced Garlic
- 2 tbsp Olive Oil
- Salt and Pepper, to taste

Cooking Direction

1. Combine the oil, herbs and spices, in a bowl.
2. Rub he mixture over the lamb.
3. Sear on all sides on SAUTE and then pour the broth around the meat.
4. Close the lid and cook for 40 minutes on HIGH.
5. Do a quick pressure release and add the potatoes.
6. Cook for 12 more minutes.
7. Release the pressure quickly and transfer the lamb and potatoes to a plate.
8. Whisk the cornstarch and water and stir the mixture into the IP.
9. Serve the gravy over the lamb and potatoes.
10. Cook on SAUTE for a few minutes.
11. Serve and enjoy!

Nutrition Values

(Calories 740| Total Fats 55g | Carbs: 19g | Protein 57g| Dietary Fiber: 1g)

Pork Tacos

(Prep Time: 5 Mins |Total Time: 45 Mins |Serves: 2)

Ingredients:

- 6 ounces ground Pork
- 1 tbsp chopped Cilantro
- ¼ tsp Salt
- ¼ Red Onion, chopped
- 1 tbsp Butter
- ½ cup Tomato Sauce
- 2 Corn Tortillas
- 1/2 cup shredded Lettuce

Cooking Direction

1. Combine the meat, onion, cilantro, butter, tomato sauce, and salt, in the Instant Pot.
2. Close the lid and cook on HIGH for 20 minutes.
3. Do a quick pressure release.
4. Divide the sauce between the tortillas and top with shredded lettuce.
5. Serve and enjoy!

Nutrition Values

(Calories 250| Total Fats 9g | Carbs: 20g | Protein 30g| Dietary Fiber: 1g)

Pork Cutlets in a Plum Sauce

(Prep Time: 5 Mins |Total Time: 40 Mins |Serves: 2)

Ingredients:

- ½ pound Ground Pork
- 1 Egg
- 2 tbsp Breadcrumbs
- 1 tsp chopped Parsley
- ½ tsp Thyme
- 1 tbsp Cornstarch
- 1 tbsp Oil
- 1 tbsp Flour
- 6 ounces Plums, pitted
- 2 tsp minced Ginger
- 1 tbsp Sugar
- 1/3 cup Lemon Juice
- 3 tbsp Water

Cooking Direction

1. In a bowl, combine the first 6 ingredients.
2. Form cutlets out of the mixture.
3. Heat the oil in the IP on SAUTE.
4. Add the cutlets and cook until they are browned on all sides.
5. In a blender, blend the remaining ingredients, until smooth.
6. Pour the plum sauce over the cutlets and close the lid.
7. Cook on HIGH for 8 minutes.
8. Do a quick pressure release.
9. Serve and enjoy!

Nutrition Values

(Calories 240| Total Fats 10g | Carbs: 15g | Protein 23g| Dietary Fiber: 1g)

Pot Roast in a Peach Sauce

(Prep Time: 5 Mins |Total Time: 45 Mins |Serves: 2)

Ingredients:

- ¼ Onion, sliced
- 1 Garlic Clove, minced
- ¾ pound Beef Roast
- 2 cups Peach Juice
- 1 tbsp Cornstarch
- 1 tbsp Olive Oil

Cooking Direction

1. Heat the oil in the IP on SAUTE.
2. Add the meat and cook until browned on all sides.
3. Add the onions and garlic and cook for two minutes.
4. Pour the juice over and close the lid.
5. Cook on MANUAL for 40 minutes.
6. Do a natural pressure release.
7. Transfer the meat t a plate.
8. Whish the cornstarch into the sauce and cook on SAUTE until thickened.
9. Serve the roast with the sauce.
10. Enjoy!

Nutrition Values

(Calories 325| Total Fats 11g | Carbs: 22g | Protein 38g| Dietary Fiber: 1g)

Gingery Lamb Shanks

(Prep Time: 5 Mins |Total Time: Mins |Serves: 2)

Ingredients:

- 2 Lamb Shanks
- ¼ Onion, sliced
- 1 ½ cups Broth
- 1 tbsp Coconut Aminos
- 1 Garlic Clove, minced
- 1 tbsp minced Ginger
- 2 tsp Fish Sauce
- 4 dried Figs, chopped
- 2 tbsp Coconut Oil

Cooking Direction

1. Melt half of the coconut oil in the IP on SAUTE.
2. Add the lamb and cook until browned on both sides. Transfer to a plate.
3. Melt the remaining oil and add the onions.
4. Cook for 2 minutes.
5. Add the garlic and ginger and cook for another minute.
6. Stir in the fish sauce, coconut aminos, figs, and broth.
7. Return the lamb to the plate and close the lid.

8. Cook on HIGH for 40 minutes.
9. Do a natural pressure release.
10. Serve the sauce over the lambs.
11. Enjoy!

Nutrition Values
(Calories 740| Total Fats 40g | Carbs: 30g | Protein 50g| Dietary Fiber: 3.3g)

Maple and Balsamic Beef
(Prep Time: 5 Mins |Total Time: 35 Mins |Serves: 2)

Ingredients:
- ¾ pound Chuck Steak
- 1 tbsp Oil
- ¼ cup Balsamic Vinegar
- ½ cup Maple Syrup
- ¾ cup Bone Broth
- ½ tsp ground Ginger
- ½ tsp Salt

Cooking Direction
1. Slice the beef into ½-inch thin slices.
2. Season with the salt and ginger.
3. Heat the oil in the IP and cook the beef until browned.
4. In a bowl, whisk together the remaining ingredients.
5. Pour over the beef and close the lid.
6. Set the Instant Pot to MANUAL.
7. Cook on HIGH for 25 minutes.
8. Do a quick pressure release.
9. Serve and enjoy!

Nutrition Values
(Calories 650| Total Fats 30g | Carbs: 36g | Protein 60g| Dietary Fiber: 0g)

Beef Lasagna
(Prep Time: 5 Mins |Total Time: 40 Mins |Serves: 2)

Ingredients:
- ½ pounds Ricotta Cheese
- 1/2 pound Ground Beef
- 4 ounces Lasagna Noodles
- 10 ounces Pasta Sauce
- ¼ cup Water
- ¼ Onion, diced
- 1 Garlic Clove, minced
- 1 Egg
- 1 tbsp Oil
- 1/3 cup shredded Mozzarella Cheese
- ¼ cup grated Parmesan Cheese
- ½ tsp Italian Seasoning

Cooking Direction
1. Heat the oil in the IP and add the onions.
2. Cook for 2 minute and then stir in the garlic.
3. Cook for 1 minute.
4. Add the beef and cook until browned.
5. Stir in the pasta sauce and water.
6. Transfers to a bowl.
7. In another bowl, combine the ricotta, egg, seasoning, and parmesan.
8. Pour some of the beef sauce at the bottom of the IP.
9. Arrange 1/3 of the noodles over and top with 1/3 of the sauce.
10. Place ½ of the ricotta over.
11. Repeat once more.
12. Top the final layer with the remaining beef sauce and sprinkle the mozzarella over.
13. Close the lid and cook on MANUAL for 7 minutes.
14. Do a quick pressure release.
15. Serve and enjoy!

Nutrition Values
(Calories 410| Total Fats 22g | Carbs: 247g | Protein 25g| Dietary Fiber: 3g)

Pork Fried Rice
(Prep Time: 5 Mins |Total Time: 40 Mins |Serves: 2)

Ingredients:
- 1 cup Rice
- 1 Egg, beaten
- 1 Carrot, shredded
- ¼ Onion, diced
- ¼ cup diced Green Bens
- 5 ounces sliced Pork Loin

- 1 tbsp Soy Sauce
- 2 tbsp Oil
- 2 cups Water

Cooking Direction
1. Heat half of the oil in the IP on SAUTE.
2. Add the pork and cook until browned.
3. Transfer the pork to a plate.
4. Heat the remaining oil and add onions and carrot.
5. Cook for 2 minutes.
6. Stir in the egg and cook until set.
7. Return the pork and stir in the rest of the ingredients.
8. Close the lid and cook on RICE for 10 minutes.
9. Do a quick pressure release.
10. Fluff with a fork before serving.
11. Serve and enjoy!

Nutrition Values
(Calories 550| Total Fats 2g | Carbs: 80g | Protein 22g| Dietary Fiber: 3g)

Meat-Stuffed Peppers

(Prep Time: 5 Mins |Total Time: 35 Mins |Serves: 2)

Ingredients:
- 2 ounces ground Chilies, chopped
- 2 tbsp Butter
- ½ Onion, chopped
- 2 Large Bell Peppers
- 1 tsp minced Garlic
- ¼ cup Corn Kernels
- 1/3 cup shredded Cheddar Cheese
- ¼ pound ground Beef
- ¼ pound ground Pork
- ¼ tsp Oregano
- 1 ½ cups Water

Cooking Direction
1. Melt the butter in the IP on SAUTE and add the onions.
2. Cook until they soften, about 5 minutes.
3. Add the garlic and cook for another minute.
4. Add the pork and beef and cook until they become browned.
5. Transfer the mixture to a bowl and stir in the chilies, cheese, and corn.
6. Divide the mixture between the peppers.
7. Pour the water into the IP and lower the rack.
8. Place the peppers on the rack and close the lid.
9. Cook on HIGH for 10 minutes.
10. Do a quick pressure release.
11. Serve and enjoy!

Nutrition Values
(Calories 395| Total Fats 32g | Carbs: 17g | Protein 34g| Dietary Fiber: 1.5g)

Tomato Pork Chops Stew

(Prep Time: 5 Mins |Total Time: 40 Mins |Serves: 6)

Ingredients:
- 6 pork chops
- 1 onion, chopped
- 1 bay leaf
- ½ cup tomato paste
- Salt and pepper to taste

Directions
1. Place all ingredients in the Instant Pot. Pour a cup of water and give a good stir.
2. Close the lid and seal off the vent.
3. Press the Meat/Stew button and adjust the cooking time to 35 minutes.
4. Do natural pressure release.

Nutrition Values
(Calories:357; Total Fat: 17.5g; Carbs: 6.5g; Dietary Fiber: 3.2g; Protein: 41.5g)

Instant Pot Pork Roast

(Prep Time: 5 Mins |Total Time: 1H 20 Mins |Serves: 9)

Ingredients:
- ½ tsp. dried thyme leaves
- 1 tbsp. minced garlic
- Salt and pepper to taste
- 4 lb. boneless pork loin roast
- 3 tbsp. extra virgin olive oil

Directions

1. Rub the thyme leaves, garlic, salt, and pepper on the surface of the pork loin.
2. Press the Sauté button on the Instant Pot and heat the oil.
3. Sear all sides of the pork until lightly golden.
4. Pour enough water into the Instant Pot such that the pork is halfway submerged.
5. Close the lid and seal off the vent.
6. Press the Manual button and adjust the cooking time to 60 minutes.
7. Do natural pressure release.

Nutrition Values
(Calories:288; Total Fat: 10.2g; Carbs: 0.9g; Dietary Fiber: 0.2g; Protein: 45.3g)

Pork Chops and Peppers

(Prep Time: 5 Mins |Total Time: 60 Mins |Serves: 4)

Ingredients:
- 4 thick pork chops
- Salt and pepper to taste
- 1 onion, chopped
- 2 cloves of garlic, minced
- 2 red and yellow bell peppers, seeded and julienned

Directions
1. Press the Sauté button on the Instant Pot and drop the pork chops in. Let pork sear for at least 3 minutes on each side. Sprinkle with salt and pepper to taste.
2. Stir in onions and garlic. Pour a cup of water and scrape the bottom to remove the browning.
3. Close the lid and make sure that the vent is sealed.
4. Press the Manual button and adjust the cooking time to 40 minutes.
5. Do natural pressure release.
6. Once the lid is open, press the Sauté button and stir in the bell peppers. Allow to simmer until the sauce thickens and the vegetables are cooked.

Nutrition Values
(Calories:145; Total Fat:3.3g; Carbs:4.3g; Dietary Fiber: 2.1g; Protein: 23.9g)

Simple Pulled Pork

(Prep Time: 5 Mins |Total Time: 60 Mins |Serves: 4)

Ingredients:
- 4 pork chops, deboned
- 1 onion, sliced
- 5 cloves of garlic, minced
- 1 ½ cups water
- Salt and pepper to taste

Directions
1. Place all ingredients in the Instant Pot.
2. Close the lid and seal off the vent.
3. Press the Meat/Stew button and adjust the cooking time to 50 minutes.
4. Do natural pressure release.
5. Once the lid is open, take out the pork chops and shred using two forks. Place the shredded meat back into the Instant Pot and press the Sauté button. Allow to simmer for 5 minutes until the sauce is absorbed by the meat.

Nutrition Values
(Calories:339; Total Fat: 17.4g; Carbs: 2.4g; Dietary Fiber: 1.6g; Protein: 40.7g)

Seared Pork Chops with Peppers

(Total Time:40 Mins |Serves: 4)

Ingredients:
- 4 pork loin chops
- 1 onion, sliced
- 3 cloves of garlic, minced
- 1 of each yellow bell pepper, red bell pepper, and green bell pepper, seeded and julienned
- 2 tbsp. capers

Directions
1. Press the Sauté button on the Instant Pot and stir in the pork. Continue stirring until the pork has rendered some of its fat.

2. Stir in the onion and garlic until fragrant. Season with salt and pepper to taste.
3. Pour a cup of water to add moisture and scrape the bottom of the pot to remove the browning.
4. Close the lid and seal the vent.
5. Press the Manual button and adjust the cooking time to 25 minutes.
6. Do natural pressure release.
7. Once the lid is open, press the Sauté button and stir in the bell peppers. Allow to simmer for 5 minutes.

Nutrition Values
(Calories:371; Total Fat: 17.7g; Carbs: 9.2g; Dietary Fiber: 5.4g; Protein: 41.8g)

Mushroom Pork Chops
(Prep Time: 5 Mins |Total Time: 50 Mins |Serves: 4)

Ingredients:
- 4 pork chops
- 3 cloves of garlic, chopped
- 1 onion, chopped
- ½ lb. fresh mushrooms, sliced
- Salt and pepper to taste
- ¾ cup water

Directions
1. Press the Sauté button on the Instant Pot and stir allow the pork chops to sear for at least 3 minutes on all sides.
2. Stir in the garlic and onions until fragrant.
3. Add the rest of the ingredients.
4. Scrape the bottom to remove the browning at the bottom of the pot.
5. Close the lid and seal the vent.
6. Press the Meat/Stew button and adjust the cooking time to 35 minutes.
7. Do natural pressure release.

Nutrition Values
(Calories:525; Total Fat: 17.9g; Carbs: 27.7g; Dietary Fiber: 19.5g; Protein: 46.8g)

Thai Coconut Pork
(Prep Time: 5 Mins |Total Time: 40 Mins |Serves: 7)

Ingredients:
- 1 tbsp. coconut oil
- 1 ¼ lb. pork shoulder, cut into chunks
- 1 thumb-size ginger, sliced
- 2 ½ cups coconut milk, freshly squeezed if possible
- 1 lemongrass stalk, pounded

Directions
1. Place all ingredients in the Instant Pot.
2. Close the lid and seal the vent.
3. Press the Meat/Stew button and adjust the cooking time to 35 minutes. Do natural pressure release.
4. Garnish with cilantro on top.

Nutrition Values
(Calories:435; Total Fat: 36.8g; Carbs: 5.6g; Dietary Fiber: 3.2g; Protein: 22.7g)

Hawaiian Kalua Pork
(Prep Time: 5 Mins |Total Time: 1H 45 Mins |Serves: 10)

Ingredients:
- 5 lb. pork shoulder, bone-in
- 1 tsp salt
- ½ cup fresh pineapples, diced
- 1 tbsp. liquid smoke
- 2 cups water

Directions
1. Place all ingredients in the Instant Pot.
2. Close the lid and seal the vent.
3. Press the Meat/Stew button and adjust the cooking time to 1 hour and 30 minutes.
4. Do natural pressure release.
5. Once the lid is open, take the meat out and shred using two forks. Return the shredded meat into the pot and press the Sauté button. Allow to simmer for 10 minutes.

Nutrition Values
(Calories:613; Total Fat: 40.3g; Carbs: 1.9g; Dietary Fiber: 0.8g; Protein: 56.9g;)

Cajun Pork

(Prep Time: 5 Mins |Total Time: 1H 5 Mins |Serves: 8)

Ingredients:
- 5 lb. pork shoulder
- Salt and pepper to taste
- 4 tbsp organic Cajun spice mix
- 1 bay leaf
- 2 cups water

Directions
1. Place all ingredients in the Instant Pot.
2. Close the lid and seal the vent.
3. Press the Meat/Stew button and adjust the cooking time to 60 minutes.
4. Do natural pressure release.

Nutrition Values
(Calories:768; Total Fat: 50.2g; Carbs: 2.6g; Dietary Fiber: 2.3g; Protein: 71.5g)

Spicy Pork Stew with Spinach

(Prep Time: 5 Mins |Total Time: 41 Mins |Serves: 4)

Ingredients:
- 1 lb. pork butt, cut into chunks
- 1 onion, chopped
- 4 cloves of garlic, minced
- 1 cup coconut milk, freshly squeezed
- 1 cup spinach leaves, washed and rinsed

Directions
1. Press the Sauté button on the Instant Pot and Add the pork butt. Stir in the onions and garlic. Keep stirring for 3 minutes until the pork becomes lightly golden.
2. Pour in the coconut milk and season with salt and pepper to taste.
3. Close the lid and seal off the vent.
4. Press the Manual button and adjust the cooking time to 30 minutes.
5. Do natural pressure release.
6. Once the lid is open, press the Sauté button and stir in the spinach leaves. Allow to simmer for 3 minutes.

Nutrition Values
(Calories:458; Total Fat: 34.4g; Carbs: 7.2g; Dietary Fiber: 4.2g; Protein: 30.5g)

Easy Thai 5-Spice Pork Stew

(Prep Time: 5 Mins |Total Time: 45 Mins |Serves: 9)

Ingredients:
- 2 lb. pork butt, cut into chunks
- 2 tbsp. 5-spice powder
- 2 cups coconut milk, freshly squeezed
- 1 ½ tbsp sliced ginger
- 1 cup chopped cilantro

Directions
1. Place all ingredients in the Instant Pot.
2. Pour a cup of water and season with salt and pepper to taste.
3. Close the lid and seal off the vent.
4. Press the Manual button and adjust the cooking time to 40 minutes.
5. Do natural pressure release.

Nutrition Values
(Calories:398; Total Fat: 30.5g; Carbs: 4.4g; Dietary Fiber: 2.1g; Protein: 398g)

Pork Adobo

(Prep Time: 5 Mins |Total Time: 50 Mins |Serves: 10)

Ingredients:
- 4 lb. pork butt, cut into chunks
- 1 cup coconut aminos
- 1/3 cup lemon juice, freshly squeezed
- 2 cloves of garlic, minced
- 1 onion, quartered

Directions
1. Place all ingredients in the Instant Pot. Give a good stir and add a cup of water for added moisture.
2. Close the lid and make sure that the vent is sealed. Press the Manual button and adjust the cooking time to 45 minutes.
3. Do natural pressure release.

Nutrition Values
(Calories:496; Total Fat: 32.2g; Carbs: 2.7g; Dietary Fiber: 0.6g; Protein: 45.8g)

Asian Gingered Pork

(Prep Time: 5 Mins |Total Time: 50 Mins |Serves: 5)

Ingredients:
- 1 lb. pork shoulder, cut into chunks
- 1 onion, chopped
- 2 tbsp. ginger root, sliced
- 1 tbsp. coconut aminos
- 1 cup water

Directions
1. Place all ingredients in the Instant Pot. Give a good stir and season with salt and pepper to taste.
2. Close the lid and make sure that the vent is sealed. Press the Manual button and adjust the cooking time to 45 minutes.
3. Do natural pressure release.
4. Garnish with toasted sesame seeds and peanut oil if desired.

Nutrition Values
(Calories:254; Total Fat: 16.1g; Carbs: 2.6g; Dietary Fiber: 1.4g; Protein: 23.5g)

Pork and Cabbage Soup

(Prep Time: 5 Mins |Total Time: 55 Mins |Serves: 10)

Ingredients:
- 3 lb. pork butt, cut into chunks
- 1 thumb-size ginger, sliced
- Salt and pepper to taste
- 1 head cabbage, cut into quarters
- 1 scallion, green part only

Directions
1. Place the pork and ginger in the Instant Pot.
2. Season with salt and pepper to taste. Pour enough water until half of the meat is submerged.
3. Close the lid and seal off the vent. Press the Manual button and adjust the cooking time to 45 minutes.
4. Do natural pressure release.
5. Once the lid is open, press the Sauté button and stir in the cabbages and scallions. Simmer for another 5 minutes.

Nutrition Values
(Calories:383; Total Fat: 24.7g; Carbs: 4.6g; Dietary Fiber: 2.4g; Protein: 35.2g)

Chapter 6 Seafood Recipes

Lemony Salmon with Chard

(Prep Time: 5 Mins |Total Time: 10 Mins |Serves: 4)

Ingredients:
- 4 Salmon Fillets
- 8 Chard Leaves
- Juice of 1 Lemon
- 1 tbsp Olive Oil
- Pinch of Garlic Powder
- Pinch of Pepper
- 1 cup Water

Cooking Direction
1. Pour the water into the IP and lower the rack.
2. Grease a baking dish with the olive oil and place the salmon inside.
3. Drizzle the lemon juice over and season with pepper and garlic powder.
4. Top with the chard.
5. Place the baking dish on the rack and close the lid.
6. Cook on HIGH for 4 minutes.
7. Do a quick pressure release.
8. Enjoy!

Nutrition Values
(Calories 195| Total Fats 9g | Carbs: 1.8g| Protein 28g | Dietary Fiber: 0.5g)

Gingery Mahi-Mahi

(Prep Time: 5 Mins |Total Time: 15 Mins |Serves: 4)

Ingredients:
- 4 Mahi-Mahi Fillets
- 1-inch piece of Ginger, grated
- Juice of 1 Lime
- 1 tsp minced Garlic
- 1 cup of Water

Cooking Direction
1. Pour the water into the IP and lower the rack.
2. Place the mahi-mahi fillets in a baking dish.
3. Whisk together the ginger, garlic, and lime juice, in a bowl.
4. Pour over the mahi-mahi.
5. Place the baking dish on the rack and close the lid.
6. Set the IP to MANUAL and cook on HIGH for 5 minutes.
7. Do a quick pressure release.
8. Serve and enjoy!

Nutrition Values
(Calories 220| Total Fats 15g | Carbs: 1g| Protein 25g | Dietary Fiber: 0g)

Pistachio-Crusted Haddock

(Prep Time: 5 Mins |Total Time: 15 Mins |Serves: 2)

Ingredients:
- 2 Haddock Fillets
- 1/3 cup sliced Pistachios
- 1 tsp Organic Dijon Mustard
- 1 ½ tbsp Olive Oil
- ¼ tsp Garlic Powder
- Pinch of Black Pepper
- 1 cup Water

Cooking Direction
1. Pour the water into the IP and lower the rack.
2. Combine the olive oil, Dijon, garlic powder, and pepper.
3. Brush the mixture over the haddock.
4. Place the pistachios in a shallow bowl and coat the haddocks with them.
5. Place the haddock fillets on a greased or lined baking dish.
6. Place the dish on the rack and close the lid of the IP.
7. Cook on HIGH for 5 minutes.
8. Do a quick pressure release.
9. Serve and enjoy!

Nutrition Values
(Calories 310| Total Fats 18g | Carbs: 5g| Protein 42g | Dietary Fiber: 3g)

Shrimp Scampi

(Prep Time: 5 Mins |Total Time: 15 Mins |Serves: 4)

Ingredients:

- 1 ½ pounds Shrimp, peeled and deveined
- 2 tbsp Coconut Oil
- 1 tbsp chopped Parsley
- ¾ cup Homemade Chicken Broth
- 1 tsp minced Garlic
- Juice of 1 Lemon

Cooking Direction

1. Place the oil in the IP and melt it on SAUTE.
2. Add garlic and cook for 1 minute.
3. Add the shrimp and pour the broth over.
4. Close the lid and set the IP on MANUAL.
5. Cook on HIGH for a minute or two.
6. Do a quick pressure release.
7. Drizzle the lemon juice and sprinkle the parsley over.
8. Serve and enjoy!

Nutrition Values

(Calories 250| Total Fats 10g | Carbs: 3.5g| Protein 35g | Dietary Fiber: 0.2g)

Tilapia with Tomatoes and Kale

(Prep Time: 5 Mins |Total Time: 15 Mins |Serves: 4)

Ingredients:

- 4 Tilapia Fillets
- 2 tbsp Ghee
- 2 cups Homemade Chicken Broth
- 1 Onion, diced
- 2 cups diced Tomatoes
- 1 Carrot, sliced
- 2 cups chopped Kale
- 1 tsp minced Garlic
- 1 tbsp chopped Parsley
- 1 tbsp chopped Basil

Cooking Direction

1. Add the IP on SAUTE and melt the ghee.
2. Add the onions and cook for 3 minutes.
3. Stir in the garlic and cook for another minute.
4. Place the tomatoes and carrots inside and pour the broth over.
5. Place the tilapia inside the steamer basket and insert it inside.
6. Close the lid and cook on HIGH for 5 minutes.
7. Release the pressure quickly and transfer the tilapia to a plate.
8. Add the kale in the IP and set it to SAUTE.
9. Cook for 2 minutes.
10. Serve the veggies and kale on the side and drizzle the fish with the juices.
11. Enjoy!

Nutrition Values

(Calories 350| Total Fats 24g | Carbs: 6g| Protein 40g | Dietary Fiber: 2.2g)

Rosemary-Flavored Salmon

(Prep Time: 5 Mins |Total Time: 15 Mins |Serves: 2)

Ingredients:

- 2 Salmon Fillets
- 2 Rosemary Sprigs
- 1 tbsp Olive Oil
- 1 cup Homemade Veggie Broth

Cooking Direction

1. Pour the broth into the IP and place the rosemary sprigs inside.
2. Place the salmon fillets inside the steamer basket and drizzle with olive oil.
3. Lower the basket into the pot and put the lid on.
4. Close and seal and set the IP to MANUAL.
5. Cook on HIGH for 4 minutes.
6. Do a quick pressure release.
7. Serve and enjoy!

Nutrition Values

(Calories 185| Total Fats 8.5g | Carbs: 0g| Protein 27g | Dietary Fiber: 0g)

Shrimp Creole

(Prep Time: 5 Mins |Total Time: 10 Mins |Serves: 4)

Ingredients:

- 1 pound frozen Jumbo Shrimp
- 1 Onion, chopped
- 2 tsp minced Garlic
- 28 ounces canned diced Tomatoes
- 2 Celery Stalks, diced
- 1 tbsp Olive Oil
- 1 tbsp Tomato Paste
- ¼ tsp Thyme
- 1 Bell Pepper, diced

Cooking Direction

1. Heat the olive oil in the IP on SAUTE.
2. Add the onion, celery, and peppers, and cook for3 minutes.
3. Add the garlic and cook for another minute.
4. Stir in the remaining ingredients and close the lid.
5. Set the IP to MANUAL.
6. Cook on HIGH for 1 minute or two.
7. Do a quick pressure release.
8. Serve and enjoy!

Nutrition Values

(Calories 280| Total Fats 17g | Carbs: 3g| Protein 35g | Dietary Fiber: 1g)

Crab Cakes

(Prep Time: 5 Mins |Total Time: 15 Mins |Serves: 2)

Ingredients:

- 1 Carrot, shredded
- 1 cup Crab Meat
- ½ cup boiled and mashed Potatoes
- ¼ Onion, grated
- ¼ cup chopped Black Olives
- ¼ cup Almond Flour
- 1 tbsp Olive Oil
- 1 ½ cup canned diced Tomatoes
- ¼ cup Homemade Chicken Broth

Cooking Direction

1. In a bowl, combine the carrots, crab meat, potatoes, onion, black olives, and almond flour.
2. Mix with your hands to combine and shape into 2 patties.
3. Heat the oil in the IP on SAUTE.
4. Add the crab cakes and cook for about a minute per side.
5. Pour the broth and tomatoes over and close the lid.
6. Set the IP to HIGH and cook for an additional minute or two.
7. Do a quick pressure release.
8. Serve the crab with the tomato sauce.
9. Enjoy!

Nutrition Values

(Calories 300| Total Fats 8g | Carbs: 5g| Protein 18g | Dietary Fiber: 2g)

Simple Broccoli Mackerel

(Prep Time: 5 Mins |Total Time: 10 Mins |Serves: 4)

Ingredients:

- 4 Mackerel Fillets
- 10 ounces Broccoli Florets
- 1 tsp Garlic Powder
- 1 ½ cup Water

Cooking Direction

1. Sprinkle the mackerel with garlic powder and arrange them inside the steamer basket.
2. Place the broccoli florets on top.
3. Pour the water into the IP.
4. Lower the steamer basket into the pot.
5. Close the lid and choose MANUAL.
6. Cook on HIGH for 2 minutes.
7. Do a quick pressure release.
8. Serve and enjoy!

Nutrition Values

(Calories 130| Total Fats 8g | Carbs: 5g| Protein 16g | Dietary Fiber: 2g)

Salmon on Veggie Noodles

(Prep Time: 5 Mins |Total Time: 15 Mins |Serves: 4)

Ingredients:

- 4 Salmon Fillets
- 1 Zucchini, Spiralized
- 1 large Carrot, Spiralized
- 2 Potatoes, Spiralized
- 1 cup of Water
- 1 Thyme Sprig
- 2 tsp Olive Oil
- Pinch of Pepper

Cooking Direction

1. Pour the water into the Instant Pot and place the thyme inside.
2. In the steamer basket, arrange the veggies.
3. Place the salmon on top.
4. Drizzle with olive oil and sprinkle with pepper.
5. Lower the basket into the pot and close the lid.
6. Close the lid and hit STEAM.
7. Cook for 5 minutes.
8. Do a quick pressure release.
9. Serve and enjoy!

Nutrition Values

(Calories 310| Total Fats 13g | Carbs: 10g| Protein 40g | Dietary Fiber: 3.5g)

Hot Lemony Instant Pot Tilapia with Asparagus

(Prep Time: 15 Mins |Total Time: 2H 15 Mins |Serves: 6)

Ingredients:

- 6 tilapia filets
- 1 bundle of asparagus
- 12 tbsp. lemon juice
- Lemon pepper seasoning
- 3 tbsp. melted coconut oil

Directions:

1. Divide asparagus into equal amounts per each fillet.
2. Place each fillet in the center of a foil and sprinkle with about 1 tsp. of lemon pepper seasoning; drizzle with about 2 tbsp. of lemon juice and about ½ tbsp. melted coconut oil.
3. Top each filet with the asparagus and fold the foil to form a packet.
4. Repeat with the remaining ingredients and then place the packets into an instant pot.
5. Lock lid and cook on high for 15 minutes.

Nutrition Values

(Calories 181| Total Fats 11.5g | Carbs: 1.8g| Protein 27.3g | Dietary Fiber: 0.7g)

Instant Pot Thai Seafood Boil

(Prep Time: 10 Mins |Total Time: 4H 10 Mins |Serves: 4)

Ingredients:

- ½ pound snow crab
- ½ pound shrimp (in shells)
- 1 stalk lemongrass, outer layer and top inch removed
- 2 tsp ginger
- ¼ fresh mint, chopped
- 1 lime, cut in half
- 2 garlic cloves, minced
- 1 small onion, cut into quarters
- 2 cups coconut milk
- 32 ounces homemade broth
- ½ tsp. cumin
- 1 tsp. salt
- 1 celery stalks, cut into 1-inch pieces
- 1 pound sweet potatoes, cut into quarters
- 1 bell pepper, cut into 1-inch pieces
- 1 ear of sweet corn, cut into 3-inch chunks

Directions:

1. Smash the end of lemongrass stalk with a rolling pin until soft;
2. Transfer to an instant pot along with ginger, mint, lime, garlic, onion, coconut milk, broth, cumin and salt.
3. Stir to combine well and then add in celery and sweet potatoes. Lock lid and cook on high for 10 minutes.

4. Quick release pressure and then corn, bell pepper and seafood; lock lid and continue cooking for 10 minutes.
5. Release pressure naturally. Strain the liquid and serve.

Nutrition Values
(Calories 595| Total Fats 31.5g | Carbs: 52.6 g| Protein 17.7g | Dietary Fiber: 9.4g)

Instant Pot Citrus Tilapia

(Prep Time: 10 Mins |Total Time: 2H 10 Mins |Serves: 4)

Ingredients:
- 4 tilapia filets
- 1 10-ounce can mandarin oranges
- 2 tbsp. minced garlic
- 2 tbsp. coconut oil
- Sea salt and pepper

Directions:
1. Arrange fish side by side onto a large piece of aluminum foil and sprinkle with garlic and coconut oil evenly.
2. Top the fish with oranges and season with salt and pepper; fold the foil to wrap the content well.
3. Place in an instant pot and lock lid; cook on high for 15 minutes.

Nutrition Values
(Calories 201| Total Fats 9.3g | Carbs: 8.2 g| Protein 22.7g | Dietary Fiber: 0.6g)

Instant Pot Coconut Curry Shrimp

(Prep Time: 5 Mins |Total Time: 20 Mins |Serves: 4)

Ingredients:
- 1 pound shelled shrimp
- 15 ounces water
- 4 cups coconut milk
- ½ cup Thai red curry sauce
- ¼ cup cilantro
- 2½ tsp. garlic-lemon seasoning

Directions:
1. In your instant pot, combine water, coconut milk, red curry paste, cilantro, and lemon garlic seasoning;
2. Stir to mix well and lock lid; cook on high for 10 minutes and then release the pressure quickly.
3. Add shrimp and continue cooking for another 5 minutes and then release pressure naturally.
4. Serve garnished with cilantro.

Nutrition Values
(Calories 624| Total Fats 52.6g | Carbs: 13.5g| Protein 30.7g | Dietary Fiber: 4.7g)

Delicious Instant Pot Seafood Stew

(Prep Time: 15 Mins ||Total Time: 35 Mins |Serves: 6)

Ingredients:
- 2 pounds seafood (1 pound large shrimp & 1 pound scallops)
- 1/2 cup chopped white onion
- 3 garlic cloves, minced
- 1 tbsp. tomato paste
- 1 can (28 oz) crushed tomatoes
- 4 cups Homemade vegetable broth
- 1 pound yellow potatoes, diced
- 1 tsp. dried basil
- 1 tsp. dried thyme
- 1 tsp. dried oregano
- 1/8 tsp. cayenne pepper
- 1/4 tsp. crush red pepper flakes
- 1/2 tsp. celery salt
- salt and pepper
- handful of chopped parsley

Cooking Direction
1. Mix all ingredients, except seafood in your instant pot and lock lid; cook on high for about 15 minutes.
2. Quick release the pressure and then stir in seafood and continue; lock lid and cook on

high for 5 minutes and then let pressure come own on its own.

3. Serve hot with crusty gluten-free bread and garnished with parsley.

Nutrition Values
(Calories 323| Total Fats 5.3g | Carbs: 7.7g| Protein 57.1g | Dietary Fiber: 0.8g)

Sweet Chili Tilapia
(Prep Time:2Mins |Cook Time:3Mins |Servings: 4)

Ingredients:
- 4 boneless, skinless tilapia fillets
- 2 teaspoons olive oil
- ¼ cup coconut aminos
- Pinch of sea salt, pepper
- 2 teaspoons crushed red pepper flakes
- Handful fresh baby spinach, finely chopped
- Topping: ¼ cup homemade lectin-free chili sauce
- 1 teaspoon organic low-sodium coconut aminos

Cooking Direction
1. In a bowl, combine coconut aminos, black pepper, salt, red pepper flakes, and baby spinach. Mix well. Fully coat the tilapia fillets with the marinade.
2. In a second bowl, combine chili sauce, coconut aminos. Stir well. Set aside.
3. Press "Sauté" function on Instant Pot. Set to lowest temperature.
4. Add olive oil in pot. Once hot, add tilapia fillets. Sauté for 2 to 3 minutes per side, until cooked through. Transfer fillets to serving plate. Top with chili sauce. Serve.

Nutrition Values
(Calories: 118, Fat: 3.4g , Carbohydrates: 1g, Dietary Fiber: 0g, Protein: 21.1g)

Ginger Tilapia
(Prep Time:7Mins |Cook Time:8Mins |Servings: 4)

Ingredients:
- 1 pound tilapia fish fillets
- 3 Tablespoons low-sodium coconut aminos
- 2 Tablespoons white vinegar or apple cider
- 2 fresh garlic cloves, finely minced
- Pinch of salt, white pepper
- 1 Tablespoon olive oil
- 2 Tablespoons fresh ginger, julienned
- ¼ cup fresh scallions, julienned
- ¼ cup fresh cilantro, finely chopped

Cooking Direction
1. In a bowl, combine coconut aminos, white vinegar, minced garlic, salt, white pepper. Mix well.
2. Add tilapia fish. Gently spoon sauce over fish to coat evenly. Marinate 2 hours.
3. Add 2 cups water, and a steamer rack to the Instant Pot.
4. Remove fillets from marinade, place on steamer rack. Reserve marinade.
5. Close, seal the lid. Press "Manual" button. Cook on LOW 2 minutes.
6. When done, quick release pressure. Remove the lid.
7. Transfer fillets to serving dish. Discard the water.
8. Press "Sauté" function on Instant Pot. Add olive oil. Once hot, add julienned ginger, sauté a few seconds. Add scallions, cilantro. Sauté 2 minutes, until soft.
9. Stir in reserved marinade, allow to heat through. Spoon sauce over the fish. Serve.

Nutrition Values
(Calories: 176, Fat: 6g, Carbohydrates: 4.98g, Dietary Fiber: 0.53g, Protein: 25g)

Steamed Crab Legs
(Prep Time:5Mins |Cook Time:5Mins |Servings: 4)

Ingredients:
- 2 pounds cleaned snow crab legs
- Juice and zest from 1 medium fresh lemon
- ½ cup organic apple cider or white vinegar
- 2 Tablespoons ghee or coconut oil, melted
- 1 teaspoon smoked paprika or regular paprika
- Pinch of sea salt, white pepper

- 4 garlic cloves, crushed
- 2 cups of water
- Fresh parsley

Cooking Direction

1. In a bowl, combine lemon juice, lemon zest, apple cider, crushed garlic, ghee, paprika, salt, and black pepper. Mix well.
2. Add 2 cups of water to Instant Pot. Place steamer rack in pot.
3. Add snow crab legs on steamer rack. Drizzle with the lemon mixture.
4. Lock, seal the lid. Press "Manual" button. Cook on HIGH 2 minutes.
5. When done, quick release pressure. Remove the lid.
6. Transfer to serving platter. Garnish with fresh parsley.

Nutrition Values

(Calories: 176, Fat: 7.9g , Carbohydrates: 5g, Dietary Fiber: 0.4g, Protein: 19.2g)

Lemon Salmon

(Prep Time:5Mins |Cook Time:6Mins |Servings: 4)

Ingredients:

- 1 pound skin-on salmon fillets
- 1 Tablespoon ghee, melted
- Pinch of salt, white pepper
- ½ medium fresh lemon, thinly sliced
- Sprigs of fresh dill, fresh parsley, fresh tarragon, fresh basil
- 1 cup of water

Cooking Direction

1. Add 1 cup water, herbs, and a steamer rack to Instant Pot.
2. Season salmon with salt, white pepper. Drizzle with melted ghee.
3. Place fillets on steamer rack. Top with lemon slices.
4. Close, seal the lid. Press "Steam" button. Cook on HIGH 3 minutes.
5. When done, manually release pressure. Remove the lid.
6. Transfer to platter. Garnish with fresh herbs. Serve.

Nutrition Values

(Calories: 180, Fat: 10.2g, Carbohydrates: 0.7g, Dietary Fiber: 0.2g, Protein: 22.1g)

Chili-Lime Halibut

(Prep Time:5Mins |Cook Time:10Mins |Servings: 2)

Ingredients:

- 2 x 5-ouunce halibut fillets
- 1 cup of water
- Pinch of sea salt, pepper

Chili-Lime Sauce Ingredients:

- 1 medium jalapeno, seeded, peeled, finely chopped
- Juice from 1 fresh lime
- 2 garlic cloves, finely minced
- 1 Tablespoon melted coconut oil
- 1 Tablespoon freshly chopped parsley
- ½ teaspoon organic cumin
- 1 teaspoon organic smoked paprika
- Small pinch of sea salt

Cooking Direction

1. In a bowl, combine chili lime sauce ingredients. Stir well. Set aside.
2. Add 1 cup of water, and steamer rack to your Instant Pot.
3. Season halibut fillets with salt and pepper. Place fillets on top of steamer rack.
4. Lock, seal the lid. Press "Steam" setting. Cook on HIGH 5 minutes.
5. When done, manually release pressure. Remove the lid.
6. Transfer fillets to serving dish. Drizzle with chili sauce. Serve.

Nutrition Values

(Calories: 419, Fat: 25.56g, Carbohydrates: 15.g, Dietary Fiber: 8.9g, Protein: 32.75g)

Cajun Tilapia

(Prep Time:6Mins |Cook Time:7Mins |Servings: 4)

Ingredients:

- 4 x 6-ounce tilapia fillets
- 1 cup ghee or non-dairy butter, melted
- 2 teaspoons cayenne pepper
- 2 Tablespoons smoked paprika
- 2 teaspoons garlic powder
- 2 teaspoons onion powder
- Pinch of salt, pepper
- 1 teaspoon dried oregano
- 1 teaspoon dried thyme
- 1 cup of water

Cooking Direction

1. In a small bowl, combine cayenne pepper, smoked paprika, garlic powder, onion powder, salt, pepper, dried oregano, and dried thyme. Add melted ghee. Mix well.
2. Dip each tilapia fillet in seasoned ghee.
3. Add 1 cup of water, and steamer rack to Instant Pot. Place seasoned fillets on rack.
4. Close, seal lid. Press "Manual" button. Cook on HIGH 5 minutes.
5. When done, manually release pressure. Remove the lid.
6. Transfer to platter. Garnish with fresh parsley, lemon wedges. Serve.

Nutrition Values

(Calories: 383 , Fat: 26g , Carbohydrates: 9.31g, Dietary Fiber: 0.98g, Protein: 28.93g)

Spicy Shrimp and Cauliflower Grits

(Prep Time:4Mins |Cook Time:23Mins |Servings: 4)

Cauliflower Grits Ingredients:

- 4 cups grated cauliflower
- 1 cup unsweetened coconut milk
- 1 Tablespoon ghee or non-dairy butter
- ¼ cup homemade low-sodium chicken broth
- 1 teaspoon olive oil
- Pinch of salt

Shrimp Ingredients:

- 1 pound shrimp, peeled and deveined
- Pinch of sea salt, pepper
- ¼ teaspoon cayenne pepper
- ¼ teaspoon paprika
- 4 bacon slices, finely chopped
- ¼ cup onion, finely chopped
- 2 Tablespoons olive oil
- 1 Tablespoon fresh lemon juice
- Garnish: green onions, 8 cups fresh swiss chard, sliced

Cooking Direction

1. Press "Sauté" function on Instant Pot. Add 1 teaspoon of olive oil.
2. Once hot, add grated cauliflower. Toast 3 minutes, stirring frequently. Turn off "Sauté" function. Add remaining grit ingredients. Stir.
3. In a bowl, combine shrimp ingredients. Stir well. Place shrimp on top of grits.
4. Lock, seal the lid. Press "Manual" button. Cook on HIGH 10 minutes.
5. When done, naturally release pressure 10 minutes. Remove the lid.
6. In a serving dish or serving platter, add the swiss chard. Top with grits and shrimp. Garnish with green onions. Serve.

Nutrition Values

(Calories: 368, Fat: 23.68g, Carbohydrates: 8.46g, Dietary Fiber: 2.1g, Protein: 30.42g)

Lemon-Dill Salmon Fillet

(Prep Time:12Mins |Cook Time:8Mins |Servings: 4)

Ingredients:

- 1 cup of water
- 1 pound organic wild-caught salmon fillet
- 3 Tablespoons of ghee.
- 2 garlic cloves, minced
- 5 large fresh sprigs of dill
- 2 medium lemon, thinly sliced
- 12 asparagus, trimmed, sliced into 1-inch pieces
- Pinch of salt, pepper

Cooking Direction

1. Drizzle ghee over both sides of salmon. Season with salt, pepper.
2. Add water, fresh dill, and minced garlic to Instant Pot Add a trivet to pot.
3. Place salmon on top of trivet. Layer lemon slices over salmon fillet.
4. Close, seal the lid. Press "Manual" button. Cook on HIGH 4 minutes.
5. When done, quick release pressure. Remove the lid.
6. Transfer salmon to serving platter. Remove the trivet and discard the liquid.
7. Press "Sauté" function on Instant Pot. Add remaining 2 Tablespoons of ghee.
8. Add asparagus. Cook 4 minutes, season with salt and pepper.
9. Cut the salmon into 4 pieces, serve with asparagus.

Nutrition Values
(Calories: 260, Fat: 16.7g, Carbohydrates: 5.4g, Dietary Fiber: 2.7g, Protein: 24.6g)

Steamed Tomato Mussels
(Prep Time: 5 Mins |Total Time: 25 Mins |Serves: 2)

Ingredients:
- 2 pound Mussels
- 2 tbsp chopped Parsley
- 14 ounces canned stewed Tomatoes
- ¼ cup Dry White Wine
- 2 tsp minced Garlic
- 2 tsp Olive Oil
- 1 tsp Lemon Juice
- 8 ounces Clam Juice

Cooking Direction
1. Scrub the mussels clean and pull off the membrane-like string. Set aside.
2. Heat the oil in the IP on SAUTE.
3. Add garlic and cook for 1 minute.
4. Stir in the wine, tomatoes, parsley, and juices.
5. Bring the mixture to a boil then place the mussels inside.
6. Cook for 4 minutes on MANUAL.
7. Release the pressure naturally.
8. Serve the mussels with the sauce.
9. Enjoy!

Nutrition Values
(Calories 295| Total Fats 9g | Carbs: 21g | Protein 25g| Dietary Fiber: 3.5g)

White Bean Shrimp
(Prep Time: 5 Mins |Total Time: 5 hours | Serves: 2)

Ingredients:
- 1/3 pound Shrimp, peeled and deveined
- 1 Bay Leaf
- 1 ½ cup Fish Stock
- 1/3 pound dried Beans
- 1 small Bell Pepper, diced
- ½ Onion, diced
- ½ Celery Stalk, diced
- 1 Garlic Clove, minced

Cooking Direction
1. Place the beans in a bowl and fill with water.
2. Let soak for 4 hours.
3. Drain and rinse the beans.
4. Grease the IP with some cooking spray and set it to SAUTE.
5. Add the onions, peppers, and celery.
6. Cook for 3 minutes.
7. Add the garlic and cook for 1 minute.
8. Add the beans, stock, and bay leaf.
9. Cook for 15 minutes on POULTRY.
10. Do a quick pressure release and stir in the shrimp.
11. Close the lid and cook for another 6 minutes.
12. Release the pressure quickly and discard the bay leaf.
13. Serve and enjoy!

Nutrition Values
(Calories 530| Total Fats 25g | Carbs: 40g | Protein 35g| Dietary Fiber: 10g)

Salmon with Tartar Sauce

(Prep Time: 5 Mins |Total Time: 12 Mins |Serves: 2)

Ingredients:
- 2 Salmon Fillets
- 1 Lemon, sliced
- ¼ cup White Wine
- ½ Onion, sliced
- 1 cup Water

Sauce:
- 1/3 cup Mayonnaise
- 1/3 cup Greek Yogurt
- 2 tbsp chopped Green Onions
- 3 tbsp Pickle Relish
- 1 tbsp Lemon Juice
- 1 tbsp chopped Capers
- 1 tbsp chopped Parsley
- 1 tsp Dijon Mustard
- Salt and Pepper, to taste

Cooking Direction
1. Pour the water into the Instant Pot and lower the rack.
2. Arrange the salmon fillets on the rack and top with onion and lemon.
3. Drizzle with the white wine.
4. Close the lid and cook for 4 minutes on MANUAL.
5. Meanwhile, whisk together all of the sauce ingredients.
6. Do a quick pressure release.
7. Serve the salmon drizzled with the sauce.

Nutrition Values
(Calories 495| Total Fats 39g | Carbs: 8g | Protein 24g| Dietary Fiber: 1g)

Honey and Orange Salmon

(Prep Time: 5 Mins |Total Time: 12 Mins |Serves: 2)

Ingredients:
- 2 Salmon Fillets
- 2 tbsp Sriracha
- 2 tbsp Honey
- 1 tbsp Nanami Togarashi
- Juice of ½ Orange
- 1 tsp minced Ginger
- 1 tsp minced Garlic
- 1 ½ cups Water

Cooking Direction
1. Pour the water into the Instant Pot and lower the trivet.
2. Mix together the juices, honey, sriracha, garlic, Nanami Togarashi, and ginger.
3. Place the salmon fillets in a greased baking dish and pour the sauce over.
4. Place the dish on the trivet and close the lid.
5. Cook for 6 minutes on POULTRY.
6. Do a quick pressure release.
7. Serve with the sauce. Enjoy!

Nutrition Values
(Calories 230| Total Fats 1g | Carbs: 23g | Protein 32g| Dietary Fiber: 1g)

Jalapeno Cod with Olives and Tomatoes

(Prep Time: 5 Mins |Total Time: 13 Mins |Serves: 2)

Ingredients:
- 2 Cod Fillets
- 8 Black Olives, chopped
- ½ Yellow Onion, chopped
- 3 tbsp Lime Juice
- 1 tbsp Olive Oil
- 1 Garlic Clove, minced
- 2 tbsp minced Jalapeno Rings
- 1 tbsp Brine from the Jalapeno Rings
- 1 tbsp chopped Capers
- ¼ cup Water

Cooking Direction
1. Heat the oil in the IP on SAUTE.
2. Add the onion and cook for 3 minutes.
3. Stir in the garlic and cook for 30 seconds.
4. Arrange the cod fillets on top.
5. Combine the remaining ingredients in a bowl and pour over the cod.
6. Close the lid and cook on MANUAL for 5 minutes.
7. Do a quick pressure release. Serve and enjoy!

Nutrition Values
(Calories 640| Total Fats 35g | Carbs: 21g | Protein 60g| Dietary Fiber: 4g)

Shrimp Scampi and Rice

(Prep Time: 5 Mins |Total Time: 20 Mins |Serves: 2)

Ingredients:
- ½ pound Frozen Shrimp
- 2 Garlic Cloves, minced
- Juice of 1 Lemon
- 2 tbsp Butter
- 2 tbsp Parsley
- ½ cup Rice
- 1 ¼ cup Water

Cooking Direction
1. Place everything in your Instant Pot and stir to combine well.
2. Set the IP to POULTRY and cook for 6 minutes.
3. Press CANCEL and do a quick pressure release.
4. Let the shrimp cool down until safe to handle.
5. Peel off the shells and serve.
6. Enjoy!

Nutrition Values
(Calories 225| Total Fats 12g | Carbs: 14g | Protein 14g| Dietary Fiber: 2g)

Tuna Noodles

(Prep Time: 5 Mins |Total Time: 8 Mins |Serves: 2)

Ingredients:
- 8 ounces Egg Noodles
- 1 can Tuna, drained
- 2 ounces shredded Cheddar
- ½ cup frozen Peas
- 1 ½ cups Water
- 2 ½ tbsp Breadcrumbs
- 14 ounces canned Mushroom Soup
- Salt and Pepper, to taste

Cooking Direction
1. Pour the water into the Instant Pot and add the noodles.
2. Stir in the soup, tuna, and peas.
3. Close the lid and set the IP to POULTRY.
4. Cook for 5 minutes and then release the pressure quickly.
5. Add the cheese and breadcrumbs and stir to combine.
6. Cook on SAUTE for a minute.
7. Serve and enjoy!

Nutrition Values
(Calories 430| Total Fats 22g | Carbs: 41g | Protein 18g| Dietary Fiber: 2g)

Caramelized Tilapia

(Prep Time: 5 Mins |Total Time: 55 Mins |Serves: 2)

Ingredients:
- 2 Tilapia Fillets
- 1 ½ tbsp Fish Sauce
- 1 Garlic Clove, minced
- 1 Spring Onion, minced
- 1 Red Chili, minced
- ¼ cup tbsp Sugar
- 1 cup Coconut Water
- Salt and Pepper, to taste
- 3 tbsp Water

Cooking Direction
1. Combine the fish sauce and garlic with some salt and pepper, and brush over the tilapia.
2. Let sit for about half an hour.
3. Place the water and sugar in the Instant Pot and cook until caramelized on SAUTE.
4. Add the tilapia and pour the coconut water over.
5. Close the lid and cook on MANUAL for 10 minutes.
6. Do a quick pressure release.
7. Serve topped with chili and spring onions. Enjoy!

Nutrition Values
(Calories 150| Total Fats 2g | Carbs: 18g | Protein 21g| Dietary Fiber: 1g)

Crunchy Tuna

(Prep Time: 5 Mins |Total Time: 5 Mins |Serves: 2)

Ingredients:

- 1 can Tuna
- 2 tbsp Butter
- 1 cup crushed Saltine Crackers
- ½ tsp minced Garlic
- ½ cup grated Cheddar Cheese
- ¼ cup Water

Cooking Direction

1. Melt the butter in your IP on saute.
2. Add the garlic and cook for 1 minute.
3. Stir in the tuna and the crackers and pour the broth over.
4. Close the lid and cook on HIGH for a minute.
5. Release the pressure quickly, stir in the cheese, and cook for an additional minute, also on HIGH.
6. Serve and enjoy!

Nutrition Values

(Calories 150| Total Fats 3g | Carbs: 13g | Protein 10g| Dietary Fiber: 0g)

Lobster Ziti Bake

(Prep Time: 5 Mins |Total Time: 35 Mins |Serves: 2)

Ingredients:

- 4 ounces dried Ziti
- ¼ cup dry White Wine
- ½ tbsp Flour
- ½ tbsp chopped Tarragon
- ½ cup shredded Gruyere Cheese
- ½ tbsp Worcestershire Sauce
- ½ cup Half and Half
- 2 Lobster Tails
- 3 cups Water
- Salt and Pepper, to taste

Cooking Direction

1. Combine the water, pasta, and lobster tails, in the Instant Pot.
2. Close the lid and cook on POULTRY for 10 minutes.
3. Release the pressure quickly and open the lid.
4. Drain the pasta and the lobster tails.
5. Let cool until safe to handle and scoop out the meat.
6. Wipe the IP clean and place the pasta and meat inside.
7. Stir in the remaining ingredients and close the lid.
8. Season with some salt and pepper.
9. Cook for a couple of minutes on SAUTE, or until thickened.
10. Serve and enjoy!

Nutrition Values

(Calories 440| Total Fats 15g | Carbs: 44g | Protein 28g| Dietary Fiber: 1g)

Wrapped Fish with Potatoes

(Prep Time: 5 Mins |Total Time: 15 Mins |Serves: 2)

Ingredients:

- 2 Fish Fillets (Salmon, Halibut, Tilapia, Cod, etc.)
- 1 Large Potato, sliced
- ½ Lemon, sliced
- ½ Onion, sliced
- 1 tbsp Olive Oil
- 1 ½ cups Water
- 1 tbsp chopped Parsley
- 1 ½ cup Water

Cooking Direction

1. Get two pieces of parchment paper and place the fish fillets at the center of each of them.
2. Top the fish with potato slices, onion, lemon, and parsley.
3. Drizzle with the olive oil.
4. Wrap them up, and then wrap in aluminum foil.
5. Pour the water into the IP and lower the rack.
6. Place the fish packets on the rack and close the lid.
7. Cook for 5 minutes on HIGH.
8. Do a quick pressure release. Serve and enjoy!

Nutrition Values

(Calories 310| Total Fats 14g | Carbs: 9g | Protein 30g| Dietary Fiber: 3g)

Canned Salmon with Corn and Olives

(Prep Time: 5 Mins |Total Time: 17 Mins |Serves: 2)

Ingredients:
- 1 can Salmon, drained
- 8 ounces dried Noodles
- ½ cup canned Corn
- ¼ cup grated Parmesan Cheese
- 4 cups Water
- ½ cup Heavy Cream
- 1 tbsp Butter
- ¼ cup chopped Black Olives

Cooking Direction
1. Combine the noodles and water in the Instant Pot and close the lid.
2. Cook on HIGH for 5 minutes.
3. Do a quick pressure release and drain the pasta.
4. Wipe the pot clean and return the pasta to the IP.
5. Add the remaining ingredients and stir to combine well.
6. Cook on SAUTE for 3 minutes.
7. Serve and enjoy!

Nutrition Values

(Calories 456| Total Fats 18g | Carbs: 41g | Protein 17g| Dietary Fiber: 1.8g)

Simple Dijon Haddock

(Prep Time: 5 Mins |Total Time: 5 Mins |Serves: 2)

Ingredients:
- 2 tbsp Haddock Fillets
- 1 ½ tbsp Dijon Mustard
- 1 ½ cup Water

Cooking Direction
1. Pour the water into the Instant Pot.
2. Brush the mustard all over the fillets and place them in the steamer basket.
3. Lower the basket and close and seal the lid.
4. Set the IP to MANUAL and cook for 3 minutes on HIGH.
5. Do a quick pressure release.
6. Serve and enjoy!

Nutrition Values

(Calories 192| Total Fats 2g | Carbs: 0.3g | Protein 42g| Dietary Fiber: 0g)

Prawn and Egg Risotto

(Prep Time: 5 Mins |Total Time: 40 Mins |Serves: 2)

Ingredients:
- 1 Egg, beaten
- 1/3 cup frozen Peas
- 2/3 cup Brown Rice
- 6 ounces pre-cooked Prawns
- 1 tbsp Sesame Oil
- 1 Garlic Clove, minced
- 1 ½ tbsp Soy Sauce
- 1/3 cup chopped Onion
- 2 cups Water

Cooking Direction
1. Heat half of the oil in the IP on SAUTE.
2. Cook the egg until set. Transfer to a plate.
3. Heat the rest of the oil and add the onions.
4. Cook for 3 minutes and add the garlic.
5. Saute for another minute.
6. Stir in the rice, peas, soy sauce, and water.
7. Close the lid and cook for 10 minutes on MANUAL.
8. Do a quick pressure release.
9. Stir in the prawns and egg.
10. Cook on SAUTE for a few minutes.
11. Serve and enjoy!

Nutrition Values

(Calories 220| Total Fats 10g | Carbs: 22g | Protein 13g| Dietary Fiber: 1g)

Teriyaki Salmon

(Prep Time: 5 Mins |Total Time: 202 Mins |Serves: 2)

Ingredients:

- 2 Salmon Fillets
- 1 tbsp Sweet Rice Wine
- ½ tbsp Sugar
- 1 Spring Onion, sliced
- ½ tbsp Sesame Oil
- 2 tbsp Spy Sauce
- 1 Bok Choy, cut in half
- 1 ounce dried Mushrooms
- 1 ½ cup Boiling Water

Cooking Direction

1. Pour the water over to mushrooms and let them sit for a few minutes.
2. Place them in the Instant Pot and stir in the remaining ingredients, except for the salmon.
3. When combined, add the salmon fillets and close the lid.
4. Cook on HIGH for 4 minutes.
5. Release the pressure naturally.
6. Serve and enjoy!

Nutrition Values

(Calories 480| Total Fats 32g | Carbs: 17g | Protein 27g| Dietary Fiber: 3g)

Trout and Farro Salad

(Prep Time: 5 Mins |Total Time: 55 Mins |Serves: 2)

Ingredients:

- 6 ounces chopped and cooked Trout
- ½ cup Farro
- 1 tbsp Dijon Mustard
- 1 ½ tbsp Lemon Juice
- ¼ cup Mayonnaise
- 2 tbsp Sour Cream
- ½ tsp Sugar
- 1/2 Fennel Bulb, shaved

Cooking Direction

1. Place the farro in the Instant Pot and add just enough water to cover.
2. Close the lid and cook on MANUAL for 17 minutes.
3. Do a quick pressure release.
4. Place the fennel in a colander and drain the farro over it.
5. Transfer to a bowl and let cool for a few minutes.
6. Stir in the trout.
7. In a bowl, whisk together the remaining ingredients and drizzle over the salad. Serve and enjoy!

Nutrition Values

(Calories 460| Total Fats 20g | Carbs: 34g | Protein 30g| Dietary Fiber: 3.3g)

Creamy Shrimp Penne

(Prep Time: 5 Mins |Total Time: 15 Mins |Serves: 2)

Ingredients:

- 6 ounces Penne Pasta
- ½ cup grated parmesan Cheese
- ¼ cup Heavy Cream
- 6 ounces peeled and deveined frozen Shrimp
- 2 cups Chicken Broth
- ½ Onion, chopped
- 1 tbsp Olive Oil
- 1 tsp Flour

Cooking Direction

1. Heat the oil in the Instant Pot on SAUTE.
2. Add the onions and cook for 3 minutes.
3. Stir in the shrimp, pasta, and broth.
4. Close the lid and cook on HIH for 7 minutes.
5. Release the pressure quickly.
6. Whisk together the heavy cream and flour and pour over.
7. Stir in the parmesan and cook on SAUTE until the sauce is thickened. Serve and enjoy!

Nutrition Values

(Calories 508| Total Fats 20g | Carbs: 45g | Protein 33g| Dietary Fiber: 1g)

Orange and Gingery Fish

(Prep Time: 5 Mins |Total Time: 20 Mins |Serves: 2)

Ingredients:
- 1 tbsp Honey
- 2 Fish Fillets
- 2 Spring Onions, chopped
- 2 tsp minced Ginger
- Juice and zest of ½ Orange
- 1 ¼ cup Fish Stock

Cooking Direction
1. Brush the fillets with honey and place in the steamer basket.
2. Combine the rest of the ingredients, except the onions, in the IP and lower the basket.
3. Close the lid and cook on HIGH for 4-5 minutes.
4. Do a quick pressure release.
5. Serve the fish garnished with spring onions and drizzled with the cooking sauce.
6. Enjoy!

Nutrition Values

(Calories 290| Total Fats 2g | Carbs: 14.3g | Protein 40g| Dietary Fiber: 3g)

Tuna Helper

(Prep Time: 5 Mins |Total Time: 15 Mins |Serves: 2)

Ingredients:
- 1 can Tuna, drained
- 6 ounces dried Pasta
- ½ cup grated Cheese
- 2 cups Chicken Broth
- ¼ cup Heavy Cream

Cooking Direction
1. Combine the water and pasta in the Instant Pot and close the lid.
2. Cook on HIGH for 7 minutes.
3. Do a quick pressure release.
4. Drain and stir in the remaining ingredients.
5. Set the IP to SAUTE and cook for 2 minutes.
6. Serve and enjoy!

Nutrition Values

(Calories 301| Total Fats 13g | Carbs: 31 | Protein 20g| Dietary Fiber: 1.5g)

Salmon and Tomato Pasta Casserole

(Prep Time: 5 Mins |Total Time: 20 Mins |Serves: 2)

Ingredients:
- 1 can Salmon, drained
- 1 tbsp Capers
- 15 ounces canned diced Tomatoes
- 1 tbsp Olive Oil
- 2 cups Pasta
- Dry White Wine
- 1 tsp minced Garlic

Cooking Direction
1. Set your IP to SAUTE.
2. Add the garlic and cook for a minute.
3. Stir in the pasta and tomatoes.
4. Fill the tomato can with white wine and pour over.
5. Close the lid and cook on MANUAL for 6 minutes.
6. Do a quick pressure release.
7. Stir in the remaining ingredients.
8. Serve and enjoy!

Nutrition Values

(Calories 650| Total Fats 20g | Carbs: 73g | Protein 25g| Dietary Fiber: 2.4g)

Shrimp Creole

(Prep Time: 5 Mins | Total Time: 20 Mins | Serves: 2)

Ingredients:

- 14 ounces canned crushed Tomatoes
- ½ Onion, chopped
- 1 Celery Stalk, diced
- ½ pound Shrimp, peeled and deveined
- 1 tsp minced Garlic
- ½ Bell Pepper, diced
- 2 tsp Creole Seasoning
- 1 tbsp Tomato Paste
- 2 tsp Olive Oil

Cooking Direction

1. Heat the oil in the IP on SAUTE.
2. Add the onions, peppers, and celery, and cook for 3 minutes.
3. Stir in the garlic and cook for another minute.
4. Whisk in the tomato paste and cook for an additional minute.
5. Stir in the remaining ingredients and close the lid.
6. Set the IP to MNUAL and cook on HIGH for 1 minute.
7. Do a quick pressure release. Serve and enjoy!

Nutrition Values

(Calories 260| Total Fats 4g | Carbs: 24g | Protein 31g| Dietary Fiber: 5g)

Seafood and Cranberry Plov

(Prep Time: 5 Mins | Total Time: 40 Mins | Serves: 2)

Ingredients:

- 8 ounces frozen Seafood Blend
- ½ Onion, chopped
- ½ Lemon, sliced
- 1 ½ tbsp Butter
- 1 Large Carrot, shredded
- ¾ cup Basmati Rice
- ½ Bell Pepper, sliced
- ¼ cup dried Cranberries
- 1 ½ cups Water

Cooking Direction

1. Melt the butter in the IP and add the onions, pepper, and carrots. Saute for 3 minutes.
2. Add the garlic and cook for 1 more minute.
3. Stir in the remaining ingredients and close the lid.
4. Set the IP to RICE and cook for 7 minutes.
5. Wait 5 minutes before doing a quick pressure release.
6. Serve and enjoy!

Nutrition Values

(Calories 430| Total Fats 7g | Carbs: 65g | Protein 22g| Dietary Fiber: 3g)

Chapter 7 Vegetarian Recipes

Coconut Cabbage in Lime Sauce

(Prep Time: 5 Mins |Total Time: 20 Mins |Serves: 4)

Ingredients:

- 1 Cabbage, shredded
- ½ cup desiccated Coconut
- 1 Carrot, sliced
- 2 Garlic Cloves, minced
- 1 tbsp Coconut Oil
- 1/3 cup Fresh Lime Juice
- 1 tsp Turmeric Powder
- ½ tsp Curry Powder
- 1 Onion, sliced

Cooking Direction

1. Place the coconut oil inside the IP and set it to SAUTE.
2. When melted, add the onions and cook for 3 minutes.
3. Add the garlic and cook for another minute.
4. Stir in the remaining ingredients and close the lid.
5. Set the IP to MANUAL.
6. Cook on HIGH for 5 minutes.
7. Do a natural pressure release.
8. Serve and enjoy!

Nutrition Values

(Calories 190| Total Fats 11g | Carbs: 20g| Protein 4.5g | Dietary Fiber: 5g)

Herbed Garlicky Potatoes

(Prep Time: 5 Mins |Total Time: 10 Mins |Serves: 2)

Ingredients:

- 1 pounds Potatoes, quartered
- 3 tbsp Coconut Oil, melted
- 4 Garlic Cloves, minced
- 1 tbsp chopped Parsley
- 1 tbsp chopped Cilantro
- 1 tbsp chopped Basil
- 1 cup Water

Cooking Direction

1. Pour the water into the IP and lower the rack.
2. Place the potatoes in a baking dish.
3. Drizzle with the melted coconut oil and sprinkle with the garlic and herbs.
4. Give it a good stir to combine.
5. Place the dish on the rack and close the lid.
6. When sealed, set the IP to MANUAL.
7. Cook on HIGH for 6 minutes.
8. Do a quick pressure release.
9. Serve and enjoy!

Nutrition Values

(Calories 320| Total Fats 15g | Carbs: 43g| Protein 6g | Dietary Fiber: 4g)

Lemony and Minty Zoodles

(Prep Time: 5 Mins |Total Time: 15 Mins |Serves: 2)

Ingredients:

- ½ tsp Lemon Zest
- 2 tbsp Lemon Juice
- 2 tbsp chopped Mint
- 2 Large Zucchini, Spiralized
- 1 Garlic Cloves, minced
- 1 tbsp Ghee
- 2 tbsp Olive Oil
- Pinch of Pepper

Cooking Direction

1. Set your Instant Pot to SAUTE and add the oil.
2. When hot, add the garlic and lemon zest and cook just for 30 seconds.
3. Stir in the remaining ingredients and cook for 2 minutes.
4. Serve immediately.
5. Enjoy!

Nutrition Values

(Calories 180| Total Fats 15g | Carbs: 12g| Protein 4g | Dietary Fiber: 1g)

Basil and Tomato 'Spaghetti'

(Prep Time: 5 Mins |Total Time: 25 Mins |Serves: 4)

Ingredients:

- ½ cup Tomato Paste
- 2 tsp minced Garlic
- 4 cups Spiralized Zucchini
- 2 cups diced Tomatoes
- ¼ cup chopped Basil
- ¼ cup Coconut Cream
- ¼ cup Homemade Veggie Broth

Cooking Direction

1. Place all of the ingredients in the Instant Pot.
2. Stir well to combine and put the lid on.
3. Turn it clockwise to seal and set the IP to MANUAL.
4. Cook on HIGH for 2 minutes.
5. Do a quick pressure release.
6. Serve and enjoy!

Nutrition Values

(Calories 70| Total Fats 4g | Carbs: 10g| Protein 2g | Dietary Fiber: 2.5g)

Sweet Potato Casserole with Walnuts and Cinnamon

(Prep Time: 5 Mins |Total Time: 35 Mins |Serves: 4)

Ingredients:

- 4 Sweet Potatoes, steamed and mashed
- 2 tbsp Coconut Milk
- 2 tbsp Fresh Orange Juice
- 1 tbsp Coconut Oil
- ¼ tsp Cinnamon
- 2 tbsp Coconut Flour
- ½ cup chopped Walnuts
- 1 cup Water

Cooking Direction

1. Place the potatoes, coconut milk, coconut oil, cinnamon, and orange juice, in a bowl.
2. Mix the ingredients to combine and then transfer the mixture to a greased baking dish.
3. Press well into the bottom.
4. Scatter the walnuts on top and sprinkle with the coconut flour.
5. Pour the water into the IP and lower the trivet.
6. Place the baking dish on the trivet and close the lid.
7. Cook on HIGH for 5 minutes.

Nutrition Values

(Calories 402| Total Fats 15g | Carbs: 67g| Protein 5g | Dietary Fiber: 8g)

Beet Borscht

(Prep Time: 5 Mins |Total Time: 65 Mins |Serves: 8)

Ingredients:

- 1 Onion, diced
- 2 Carrots, sliced
- 3 Celery Stalks, diced
- 8 cups diced Beets
- 3 cups Homemade Veggie Stock
- 3 cups shredded Cabbage
- 1 tsp minced Garlic
- 1 tsp Thyme
- 1 tbsp chopped Parsley

Cooking Direction

1. Pour the water into the IP.
2. Place the beets inside the steamer basket and lower it into the pot.
3. Close the lid and set the IP to MANUAL.
4. Cook on HIGH for 7 minutes.
5. Do a quick pressure release.
6. Open the lid and stir in the remaining ingredients.
7. Seal the lid and set the IP to SOUP.
8. Cook for 45 minutes.
9. Let the pressure drop naturally.
10. Serve and enjoy!

Nutrition Values

(Calories 110| Total Fats 2g | Carbs: 24g| Protein 4g | Dietary Fiber: 5g)

Baby Root Veggie Casserole

(Prep Time: 5 Mins |Total Time: 25 Mins |Serves: 6)

Ingredients:

- 2 pounds Baby Carrots
- 4 pounds Baby Potatoes, halved
- 1 Onion, diced
- 1 tsp minced Garlic Clove
- ½ cup Homemade Veggie Broth
- 2 tbsp Olive Oil

Cooking Direction

1. Heat the oil in the IP on SAUTE.
2. Add the onions and cook for 3 minutes.
3. Then, add the carrots and cook for another 3 minutes.
4. Add the remaining ingredients and stir to combine.
5. Close the lid and set the IP to MANUAL.
6. Cook on HIGH for 10 minutes.
7. Do a natural pressure release.
8. Serve and enjoy!

Nutrition Values

(Calories 330| Total Fats 5g | Carbs: 65g| Protein 7g | Dietary Fiber: 8g)

Creamy Spinach Risotto

(Prep Time: 5 Mins |Total Time: 30 Mins |Serves: 4)

Ingredients:

- 6 cups ground Cauliflower
- 1 cup Homemade Vegetable Broth
- 2 cups chopped Spinach
- 1 tbsp Olive Oil
- ¼ cup Coconut Cream
- ½ Onion, diced
- 1 tsp minced Garlic

Cooking Direction

1. Set your IP to SAUTE and heat the oil in it.
2. Add onions and cook them for 3 minutes.
3. Add the garlic and cook for one more minute.
4. Stir in the remaining ingredients and put the lid on.
5. Seal and set the IP to MANUAL.
6. Cook on HIGH for 5 minutes.
7. Do a quick pressure release.
8. Serve and enjoy!

Nutrition Values

(Calories 120| Total Fats 5g | Carbs: 7g| Protein 3g | Dietary Fiber: 2g)

Herbed Cauliflower Tabbouleh

(Prep Time: 5 Mins |Total Time: 15 Mins |Serves: 6)

Ingredients:

- 1/3 cup chopped Spring Onions
- 2 cups Cauliflower Rice (ground cauliflower in a food processor)
- 4 tbsp Olive Oil
- 1 cup chopped Parsley
- ½ Cucumber, diced
- 1 Garlic Clove, minced
- 1 cup diced Tomatoes
- 3 tbsp Lemon Juice
- ¼ cup chopped

Cooking Direction

1. Heat some of the olive oil in the IP on SAUTE.
2. Add the garlic and cook for 30 seconds.
3. Add the cauliflower and tomatoes and cook on SAUTE for 2 minutes.
4. Transfer to a bowl.
5. Stir in the remaining ingredients.
6. Serve and enjoy!

Nutrition Values

(Calories 110| Total Fats 9g | Carbs: 2g| Protein 1g | Dietary Fiber: 1.5g)

Mashed Chili Carrots

(Prep Time: 5 Mins |Total Time: 25 Mins |Serves: 4)

Ingredients:

- 1 ½ pounds Carrots, chopped
- 1 tsp Chili Powder
- 1 tbsp Coconut Cream
- 1 tbsp Coconut Oil
- 1 ½ cups Water

Cooking Direction

1. Pour the water into the IP.
2. Place the carrots inside the basket and then lower it into the pot.
3. Put the lid on and seal.
4. Set the Instant Pot to MANUAL.
5. Cook on HIGH for 4 minutes.
6. Release the pressure quickly.
7. Open the lid and transfer the carrots to a food processor.
8. Add the coconut cream, coconut oil, and chili powder.
9. Process until the mixture becomes smooth and creamy.
10. Serve and enjoy!

Nutrition Values

(Calories 45| Total Fats 1g | Carbs: 11g| Protein 1g | Dietary Fiber: 1g)

Tasty Pepper Salad

(Prep Time: 5 Mins |Total Time: 15 Mins |Serves: 4)

Ingredients:

- 2 red capsicums, sliced into strips
- 2 yellow capsicums, sliced into strips
- 1 green capsicum, sliced into strips
- ½ teaspoon olive oil
- 1 red onion
- 2 garlic cloves
- 3 tomatoes, chopped
- basil, chopped
- salt and pepper

Directions

1. Add oil to your instant pot and sauté onions until tender; add 1 garlic clove, and capsicums and cook until browned.
2. Add the chopped tomatoes, salt and pepper and stir to mix; lock lid and cook on high pressure for 5 minutes and then release pressure naturally.
3. Press the remaining garlic clove and set aside.
4. Remove capsicums into a bowl and add olive oil, garlic and chopped basil; mix well and serve.

Nutrition Values

(Calories 48| Total Fats 1.1g | Carbs: 9.2g| Protein 1.8g | Dietary Fiber: 2.9g)

Instant Pot Coconut Cabbage

(Prep Time: 15 Mins |Total Time: 25 Mins |Serves: 7)

Ingredients:

- 1 tablespoon coconut oil
- 1 tablespoon olive oil
- ½ cup desiccated unsweetened coconut
- 2 tablespoons lemon juice
- 1 medium carrot, sliced
- 1 medium brown onion, sliced
- 1 medium cabbage, shredded
- 1 tablespoon turmeric powder
- 1 tablespoon mild curry powder
- 1 teaspoon mustard powder
- ½ long red chili, sliced
- 2 large cloves of garlic, diced
- 1 + ½ teaspoons salt
- ⅓ cup water

Directions:

1. Turn your instant pot on sauté mode and add coconut oil; stir in onion and salt and cook for about 4 minutes.
2. Stir in spices, chili and garlic for about 30 seconds.
3. Stir in the remaining ingredients and lock the lid; set on manual high for 5 minutes.
4. When done, natural release the pressure and stir the mixture. Serve with beans or rice.

Nutrition Values

(Calories 231| Total Fats 2.5g | Carbs: 15.9g| Protein 5.9g | Dietary Fiber: 8.5g)

Instant Pot Garlicky Mashed Potatoes

(Prep Time: 5 Mins |Total Time: 9 Mins |Serves: 4)

Ingredients:

- 6 cloves garlic, chopped
- 1 cup Homemade vegetable broth
- 4 Yukon gold potatoes, diced
- 1/2 cup almond milk
- 1/4 cup chopped parsley
- 1/8 teaspoon sea salt

Directions:

1. In your instant pot, mix garlic, broth and potatoes and lock the lid; set to manual for 4 minutes and then release the pressure naturally.
2. Transfer the potato mixture to a large bowl and mash with a potato masher until smooth.
3. Add soy milk to your desired consistency and then stir in parsley and salt. Serve hot!

Nutrition Values

(Calories 243| Total Fats 0.8g | Carbs: 24.7g| Protein 4.5g | Dietary Fiber: 11.2g)

Instant Pot Ratatouille

(Prep Time: 15 Mins |Total Time: 35 Mins |Serves: 4)

Ingredients:

- 1 egg plant, halved then sliced
- 1 green pepper, cut in strips (deseeded)
- 1 onion, halved then sliced
- 1 tomatoes, wedged
- 2 small zucchinis, sliced
- 75 ml tomato paste
- 1/8 cup olive oil
- 2tbsp fresh parsley
- 1tsp dried basil
- ½ tsp. oregano
- ½ tsp. freshly ground black pepper
- Salt and red pepper flakes to taste

Directions:

1. Layer the vegetables on your instant pot by starting with onions, eggplant, zucchini, garlic, followed by the peppers and finally the tomatoes.
2. Sprinkle with half the dried herbs, parsley, salt and the pepper flakes.
3. Add half the tomato paste and repeat the layering in the same order.
4. Next, drizzle with the olive oil and lock lid and cook on high pressure for 20 minutes. Release the pressure naturally and serve.

Nutrition Values

(Calories 137| Total Fats 6.9g | Carbs: 19.1g| Protein 3.7g | Dietary Fiber: 7.2g)

Arugula, Orange & Kamut Salad

(Prep Time: 10 Mins |Total Time: 40 Mins |Serves: 7)

Ingredients:

- 1 cup whole Kamut grains, rinsed
- 1 teaspoon vegetable oil
- 2 cups water
- 1 teaspoon sea salt
- ½ lemon
- ¼ cup chopped walnuts
- 1 tablespoon extra-virgin olive oil
- 2 medium blood oranges, sliced
- 2 cups rocket Arugula

Directions:

1. In a bowl, combine kamut grains, lemon juice and 4 cups of water; soak overnight.
2. Strain the kamut and add to an instant pot along with oil, salt and water; lock the lid and cook on high pressure for 18 minutes.
3. Release the pressure naturally and then transfer to a serving bowl; stir in olive oil, walnuts, orange pieces and arugula.
4. Serve right away.

Nutrition Values

(Calories 63| Total Fats 8.6g | Carbs: 11.7g| Protein 2.8g | Dietary Fiber: 2.1g)

Sage-Infused Butternut Squash Zucchini Noodles

(Prep Time: 10 Mins |Total Time: 25 Mins |Serves: 4)

Ingredients:

- 3 large zucchinis, Spiralized or julienned into noodles
- 3 cups cubed butternut squash
- 2 cloves garlic, finely chopped
- 1 yellow onion, chopped
- 2 tablespoons olive oil
- 2 cups homemade vegetable broth
- ¼ teaspoon red pepper flakes
- Freshly ground black pepper
- 1 tablespoon fresh sage, finely chopped
- Salt, to taste and smoked salt for garnish

Directions:

1. Add the oil to a pan over medium heat and sauté the sage once it's hot until it turns crisp.
2. Transfer to a small bowl and season lightly with salt then set aside.
3. Add the onion, butternut, garlic, broth, salt and pepper flakes to in instant pot and lock the lid; cook on high pressure for 10 minutes and then release pressure naturally.
4. Meanwhile, steam the zucchini noodles in your microwave or steamer until crisp-tender.
5. Once the butternut mixture is ready, remove from heat and let cool off slightly then transfer to a blender and process until smooth.
6. Combine the zucchini noodles and the butternut puree in the skillet over medium heat and cook until heated through and evenly coated for 2 minutes.
7. Sprinkle with fried sage and smoked salt and serve hot.

Nutrition Values

(Calories 301| Total Fats 28.5g | Carbs: 13.8g| Protein 1.9g | Dietary Fiber: 3.4g)

Cauliflower Tikka Masala

(Prep Time:3Mins |Cook Time:7Mins |Servings: 4)

Ingredients:

- 1 large cauliflower head, chopped into florets
- ½ cup unsweetened coconut cream or unsweetened non-dairy yogurt
- 1 medium beet, peeled, peeled, diced
- ½ cup pumpkin puree
- ½ cup organic low-sodium bone broth
- 2 Tablespoons ghee or non-dairy butter
- 1 medium red onion, finely chopped, 4 garlic cloves, minced
- 1 1-inch fresh ginger, peeled, grated, 1 Tablespoon dried fenugreek leaves
- 1 Tablespoon fresh parsley, finely chopped
- 1 Tablespoon garam masala
- 1 teaspoon smoked or regular paprika
- 1 teaspoon organic ground turmeric
- 1 teaspoon organic chili powder
- Garnish: roasted cashews, finely chopped cilantro

Cooking Direction

1. Press "Sauté" function on Instant Pot. Add the ghee.
2. Once melted, add onion. Cook 3 minutes. Add garlic, grated ginger. Cook 2 minutes more. Add fenugreek, paprika, chili powder, turmeric, garam masala, and parsley. Cook 1 minute, stirring frequently.
3. In a blender, combine the beet, pumpkin puree, and bone broth. Blend until slightly chunky. Add to ingredients in the Instant Pot. Stir in the cauliflower.
4. Lock, seal the lid. Press "Manual" button. Cook on HIGH 2 minutes.
5. When done, allow to sit for 1 minute before quick releasing pressure. Remove lid.
6. Stir in cream until well combined. Ladle in bowls. Garnish with roasted cashews, cilantro. Serve.

Nutrition Values

(Calories: 243 , Fat: 8.3g , Carbohydrates: 33.23g, Dietary Fiber: 11.96g, Protein: 13.4g)

Barbecue Jackfruit

(Prep Time:5Mins |Cook Time:10Mins |Servings: 4)

Ingredients:

- 2 x 8-ounce cans jackfruit, drained, chopped
- 1/2 cup homemade low-sodium vegetable broth
- 1/2 cup ghee or non-dairy butter, melted
- ½ cup vinegar
- Juice from 1 fresh lemon
- 1/2 Tablespoon Worcestershire sauce
- 1/2 teaspoons paprika
- 1/4 teaspoon onion powder
- 1/4 teaspoon garlic powder
- 1/2 teaspoons salt
- 1/4 teaspoon pepper
- Lettuce leaves for serving

Cooking Direction

1. Add jackfruit and vegetable broth to Instant Pot.
2. Lock, seal the lid. Press "Manual" button. Cook on HIGH 5 minutes.
3. When done, naturally release pressure. Remove the lid.
4. Using a colander, drain liquid from jackfruit. Return fruit to Instant Pot. Using a potato masher, smash the fruit slightly.
5. In a bowl, combine melted ghee, vinegar, lemon juice, Worcestershire sauce, paprika, garlic powder, onion powder, salt, and black pepper. Stir well. Pour mixture over the jackfruit.
6. Press "Sauté" function. Warm for 5 minutes. Ladle over lettuce leaves. Serve.

Nutrition Values

(Calories: 488, Fat: 34.8g , Carbohydrates: 45.7g, Dietary Fiber: 3g, Protein: 3.7g)

Cauliflower Risotto

(Prep Time:10Mins |Cook Time:27Mins |Servings: 4)

Ingredients:

- 12 asparagus, remove woodsy stem, diced
- 1 cup organic fresh broccoli florets, 1 cup organic baby carrots
- 1 cup fresh leeks, finely chopped, 2 garlic cloves, minced
- 1 cup fresh baby spinach, ½ bunch chives, thinly sliced
- 1 medium yellow onion, finely chopped
- 1½ cups cauliflower rice
- 4 cups homemade low-sodium vegetable broth
- 2 Tablespoons olive oil
- 1 teaspoon fresh thyme, ½ teaspoon garlic powder, ¼ teaspoon red pepper flakes
- 1 teaspoon fresh lemon zest, 2 Tablespoons fresh lemon juice
- ¼ cup ghee or non-dairy butter
- Pinch of salt, pepper

Cooking Direction

1. Line a baking sheet with parchment paper. Place asparagus, broccoli, and carrots in a single layer on the tray. Drizzle olive oil. Season with salt and pepper.
2. Place baking sheet in 400°F oven 15 minutes, until broccoli is tender. Remove, set aside. Once cooled, dice in small pieces.
3. Press "Sauté" function on Instant Pot. Add 1 tablespoon of olive oil.
4. Once hot, add onion. Cook 4 minutes. Add garlic, leeks. Cook 2 minutes. Add cauliflower rice. Sauté 1 minute.
5. Stir in vegetable broth, ghee or non-dairy butter, and fresh thyme.
6. Lock, seal the lid. Press "Manual" button. Cook on HIGH 7 minutes.
7. When done, quick release pressure. Remove the lid.
8. Press "Sauté" function. Stir in asparagus, broccoli, carrots, leeks, spinach, garlic powder, red pepper flakes, lemon zest, and lemon juice. Sauté 1 minute, until spinach wilts. Ladle in bowls. Garnish with chives. Serve.

Nutrition Values

(Calories: 278, Fat: 21.5g, Carbohydrates: 15.3g, Dietary Fiber: 4.3g, Protein: 8.4g)

Mexican-Inspired Posole

(Prep Time:20Mins |Cook Time:30Mins |Servings: 4)

Ingredients:

- 1/2 large head cauliflower, finely chopped
- 1/2 medium yellow onion, finely chopped
- 4 garlic cloves, minced
- 2 x 10-ounce cans jackfruit
- ½ cup coconut oil or olive oil
- ½ cup New Mexico red chile powder
- 1/2 teaspoon organic ground cumin powder
- 1/2 teaspoon organic Mexican dried oregano
- ¾ cup coconut flour or almond flour
- 3 cups homemade low-sodium vegetable broth
- Pinch of salt, pepper

Cooking Direction

1. Press "Sauté" function on Instant Pot. Add coconut oil.
2. Once hot, add onion. Cook 4 minutes. Add garlic. Cook 1 minute.
3. Stir in coconut flour, red chile powder, cumin, oregano, salt, pepper. Cook 3 minutes. Stir in 2 cups of the vegetable broth, jackfruit, and cauliflower florets.
4. Break the jackfruit and cauliflower florets apart using a potato masher. Stir in remaining vegetable broth.
5. Close, seal the lid. Press "Manual" button. Cook on HIGH 10 minutes.
6. When done, naturally release pressure. Remove the lid. Stir ingredients.
7. Ladle into bowls. Serve.

Nutrition Values
(Calories: 314, Fat: 17.4g, Carbohydrates: 39.3g, Dietary Fiber: 3.7g, Protein: 7.3g)

Mushroom Stir-Fry

(Prep Time:4Mins |Cook Time:|30Mins |Servings: 2)

Ingredients:

- 4 cups mushrooms, finely sliced
- 2 Tablespoons of olive oil
- 1 teaspoon of cumin seeds
- 1 strand curry leaves
- 3 Tablespoons homemade low-sodium vegetable broth
- ½ teaspoon mustard seeds
- ¼ teaspoon turmeric powder
- Pinch of salt, pepper

Cooking Direction

1. Press "Sauté" function on Instant Pot. Add the olive oil.
2. Once hot, add cumin seeds, mustard seeds, curry leaves, turmeric, salt, pepper. Stir. Add the mushrooms and vegetable broth. Turn off "Sauté" function.
3. Close, seal the lid. Press "Steam" function. Cook on HIGH 2 minutes.
4. When done, quick release pressure. Remove the lid.
5. Press "Sauté" function. Simmer until all liquid has evaporated.
6. Ladle in bowls. Garnish with fresh parsley. Serve.

Nutrition Values
(Calories: 150, Fat: 14.4g, Carbohydrates: 4.7g, Dietary Fiber: 1.4g, Protein: 4.4g)

Mashed Cauliflower with Spinach

(Prep Time:5Mins |Cook Time:31Mins |Servings: 4)

Ingredients:

- 1 large head of cauliflower, cut into florets
- 1 Tablespoon flavorless oil
- 1 small yellow onion, finely chopped
- 2 cups organic baby spinach
- 2 garlic cloves, minced
- 2 Tablespoons ghee or non-dairy butter
- ½ cup unsweetened coconut cream or organic heavy cream
- Pinch of salt, pepper
- 1 cup homemade vegetable broth
- 6 sprigs fresh thyme

Cooking Direction

1. Press "Sauté" function on Instant Pot. Add the oil.
2. Add onion. Cook 4 minutes. Add garlic. Cook 2 minutes. Stir in thyme.
3. Add 1 cup of water, and trivet to Instant Pot. Place cauliflower on top.
4. Lock, seal the lid. Press "Manual" button. Cook on HIGH 15 minutes.
5. When done, naturally release pressure 10 minutes, then quick release remaining pressure. Remove the lid.
6. Remove trivet. Discard liquid. Return cauliflower to pot.
7. While pot is still hot, add ghee, spinach, salt, black pepper, and cream. Using potato masher, mash ingredients until combined. Season. Transfer to bowl. Serve.

Nutrition Values
(Calories: 111, Fat: 4.3g, Carbohydrates: 9.8g, Dietary Fiber: 4.1g, Protein: 9.83g)

Pesto Farfale
(Prep Time: 5 Mins |Total Time: 10 Mins |Serves: 2)

Ingredients:
- 7 ounces pasta Farfale
- 2/3 cup Pesto Sauce
- 3 cups Water
- ½ cup halved Cherry Tomatoes
- 1 tbsp chopped Basil
- 2 tbsp grated Parmesan Cheese

Cooking Direction
1. Combine the pasta and water in the IP and close the lid.
2. Cook for 7 minutes on HIGH.
3. DO a quick pressure release.
4. Drain and return to the IP.
5. Stir in the cherry tomatoes and pesto and cook for 1 more minute.
6. Divide between two plates.
7. Top with basil and parmesan.
8. Serve and enjoy!

Nutrition Values
(Calories 395| Total Fats 10g | Carbs: 40g | Protein 8g| Dietary Fiber: 1g)

Spinach and Mushroom Risotto
(Prep Time: 5 Mins |Total Time: 25 Mins |Serves: 2)

Ingredients:
- ¼ Onion, diced
- 1 cup Spinach
- 2 tbsp Lemon Juice
- 4 ounces Mushrooms, sliced
- ¼ cup dry White Wine
- 1 tbsp Butter
- 2/3 cup Arborio Rice
- 1 tbsp Nutritional Yeast
- 2 ½ cups Vegetable Broth
- 1 tbsp Olive Oil

Cooking Direction
1. Heat the oil in the IP on SAUTE.
2. Add the onions and cook for 3 minutes.
3. Stir in the rice, and mushrooms, and cook for 2 minutes.
4. Add broth and wine and stir to combine.
5. Close the lid and set the IP to MANUAL.
6. Cook on HIGH for 6 minutes.
7. Do a quick pressure release.
8. Stir in the butter, spinach, and yeast.
9. Let sit for 2 minutes before serving.
10. Enjoy!

Nutrition Values
(Calories 320| Total Fats 8g | Carbs: 45g | Protein 10g| Dietary Fiber: 6g)

Stuffed Eggplant
(Prep Time: 5 Mins |Total Time: 50 Mins |Serves: 2)

Ingredients:
- 2 Eggplants
- ½ pound Mushrooms, chopped
- ½ cup diced Celery
- 1 tbsp Oil
- ½ Onion, diced
- ¾ cup grated Cheddar Cheese

- 1 tbsp chopped Parsley
- 1 ½ cups Water

Cooking Direction

1. Cut the eggplants in half lengthwise and scoop out the flesh. Reserve it.
2. Pour the water into the IP and lower the rack.
3. Place the eggplants on the rack and drizzle with oil.
4. Close the lid and cook on HIGH for 5 minutes.
5. In a bowl, combine the remaining ingredients, including the reserved flesh.
6. Do a quick pressure release and divide the mixture between the eggplants.
7. Return the eggplants to the rack and cook for 10 minutes on HIGH.
8. Release the pressure quickly.
9. Serve and enjoy!

Nutrition Values

(Calories 175| Total Fats 7g | Carbs: 25g | Protein 6g| Dietary Fiber: 3g)

Veggie Patties

(Prep Time: 5 Mins |Total Time: 30 Mins |Serves: 2)

Ingredients:

- ½ Zucchini, grated
- 1 Carrot, grated
- 1 cup Broccoli Florets
- 1 cup Sweet Potato cubes
- 2 tbsp Olive Oil
- ½ tsp Turmeric
- 1 ½ cups Cauliflower Florets
- 2/3 cup Veggie Broth

Cooking Direction

1. Heat half of the oil in the IP on SAUTE.
2. Add the onions and cook for 3 minutes.
3. Add carrots and cook for another minute.
4. Stir in the potatoes and broth and close the lid.
5. Cook for 6 minutes on HIGH.
6. Do a quick pressure release.
7. Stir in the remaining vegetables.
8. Close the lid and cook for 3 more minutes.
9. Release the pressure quickly and mash the veggies with a potato masher.
10. Let cool until safe to handle and shape into patties.
11. Wipe the pot clean and heat the remaining oil in it.
12. Add the patties and cook on SAUTE until golden.
13. Serve and enjoy!

Nutrition Values

(Calories 220| Total Fats 7g | Carbs: 34g | Protein 4g| Dietary Fiber: 6.5g)

Leafy Risotto

(Prep Time: 5 Mins |Total Time: 20 Mins |Serves: 2)

Ingredients:

- 2/3 cup Arborio Rice
- ½ cup chopped Spinach
- ½ cup chopped Kale
- ¼ cup grated Parmesan Cheese
- ¼ cup diced Onion
- 1 tsp minced Garlic
- 2 ½ cups Veggie Broth
- 1 tbsp Oil
- 1 tbsp Butter

Cooking Direction

1. Heat the oil in the IP on SAUTE.
2. Add the onions and cook for 3 minutes.
3. Add garlic and cook for 1 minute.
4. Stir in the rice and cook for an additional minute.
5. Pour the broth over, stir to combine, and close the lid.
6. Cook on RICE for 6 minutes.
7. Do a quick pressure release.
8. Drain if there is excess liquid.
9. Stir in the butter, parmesan, and greens.
10. Serve after 2 minutes.
11. Enjoy!

Nutrition Values

(Calories 272| Total Fats 11g | Carbs: 140g | Protein 6g| Dietary Fiber: 3g)

Spaghetti "Bolognese"

(Prep Time: 5 Mins |Total Time: 25 Mins |Serves: 2)

Ingredients:

- 2 cups cooked Spaghetti
- 1 tbsp Tomato Paste
- ½ cup Cauliflower Florets
- 1 tbsp Balsamic Vinegar
- 5 ounces Mushrooms
- 14 ounces canned diced Tomatoes
- 1 tsp dried Basil
- ¼ tsp Oregano
- 1 tbsp Agave Nectar
- ¼ cup chopped Eggplant

Cooking Direction

1. Place the cauliflower, eggplants, and mushrooms, in your food processor. Pulse until ground.
2. Transfer the mixture to the Instant Pot.
3. Stir in the rest of the ingredients, except the spaghetti.
4. Close the lid and cook on HIGH for 6 minutes.
5. Do a quick pressure release.
6. Stir in the spaghetti. Serve and enjoy!

Nutrition Values

(Calories 360| Total Fats 2.3g | Carbs: 72g | Protein 14g| Dietary Fiber: 8g)

Bean and Rice Bake

(Prep Time: 5 Mins |Total Time: 40 Mins |Serves: 2)

Ingredients:

- ½ cup Beans, soaked and rinsed
- 2 ½ cups Water
- 1 cup Brown Rice
- 1 tsp Chili Powder
- 3 ounces Tomato Sauce
- 1 Garlic Clove, minced
- 1 tsp Onion Powder
- ¼ tsp Salt

Cooking Direction

1. Place all of the ingredients in your IP.
2. Close the lid and set it to POULTRY.
3. Cook for 27 minutes.
4. Do a quick pressure release.
5. Serve and enjoy!

Nutrition Values

(Calories 320| Total Fats 2g | Carbs: 63g | Protein 6g| Dietary Fiber: 9g)

Broccoli & Tofu in a Tamari Sauce

(Prep Time: 5 Mins |Total Time: 15 Mins |Serves: 2)

Ingredients:

- ½ pound Tofu, cubed
- 2 tsp Rice Vinegar
- 1 tbsp Tahini
- 2 tbsp Tamari
- 1 Garlic Clove, minced
- 1/3 cup Veggie Stock
- 1 cup Onion Slices
- 1 tbsp Sriracha
- 2 tsp Sesame Oil
- 1 tbsp Sesame Seeds
- 1 cup Broccoli Florets
- ½ cup diced Sweet Potato

Cooking Direction

1. Heat the oil in the IP.
2. Add the sweet potatoes and onions and cook for 3 minutes.
3. Add garlic and cook for a minute.
4. Stir in the tofu, tamari, vinegar, and broth.
5. Close the lid and cook for 2 minutes on HIGH.
6. So a quick pressure release and stir in the broccoli.
7. Cook for another 2 minutes.
8. Release the pressure quickly, again, and stir in the sriracha.
9. Serve and enjoy!

Nutrition Values

(Calories 250| Total Fats 12g | Carbs: 22g | Protein 17g| Dietary Fiber: 2g)

Carrot and Sweet Potato Medley

(Prep Time: 5 Mins |Total Time: 30 Mins |Serves: 2)

Ingredients:
- ½ Onion, chopped
- 1 pound Baby Carrots, halved
- 1 pound Sweet Potatoes, cubed
- 2 tbsp Olive Oil
- ½ tsp Italian Seasoning
- 1 cup Vegetable Broth
- ¼ tsp Garlic Salt

Cooking Direction
1. Heat the oil in the IP on SAUTE.
2. Add the onions and cook for about 3-4 minutes.
3. Add the carrots and cook for another 3-4 minutes.
4. Stir in the remaining ingredients.
5. Close the lid and set the IP to MANUAL.
6. Cook for 8 minutes on HIGH.
7. Serve and enjoy!

Nutrition Values
(Calories 413| Total Fats 7g | Carbs: 74g | Protein 7g| Dietary Fiber: 12g)

Fruity Wild Rice Casserole with Almonds

(Prep Time: 5 Mins |Total Time: 55 Mins |Serves: 2)

Ingredients:
- 1/3 cup dried Fruit
- 2 tbsp Apple Juice
- ½ Pear, chopped
- 1 Apple, chopped
- ½ tbsp Maple Syrup
- ¼ cup Slivered Almonds
- ¾ cup Wild Rice
- 2 cups Water
- 1 tsp Oil
- Pinch of Cinnamon

Cooking Direction
1. Place the rice and water in the IP and close the lid.
2. Cook on HIGH for 20 minutes.
3. Meanwhile combine the dried fruit and apple juice and let sit for 20 minutes.
4. Drain the fruits and chop them.
5. Do a quick pressure release and stir in the remaining ingredients.
6. Close the lid again and cook for 2 minutes on HIGH.
7. Serve and enjoy!

Nutrition Values
(Calories 410| Total Fats 5g | Carbs: 70g | Protein 9g| Dietary Fiber: 19g)

Basil Risotto

(Prep Time: 5 Mins |Total Time: 30 Mins |Serves: 2)

Ingredients:
- ¼ Onion, chopped
- 1 cup Rice
- 2 ¼ cup Chicken Broth
- 2 tbsp grated Parmesan Cheese
- 1 tbsp Oil
- A handful of Basil, chopped

Cooking Direction
1. Set your Instant Pot to SAUTE and heat the oil in it.
2. Add the onions and cook for 2 minutes.
3. Add the rice and cook for an additional minute.
4. Pour the broth over, stir to combine, and close the lid.
5. Cook on RICE for 10 minutes.
6. Do a quick pressure release.
7. Drain if there is excess liquid.
8. Stir in the basil and serve topped with parmesan.
9. Enjoy!

Nutrition Values
(Calories 510| Total Fats 7g | Carbs: 80g | Protein 12| Dietary Fiber: 20g)

Wheat Berries with Tomatoes

(Prep Time: 5 Mins |Total Time: 45 Mins |Serves: 2)

Ingredients:
- ¾ cup Wheat Berries
- 1 tbsp Butter
- 8 ounces diced canned Tomatoes
- ½ cup Chicken Broth

Cooking Direction
1. Melt the butter in your Instant Pot on SAUTE.
2. Add the wheat berries and cook for about 2 minutes.
3. Stir in the remaining ingredients.
4. Close the lid and set the IP to MANUAL.
5. Cook on HIGH for 25 minutes.
6. Do a natural pressure release.
7. Serve and enjoy!

Nutrition Values
(Calories 140| Total Fats 7g | Carbs: 15 g | Protein 4g| Dietary Fiber: 4g)

Black Bean Hash

(Prep Time: 5 Mins |Total Time: 10 Mins |Serves: 2)

Ingredients:
- 2 cups cubed Sweet Potatoes
- ½ cup chopped Onions
- 1 tsp Chili Powder
- 1/3 cup Veggie Broth
- 1 cup canned Black Beans, drained
- ¼ cup chopped Scallions
- 1 tbsp Olive Oil

Cooking Direction
1. Heat the oil in your IP on SAUTE.
2. Add the onions and cook for 3 minutes.
3. Add the rest of the ingredients.
4. Give it a good stir to combine well.
5. Close the lid and set the IP to MANUAL.
6. Cook for 3 minutes on HIGH.
7. Release the pressure quickly.
8. Serve and enjoy!

Nutrition Values
(Calories 266| Total Fats 9g| Carbs: 28g | Protein 5g| Dietary Fiber: 6g)

Rich Veggie Risotto

(Prep Time: 5 Mins |Total Time: 30 Mins |Serves: 2)

Ingredients:
- 1 cup Arborio Rice
- 1 Carrot, shredded
- 1 tbsp Olive Oil
- 2 tbsp Butter
- ¼ Onion, chopped
- ¼ cup Heavy Cream
- 5 ounces Mushrooms, sliced
- 2 tbsp grated Parmesan Cheese
- 1 Bell Pepper, diced
- 1 2/3 cup Veggie Stock
- ½ tsp minced Garlic

Cooking Direction
1. Set your Instant Pot to SAUTE and heat the oil in it.
2. Add the onions and peppers and cook for 3 minutes.
3. Add garlic and cook for one more minute.
4. Stir in the carrots and mushrooms. Cook for 3 minutes.
5. Stir in the rice and broth and close the lid.
6. Choose the MANUAL cooking mode.
7. Cook for 10 minutes on HIGH.
8. Do a quick pressure release.
9. Stir in the heavy cream and butter.
10. Sprinkle with parmesan cheese.
11. Serve and enjoy!

Nutrition Values
(Calories 300| Total Fats 4g | Carbs: 47g | Protein 5g| Dietary Fiber: 12g)

Instant Mac and Cheese

(Prep Time: 5 Mins |Total Time: 10 Mins |Serves: 2)

Ingredients:
- 1 tbsp Butter
- 2 cups Elbow Macaroni
- ½ cup Milk
- 2 cups Chicken Stock
- ¾ cup shredded Pepper Jack Cheese
- 2 tbsp Parmesan Cheese
- ¼ tsp Pepper
- Pinch of Salt

Cooking Direction
1. Place all of the ingredients, except the cheese, in the IP.
2. Stir to combine well.
3. Close the lid and choose MANUAL.
4. Cook on HIGH for 7 minutes.
5. Do a quick pressure release.
6. Stir in the shredded cheese and wait to melt before serving.
7. Sprinkle with the parmesan cheese.
8. Serve and enjoy!

Nutrition Values

(Calories 650| Total Fats 49g | Carbs: 48g | Protein 30g| Dietary Fiber: 5g)

Caprese Pasta

(Prep Time: 5 Mins |Total Time: 20 Mins |Serves: 2)

Ingredients:
- 2 cups Penne Pasta
- 2 tsp minced Garlic
- ½ cup halved Grape Tomatoes
- A handful of Basil Leaves
- ½ cup Mozzarella Balls
- 8 ounces Tomato Sauce
- ¼ Onion, diced
- 1 tbsp Balsamic Vinegar
- 2 cups Water
- 1 tbsp Olive Oil

Cooking Direction
1. Heat the oil in the IP on SAUTE.
2. Add the garlic and cook for a minute.
3. Add the sauce, tomatoes, pasta, water, and half of the basil.
4. Stir to combine and close the lid.
5. Set the IP to MANUAL and cook for 5 minutes on HIGH.
6. Do a natural pressure release.
7. Stir in the mozzarella and remaining basil.
8. Serve and enjoy!

Nutrition Values

(Calories 480| Total Fats 9g | Carbs: 80g | Protein 18g| Dietary Fiber: 8g)

Nutty and Minty Barley Salad

(Prep Time: 5 Mins |Total Time: 3 hours and 30 Mins |Serves: 2)

Ingredients:
- 2/3 cup Barley
- ¼ cup chopped Pine Nuts
- 2 tbsp Sparkling Wine
- ¼ tsp Onion Powder
- 1 tsp Lemon Zest
- 2 tbsp chopped Mint
- 1 Spring Onion, chopped
- ¼ tsp Red Pepper Flakes
- 1 tbsp Olive Oil
- 2 cups Water

Cooking Direction
1. Combine the water and barley in the IP and close the lid.
2. Cook on RICE for 17 minutes.
3. Do a quick pressure release.
4. Stir in the remaining ingredients.
5. Transfer the barley to a bowl and cover.
6. Refrigerate for 3 hours.
7. Divide between 2 bowls.
8. Sprinkle with some grated cheese, if desired.
9. Serve and enjoy!

Nutrition Values

(Calories 370| Total Fats 14g | Carbs: 54g | Protein 8g| Dietary Fiber: 18g)

Cheesy Kamut

(Prep Time: 5 Mins |Total Time: 20 Mins |Serves: 2)

Ingredients:
- 2/3 cup Kamut
- 1 Bell Pepper, chopped
- ½ cup halved Cherry Tomatoes
- 2 tbsp Parmesan Cheese
- ¼ cup Haloumi Cheese, chopped
- 2 tbsp Olive Oil
- 1 tsp Honey
- 2 tsp Lemon Juice
- Pinch of Salt
- 2 cups Water

Cooking Direction

1. Combine the kamut and water in your IP.
2. Close the lid and set the IP on SOUP.
3. Cook for about 25 minutes.
4. Do a quick pressure release.
5. Stir in the veggies and cheeses.
6. In a bowl, whisk together the salt, lemon juice, oil, and honey.
7. Drizzle the vinaigrette over the salad. Serve and enjoy!

Nutrition Values

(Calories 280| Total Fats 13g | Carbs: 32g | Protein 8g| Dietary Fiber: 11g)

Black Eyed Pea Lunch Cakes

(Prep Time: 5 Mins |Total Time: 45 Mins |Serves: 2)

Ingredients:
- 1 cup Black Eyed Peas, soaked and rinsed
- 1 Onion, chopped
- 1 Roasted Red Pepper
- 1 tbsp Tomato Paste
- ¼ cup Veggie Broth
- 1 tsp Old Bay Seasoning

Cooking Direction
1. Place the drained beans in a food processor.
2. Place in a bowl with water and remove the skin.
3. Drain and return to the food processor.
4. Add the remaining ingredients. Pulse until smooth.
5. Grease two large ramekins and divide the mixture between them.
6. Wrap the ramekins in foil.
7. Pour some water into your IP (about 1-2 cups) and lower the trivet.
8. Place the ramekins on the trivet and close the lid.
9. Cook for 30 minutes on POULTRY.
10. Do a quick pressure release. Serve and enjoy!

Nutrition Values

(Calories 320| Total Fats 2g | Carbs: 19g | Protein 18g| Dietary Fiber: 5g)

Lentil Sloppy Joe's

(Prep Time: 5 Mins |Total Time: 55 Mins |Serves: 2)

Ingredients:
- 1 cup Green Lentils
- 1 Red Bell Pepper, chopped
- ¼ Onion, chopped
- 1 tbsp Soy Sauce
- 1 tbsp Coconut Sugar
- 1 tbsp Olive Oil
- 1 tbsp Dijon Mustard
- 2 cups Veggie Broth
- 8 ounces canned crushed Tomatoes

Cooking Direction

1. Heat the oil in the IP on SAUTE.
2. Add the onions and peppers and cook for 3 minutes.
3. Stir in the remaining ingredients.
4. Close the lid and select MANUAL.
5. Cook for 22 minutes on HIGH.
6. Do a natural pressure release.
7. Serve and enjoy!

Nutrition Values

(Calories 350| Total Fats 6.5g | Carbs: 75g | Protein 18g| Dietary Fiber: 7g)

Eggplant Burgers

(Prep Time: 5 Mins |Total Time: 25 Mins |Serves: 2)

Ingredients:

- ½ Eggplant, cut in half
- 1 tbsp Mustard
- 1 tbsp Olive Oil
- ¼ cup Panko Breadcrumbs
- 1 cup Water

Cooking Direction

1. Pour the water into the IP and place the eggplants inside.
2. Close the lid and cook for 2 minutes on HIGH.
3. Drain the liquid and pat the eggplants dry with some paper towels.
4. Brush with mustard and coat with breadcrumbs.
5. Wipe the IP clean and heat the oil in it.
6. Add the burgers and cook until golden on all sides.
7. Serve in buns.
8. Serve and enjoy!

Nutrition Values

(Calories 130| Total Fats 2g | Carbs: 9g | Protein 2g| Dietary Fiber: 1g)

Vegetarian Shepherd's Pie

(Prep Time: 5 Mins |Total Time: 17 Mins |Serves: 2)

Ingredients:

- ½ cup diced Onion
- ¼ cup diced Celery
- 1 tbsp Olive Oil
- ¼ cup diced Turnip
- ½ cup diced Tomatoes
- ½ cup grated Potatoes
- ¼ cup diced Carrots
- 1 cup cooked and mashed Cauliflower
- 1 cup Water
- 1 cup Vegie Broth

Cooking Direction

1. Heat the oil in the IP on SAUTE.
2. Add the onions, celery, and carrots. Saute for about 3 minutes.
3. Add the potatoes and turnips and pour the broth over.
4. Close the lid and cook on HIGH for 7 minutes.
5. Do a quick pressure release.
6. Grease a baking dish with cooking spray and transfer the drained veggies to it.
7. Top with the mashed cauliflower.
8. Pour the water into the IP and lower the trivet.
9. Place the baking dish on the trivet and close the lid.
10. Cook on HIGH for 5 minutes.
11. Release the pressure quickly.
12. Serve and enjoy!

Nutrition Values

(Calories 224| Total Fats 14g | Carbs: 6g | Protein 16g| Dietary Fiber: 0g)

Asparagus and Mushrooms

(Prep Time: 5 Mins |Total Time: 9 Mins |Serves: 4)

Ingredients:

- 1 tbsp. coconut oil
- 2 cloves of garlic, minced
- 1 lb. asparagus spears, trimmed
- ½ cup fresh mushrooms
- Salt and pepper to taste

Directions

1. Press the Sauté button on the Instant Pot and heat the oil.
2. Stir in the garlic until fragrant and stir in the asparagus spears and mushrooms. Season with salt and pepper to taste. Add ¼ cup of water.
3. Close the lid and make sure that the vent is sealed.
4. Press the Manual button and adjust the cooking time to 5 minutes.
5. Do natural pressure release.

Nutrition Values

(Calories:61; Total Fat: 3.6g; Carbs: 6.5g; Dietary Fiber: 4.9g; Protein: 3.1g)

Instant Pot Steamed Asparagus

(Prep Time: 5 Mins |Total Time: 10 Mins |Serves: 1)

Ingredients:
- 7 asparagus spears, washed and trimmed
- A pinch of salt
- A dash of pepper
- Juice from ¼ lemon, freshly squeezed
- 1 tbsp. extra virgin olive oil

Directions
1. Place a trivet or the steamer rack in the Instant Pot and pour a cup of water.
2. In a mixing bowl, combine the asparagus spears, salt, pepper, and lemon juice.
3. Place on top of the trivet.
4. Close the lid and seal off the vent.
5. Press the Steam button and adjust the cooking time to 5 minutes.
6. Do natural pressure release.
7. Drizzle the asparagus with olive oil.

Nutrition Values
(Calories:80; Total Fat: 6.2g; Carbs: 6.4g; Dietary Fiber: 4.7g; Protein: 1.5g)

Summer Beet Salad

(Prep Time: 5 Mins |Total Time: 16 Mins |Serves: 6)

Ingredients:
- 4 medium-sized red beets
- 2 tbsp. extra virgin olive oil
- 1 large tomatoes (red and yellow), chopped
- 1 cup baby arugula
- Salt and pepper to taste

Directions
1. Wash the beets and peel. Cut the beets into cubes.
2. Place a trivet or the steamer rack in the Instant Pot and pour a cup of water.
3. Place the beets on the trivet.
4. Close the lid and seal off the vent.
5. Press the Steam button and adjust the cooking time to 6 minutes.
6. Do quick pressure release.
7. Take the beets out and allow to cool for a few minutes.
8. Assemble the salad by combining the steamed beets with the rest of the ingredients.
9. Serve chilled.

Nutrition Values
(Calories:51; Total Fat: 2.2g; Carbs: 7.2g; Dietary Fiber: 5.8g; Protein: 1.4g)

Sautéed Brussels Sprouts And Pecans

(Prep Time: 5 Mins |Total Time: 10 Mins |Serves: 4)

Ingredients:
- 1 tbsp. coconut oil
- 2 cloves of garlic, minced
- 2 cups baby Brussels sprouts
- Salt and pepper to taste
- ¼ cup pecans, chopped

Directions
1. Press the Sauté button on the Instant Pot and heat the oil.
2. Sauté the garlic until fragrant.
3. Stir in the Brussels sprouts and season with salt and pepper to taste.
4. Pour a few tablespoons of water to add moisture.
5. Close the lid and seal off the vent.
6. Press the Manual button and adjust the cooking time to 3 minutes.
7. Do quick pressure release.
8. Once the lid is open, stir in the pecans for 3 minutes.

Nutrition Values
(Calories:98; Total Fat: 8.1g; Carbs: 6.3g; Dietary Fiber: 4.5g; Protein: 2.3g)

Vegetables Casserole

(Prep Time: 15 Mins |Total Time: 45 Mins |Serves: 6)

Ingredients
- 2 medium green bell pepper, seeded and chopped
- 2 cups tomatoes, chopped
- 2 medium zucchinis, chopped
- 16 large eggs
- 1 cup almond flour

- 1 cup almond milk
- 1½ cups mozzarella cheese, shredded
- Salt and black pepper, to taste

Cooking Direction
1. Place the steamer trivet in the bottom of Instant Pot and add water.
2. Mix together almond flour, almond milk, eggs, salt and black pepper in a bowl.
3. Beat well and add vegetables and cheese.
4. Put the bowl on the trivet and close the lid.
5. Set the Instant Pot to "Manual" at high pressure for 25 minutes.
6. Release the pressure naturally and dish out.

Nutrition Values
(Calories: 443; Total Fat: 33.7g; Carbs: 15g; Sugars: 7.7g; Protein: 25.4g)

Coconut Cabbage

(Prep Time: 5 Mins |Total Time: 25 Mins |Serves: 4)

Ingredients:
- 1 head of cabbage, shredded
- 1 onion, halved
- 1 bulb of garlic, crushed
- 1 thumb-size ginger, sliced
- 2 cups of coconut milk, freshly squeezed

Directions
1. Place all ingredients in the Instant Pot and give a good stir. Season with salt and pepper to taste.
2. Close the lid and seal off the vent.
3. Press the Manual button and adjust the cooking time to 20 minutes.
4. Do quick pressure release.

Nutrition Values
(Calories:331; Total Fat: 28.9g; Carbs: 19.7g; Dietary Fiber: 15.3g; Protein: 5.1g)

Steamed Paprika Broccoli

(Prep Time: 5 Mins |Total Time: 11 Mins |Serves: 2)

Ingredients:
- 1 broccoli head, cut into florets
- A dash of salt
- A dash of ground black pepper
- 1 tbsp. paprika
- 1 tbsp. lemon juice, freshly squeezed

Directions
1. Place a trivet or the steamer rack in the Instant Pot and pour a cup of water.
2. Place the broccoli florets on the trivet and sprinkle salt, pepper, paprika, and lemon juice.
3. Close the lid and seal off the vent.
4. Press the Steam button and adjust the cooking time to 6 minutes.
5. Do quick pressure release.

Nutrition Values
(Calories:22; Total Fat: 0.5g; Carbs: 4.7g; Dietary Fiber: 3.6g; Protein: 1.3g)

Cauliflower Mushroom Risotto

(Prep Time: 5 Mins |Total Time: 17 Mins |Serves: 3)

Ingredients:
- 1 tbsp. coconut oil
- 1 onion, chopped
- 1 head cauliflower, grated
- 1 lb. shiitake mushrooms, sliced
- 1 cup coconut milk, freshly squeezed

Directions
1. Press the Sauté button and heat the coconut oil.
2. Sauté the onions until fragrant. Stir in the cauliflower and shiitake mushrooms. Season with salt and pepper to taste.
3. Add the coconut milk in three batches.
4. Allow to simmer for 10 minutes.
5. Garnish with chopped parsley if desired.

Nutrition Values
(Calories:344; Total Fat: 24.2g; Carbs: 34g; Dietary Fiber: 26.4g; Protein: 6.3g)

Vegetarian Smothered Cajun Greens

(Prep Time: 5 Mins |Total Time: 9 Mins |Serves: 4)

Ingredients:

- 1 tbsp. coconut oil
- 1 onion, chopped
- 2 tsp. crushed garlic
- 6 cups raw greens (mustard, collard, spinach, and kale)
- Salt and pepper to taste

Directions

1. Press the Sauté button on the Instant Pot and heat the coconut oil.
2. Sauté the onion and garlic until fragrant.
3. Stir in the greens and season with salt and pepper to taste.
4. Add a cup of water.
5. Close the lid and seal the vent.
6. Press the Manual button and adjust the cooking time to 3 minutes.
7. Do quick pressure release.
8. Sprinkle with red chilli flakes if desired.

Nutrition Values

(Calories:70; Total Fat: 3.8g; Carbs: 8.2g; Dietary Fiber: 5.8g; Protein: 3.2g)

Caramelized Onions

(Prep Time: 5 Mins |Total Time: 40 Mins |Serves: 2)

Ingredients:

- 3 tbsp. coconut oil
- 3 large white onions, sliced
- Salt to taste
- A dash of pepper
- 1 tbsp. lemon juice, freshly squeezed

Directions

1. Press the Sauté button on the Instant Pot and heat the coconut oil.
2. Sauté the onions for 5 minutes and season with the remaining ingredients.
3. Add a cup of water and mix.
4. Close the lid and seal off the vent.
5. Press the Manual button and adjust the cooking time to 20 minutes.
6. Do natural pressure release.
7. Once the lid is open, press the Sauté button and continue cooking for another 10 minutes.

Nutrition Values

(Calories:277; Total Fat: 20.7g; Carbs: 23.8g; Dietary Fiber: 19.3g; Protein: 2.8g)

Zucchini and Tomato Melange

(Prep Time: 5 Mins |Total Time: 23 Mins |Serves: 4)

Ingredients:

- 1 lb. tomatoes, pureed
- 1 tbsp. coconut oil
- 5 cloves of garlic, minced
- 1 onion, chopped
- 3 medium zucchinis, chopped

Directions

1. Place the tomatoes in a food processor and blend until smooth.
2. Press the Sauté button on the Instant Pot and heat the oil.
3. Sauté the garlic and onions until fragrant.
4. Add the zucchini and tomato puree. Season with salt and pepper to taste. Add a cup of water to add more moisture.
5. Close the lid and seal off the vent.
6. Press the Manual button and adjust the cooking time to 10 minutes.
7. Do quick pressure release.

Nutrition Values

(Calories:66; Total Fat: 3.8g; Carbs: 7.5g; Dietary Fiber: 3.9g; Protein: 2.1g)

Instant Pot Veggie Stew

(Prep Time: 5 Mins |Total Time: 15 Mins |Serves: 5)

Ingredients:

- 1 onion, chopped
- 1 stalk celery, minced
- 1 lb. mushrooms, sliced
- 2 zucchinis, chopped
- ½ cup chopped tomatoes

Directions

1. Place all ingredients in the Instant Pot.
2. Season with salt and pepper to taste. Pour in water until half of the vegetables are submerged.
3. Close the lid and seal off the vent.
4. Press the Manual button and adjust the cooking time to 10 minutes.
5. Do natural pressure release.

Nutrition Values
(Calories:281; Total Fat: 0.9g; Carbs: 71.2g; Dietary Fiber: 50.3g; Protein: 9.2g)

Zucchini and Bell Pepper Stir Fry

(Prep Time: 5 Mins |Total Time: 11 Mins |Serves: 6)

Ingredients:
- 1 tbsp. coconut oil
- 1 onion, chopped
- 4 cloves of garlic, minced
- 2 large zucchinis, sliced
- 2 red sweet bell peppers, julienned

Directions
1. Press the Sauté button on the Instant Pot.
2. Heat the coconut oil and sauté the onion and garlic until fragrant.
3. Stir in the zucchini and red bell peppers. Season with salt and pepper to taste.
4. Pour ¼ cup of water.
5. Close the lid and seal off the vent.
6. Press the Manual button and adjust the cooking time to 5 minutes.
7. Do quick pressure release.

Nutrition Values
(Calories:54; Total Fat: 2.7g; Carbs: 7.2g; Dietary Fiber: 4.6g; Protein: 1.8g)

Eggplant, Zucchini, And Tomatoes

(Prep Time: 5 Mins |Total Time: 14 Mins |Serves: 6)

Ingredients:
- 3 tbsp. olive oil
- 1 onion, diced
- 1 eggplant, chopped
- 3 tomatoes, sliced
- 3 zucchinis, sliced

Directions
1. Press the Sauté button on the Instant Pot and heat the olive oil.
2. Sauté the onions until fragrant and Add the eggplants. Stir for another 2 minutes.
3. Add the tomatoes and zucchini.
4. Season with salt and pepper to taste.
5. Add ¼ cup of water.
6. Close the lid and seal off the vent.
7. Press the Manual button and adjust the cooking time to 6 minutes.

Nutrition Values
(Calories:92; Total Fat: 6.8g; Carbs: 7.9g; Dietary Fiber: 5.3g; Protein: 1.3g)

Instant Pot Baby Bok Choy

(Prep Time: 5 Mins |Total Time: 11 Mins |Serves: 6)

Ingredients:
- 1 tsp. peanut oil
- 4 cloves of garlic, minced
- 1 lb. baby bok choy, trimmed and washed
- Salt and pepper to taste
- ½ cup water

Directions
1. Press the Sauté button on the Instant Pot.
2. Heat the oil and sauté the garlic until fragrant.
3. Add the bok choy and season with salt and pepper to taste.
4. Pour in water.
5. Close the lid and seal off the vent.
6. Press the Manual button and adjust the cooking time to 4 minutes.
7. Do quick pressure release.
8. Sprinkle with red pepper flakes if desired.

Nutrition Values
(Calories:273; Total Fat: 4.7g; Carbs: 53.2g; Dietary Fiber: 42.1g; Protein: 4.3g)

Instant Pot Artichokes

(Prep Time: 5 Mins |Total Time: 35 Mins |Serves: 8)

Ingredients:

- 4 large artichokes, trimmed and cleaned
- 1 cloves of garlic, crushed
- 1 onion, chopped
- ½ cup organic chicken broth
- Salt and pepper to taste

Directions

1. Place all ingredients in the Instant Pot.
2. Close the lid and seal off the vent.
3. Press the Manual button and adjust the cooking time to 30 minutes.
4. Do quick pressure release.
5. Serve the artichokes with lemon juice.

Nutrition Values

(Calories:47; Total Fat: 0.2g; Carbs: 10.5g; Dietary Fiber: 7.6g; protein: 3.1g)

Coconut Cauliflower Rice

(Prep Time: 5 Mins |Total Time: 15 Mins |Serves: 3)

Ingredients:

- 1 head cauliflower, grated
- 3 cloves of garlic, minced
- 1 onion, chopped
- 1 cup coconut milk, freshly squeezed
- Salt and pepper to taste

Directions

1. Place all ingredients in the Instant Pot.
2. Close the lid and seal off the vent.
3. Press the Manual button and adjust the cooking time to 10 minutes.
4. Do quick pressure release.

Nutrition Values

(Calories:231; Total Fat: 19.4g; Carbs: 14.6g; Dietary Fiber: 10.3g; Protein: 4.4g)

Cauliflower Mash

(Prep Time: 5 Mins |Total Time: 20 Mins |Serves: 4)

Ingredients:

- 1 head of cauliflower
- ¼ tsp. garlic powder
- ¼ tsp. salt
- ¼ tsp. ground black pepper
- 1 handful of chives, chopped

Directions

1. Place a trivet or steamer basket in the Instant Pot and pour a cup of water.
2. Place the cauliflower head and close the lid.
3. Make sure that the vent is sealed.
4. Press the Steam button and adjust the cooking time to 10 minutes.
5. Do natural pressure release.
6. Place the cauliflower in a food processor and pulse.
7. Stir in the garlic powder, salt, and pepper.
8. Garnish with chives.

Nutrition Values

(Calories:18; Total Fat: 0.2g; Carbs: 3.7g; Dietary Fiber: 2.4g; Protein: 1.3g)

Brussels Sprout Salad

(Prep Time: 10 Mins |Total Time: 15 Mins |Serves: 4)

Ingredients

- 1 pound Brussels sprouts, trimmed and halved
- 1 cup pomegranate seeds
- ¼ cup cashew nuts, chopped
- ½ tablespoon unsalted butter, melted
- ¼ cup almonds, chopped
- 1 cup water
- Salt and black pepper, to taste

Directions

1. Place the steamer trivet in the bottom of Instant Pot and add water.
2. Put the Brussels sprout on the trivet.
3. Set the Instant Pot to "Manual" at high pressure for 4 minutes.
4. Release the pressure naturally and top with melted butter, almonds, cashew nuts and pomegranate seeds.

Nutrition Values

(Calories: 170; Total Fat: 8.8g; Carbs: 20.4g; Sugars: 6.1g; Protein: 6.7g)

Whole Garlic Roast

(Prep Time: 2 Mins |Total Time: 11 Mins |Serves: 4)

Ingredients

- 4 large garlic bulbs
- 2 tablespoons herbed butter
- 1 cup water
- Salt and black pepper, to taste

Directions

1. Place the steamer trivet in the bottom of Instant Pot and add water.
2. Season the garlic bulbs with salt and pepper.
3. Put the seasoned garlic bulbs on the trivet.
4. Set the Instant Pot to "Manual" at high pressure for 6 minutes.
5. Release the pressure naturally and remove the trivet.
6. Put the herbed butter and garlic bulbs and select "Sauté".
7. Sauté for 3 minutes and dish out.

Nutrition Values

(Calories: 66; Total Fat: 5.8g; Carbs: 3g; Sugars: 0g; Protein: 0.1g)

Tangy Lemon Potatoes

(Prep Time: 3 Mins |Total Time: 15 Mins |Serves: 6)

Ingredients

- 10 medium potatoes, scrubbed and cubed
- 4 tablespoons fresh lemon juice
- 2 tablespoons olive oil
- 4 tablespoons fresh rosemary, chopped
- 2 cups vegetable broth
- Salt and black pepper, to taste

Cooking Direction

1. Put the olive oil and potatoes in the Instant Pot and select "Sauté".
2. Sauté for 4 minutes and add the rosemary, salt and black pepper.
3. Sauté for 2 minutes and stir in the lemon juice and broth.
4. Set the Instant Pot to "Manual" at high pressure for 6 minutes.
5. Release the pressure naturally and serve warm.

Nutrition Values

(Calories: 307; Total Fat: 5.9g; Carbs: 57.7g; Sugars: 4.5g; Protein: 7.8g)

Caramelised Onions

(Prep Time: 3 Mins |Total Time: 12 Mins |Serves: 2)

Ingredients

- 3 large onion bulbs
- 1 cup water
- 1 tablespoon butter
- Salt and black pepper, to taste

Cooking Direction

1. Place the steamer trivet in the bottom of Instant Pot and add water.
2. Season the onion bulbs with salt and pepper.
3. Put the seasoned onion bulbs on the trivet.
4. Set the Instant Pot to "Manual" at high pressure for 6 minutes.
5. Release the pressure naturally and remove the trivet.
6. Put the butter and garlic bulbs and select "Sauté".
7. Sauté for 3 minutes and dish out.

Nutrition Values

(Calories: 63; Total Fat: 5.8g; Carbs: 2.8g; Sugars: 0.9g; Protein: 0.8g)

Tomato Sauce Spinach

(Prep Time: 5 Mins |Total Time: 18 Mins |Serves: 4)

Ingredients

- 1 tablespoon olive oil
- 1 small onion, chopped
- 1 teaspoon garlic, minced
- ½ teaspoon red pepper flakes, crushed
- 5 cups fresh spinach, chopped
- ½ cup tomatoes, chopped

- ¼ cup homemade tomato puree
- ¼ cup white wine
- ½ cup vegetable broth

Cooking Direction
1. Put the olive oil and onions in the Instant Pot and select "Sauté".
2. Sauté for 4 minutes and add garlic, spinach and red pepper flakes.
3. Sauté for 3 minutes and stir in the remaining ingredients.
4. Set the Instant Pot to "Manual" at high pressure for 6 minutes.
5. Release the pressure quickly and serve warm.

Nutrition Values
(Calories: 72; Total Fat: 3.9g; Carbs: 5.5g; Sugars: 2.2g; Protein: 2.3g)

Steamed Tomatoes

(Prep Time: 3 Mins |Total Time: 10 Mins |Serves: 4)

Ingredients
- 4 large tomatoes
- 1 cup water
- 1 tablespoon herbed butter
- 1 cup mozzarella cheese, shredded

Cooking Direction
1. Place the steamer trivet in the bottom of Instant Pot and add water.
2. Scoop out the inner filling of the tomato and stuff with the mozzarella cheese.
3. Put the stuffed tomatoes on the trivet.
4. Set the Instant Pot to "Manual" at high pressure for 5 minutes.
5. Release the pressure naturally and remove the trivet.
6. Put the herbed butter and stuffed tomatoes and select "Sauté".
7. Sauté for 2 minutes and dish out.

Nutrition Values
(Calories: 75; Total Fat: 3.2g; Carbs: 7.5g; Sugars: 4.9g; Protein: 5g)

Glazed Carrots

(Prep Time: 5 Mins |Total Time: 10 Mins |Serves: 3)

Ingredients
- 1 pound carrots, peeled and sliced diagonally
- ½ cup water
- 1 tablespoon honey
- ¼ cup golden raisins
- 1 tablespoon unsalted butter, melted
- ½ teaspoon red pepper flakes, crushed
- Pinch of salt

Directions
1. Put the carrots, water and raisins in the Instant Pot.
2. Set the Instant Pot to "Manual" at low pressure for 5 minutes.
3. Release the pressure naturally and transfer he carrots into a bowl.
4. Stir in the remaining ingredients and mix well to serve.

Nutrition Values
(Calories: 154; Total Fat: 4g; Carbs: 30.4g; Sugars: 20.4g; Protein: 1.7g)

Chili Polenta

(Prep Time: 5 Mins |Total Time: 15 Mins |Serves: 6)

Ingredients
- 3 cups coarse polenta
- 10 cups water
- 3 teaspoons salt
- 3tablespoons red paprika flakes

Cooking Direction
1. Put the water, salt, red paprika flakes and polenta flour in the Instant Pot.
2. Set the Instant Pot to "Manual" at high pressure for 9 minutes.
3. Release the pressure naturally and dish out.

Nutrition Values
(Calories: 310; Total Fat: 9.7g; Carbs: 66.8g; Sugars: 0.8g; Protein: 5.8g)

Rosemary Baby Potatoes

(Prep Time: 5 Mins |Total Time: 20 Mins |Serves: 7)

Ingredients

- 20 baby potatoes
- 2 cups water
- 1 cup fresh rosemary
- 4tablespoons herb butter

Cooking Direction

1. Place the steamer trivet in the bottom of Instant Pot and add water.
2. Put the baby potatoes and rosemary on the trivet.
3. Set the Instant Pot to "Manual" at high pressure for 10 minutes.
4. Release the pressure naturally and remove the trivet.
5. Put the herbed butter and baby potatoes and select "Sauté".
6. Sauté for 5 minutes and dish out.

Nutrition Values

(Calories: 108; Total Fat: 1.7g; Carbs: 22.1g; Sugars: 0g; Protein: 3.6g)

Steamed Cabbage Sheets

(Prep Time: 6 Mins |Total Time: 15 Mins |Serves: 4)

Ingredients

- 12 sheets of fresh cabbage
- 3 teaspoons fresh basil
- 3 teaspoons olive oil
- 2 cups water
- Salt and pepper

Cooking Direction

1. Place the steamer trivet in the bottom of Instant Pot and add water.
2. Put the cabbage sheets and basil on the trivet.
3. Set the Instant Pot to "Manual" at high pressure for 6 minutes.
4. Release the pressure naturally and remove the trivet.
5. Put the olive oil, cabbage sheets, salt and black pepper and select "Sauté".
6. Sauté for 3 minutes and dish out.

Nutrition Values

(Calories: 55; Total Fat: 3.6g; Carbs: 5.8g; Sugars: 3.2g; Protein: 1.3g)

Corn Kernels

(Prep Time: 5 Mins |Total Time: 13 Mins |Serves: 4)

Ingredients

- 1½ cups corn kernels
- 2 cups water
- 1 tablespoons lemon juice
- 2 tablespoons butter
- 1 teaspoon red pepper powder
- Salt and black pepper, to taste

Cooking Direction

1. Season the corn kernels with red pepper powder, salt and black pepper
2. Place the steamer trivet in the bottom of Instant Pot and add water.
3. Put the seasoned corn kernels on the trivet.
4. Set the Instant Pot to "Manual" at high pressure for 5 minutes.
5. Release the pressure naturally and remove the trivet.
6. Put the butter and corn kernels and select "Sauté".
7. Sauté for 3 minutes and stir in the lemon juice.

Nutrition Values

(Calories: 188; Total Fat: 6.7g; Carbs: 32.2g; Sugars: 5.6g; Protein: 5.6g)

Steamed French and Broad Beans

(Prep Time: 5 Mins |Total Time: 23 Mins |Serves: 6)

Ingredients

- 1 cup French beans, washed
- 1 cup broad beans, washed
- 1 teaspoon ginger powder
- 3 cups water
- 3 tablespoons olive oil
- Salt and black pepper, to taste

Cooking Direction

1. Season the French beans and broad beans with ginger powder, salt and black pepper
2. Place the steamer trivet in the bottom of Instant Pot and add water.
3. Put the seasoned beans on the trivet.
4. Set the Instant Pot to "Manual" at high pressure for 12 minutes.
5. Release the pressure naturally and remove the trivet.
6. Put the olive oil and beans and select "Sauté".
7. Sauté for 5 minutes and stir in the lemon juice.

Nutrition Values

(Calories: 260; Total Fat: 8g; Carbs: 37.2g; Sugars: 0.7g; Protein: 11.1g)

Thai Sweet Potatoes

(Prep Time: 5 Mins |Total Time: 15 Mins |Serves: 5)

Ingredients

- 3 cups sweet potatoes
- 1 tablespoon butter
- 1 cup water
- ¼ cup Thai red sauce
- 1 tablespoon brown sugar
- 1½ cups brown rice, cooked
- ½ cup pecans, chopped
- ¾ cup cheddar cheese, shredded

Cooking Direction

1. Put the water and sweet potatoes in the Instant Pot.
2. Set the Instant Pot to "Manual" at high pressure for 7 minutes.
3. Release the pressure naturally and add rest of the ingredients except rice and cheese.
4. Let it simmer for 3 minutes and dish out over the cooked rice.
5. Garnish with shredded cheddar cheese and serve.

Nutrition Values

(Calories: 441; Total Fat: 12.7g; Carbs: 71.5g; Sugars: 2.7g; Protein: 10.4g)

Mixed Veggies

(Prep Time: 10 Mins |Total Time: 22 Mins |Serves: 3)

Ingredients

- 1 tablespoon olive oil
- 8 oz. mushrooms, sliced
- 1 zucchini, sliced
- 1 bell pepper, diced
- 1 Japanese eggplant, peeled and sliced
- 1 medium potato, peeled and diced
- 1 small onion, thinly sliced
- 1 garlic clove, minced
- 1 tablespoon tomato paste
- 1 teaspoon oregano
- 1 teaspoon basil
- 3 tablespoons water
- ¼ teaspoon red pepper flakes
- ½ cup Parmigiano-Reggiano cheese, grated
- Salt and pepper, to taste

Cooking Direction

1. Put the olive oil, onions, garlic and potatoes in the Instant Pot and select "Sauté".
2. Sauté for 3 minutes and add rest of the ingredients except cheese.
3. Set the Instant Pot to "Manual" at high pressure for 10 minutes.
4. Release the pressure naturally and add Parmigiano-Reggiano cheese.

Nutrition Values

(Calories: 212; Total Fat: 6.6g; Carbs: 34.9g; Sugars: 12.2g; Protein: 8.9g)

Delicious Succotash

(Prep Time: 7 Mins |Total Time: 20 Mins |Serves: 6)

Ingredients
- 1 cup bell peppers
- 2 cups complete corn kernels
- 2 cups water
- 3 tablespoons butter
- 2 cups lima beans
- 2 cups tomatoes
- 2 teaspoons salt

Cooking Direction

1. Put the butter and bell peppers in the Instant Pot and select "Sauté".
2. Sauté for 3 minutes and add rest of the ingredients.
3. Set the Instant Pot to "Manual" at high pressure for 10 minutes.
4. Release the pressure naturally and serve hot.

Nutrition Values
(Calories: 153; Total Fat: 6.7g; Carbs: 19.7g; Sugars: 5.4g; Protein: 5g)

Vegetable Medley

(Prep Time: 5 Mins |Total Time: 14 Mins |Serves: 3)

Ingredients
- 1 small sweet potato, peeled and diced
- 2 carrots, peeled and diced
- 3 pink potatoes, quartered
- 1½ cups butternut squash
- 1 tablespoon olive oil
- 1 sprig rosemary
- ½ cup water
- Salt and pepper, to taste

Cooking Direction

1. Put the olive oil and rosemary sprig in the Instant Pot and select "Sauté".
2. Sauté for 2 minutes and add rest of the ingredients.
3. Set the Instant Pot to "Manual" at high pressure for 7 minutes.
4. Release the pressure naturally and serve hot.

Nutrition Values
(Calories: 202; Total Fat: 5.2g; Carbs: 40.6g; Sugars: 9g; Protein: 3.6g)

Couscous Stuffed Peppers

(Prep Time: 10 Mins |Total Time: 46 Mins |Serves: 4)

Ingredients
- 1 cup couscous
- 4 tablespoons pine nuts, roasted
- 4 large red bell peppers
- 2 cups water
- 2 teaspoons dried oregano
- 1 teaspoon salt
- ½ teaspoon black pepper
- ¼ cup feta cheese, crumbled

Cooking Direction

1. Put the water and couscous in the Instant Pot.
2. Set the Instant Pot to "Manual" at high pressure for 3 minutes.
3. Release the pressure naturally and add rest of the ingredients.
4. Sauté for 3 minutes and fill this stuffing evenly in the bell peppers.
5. Bake in a pre-heated oven at 375ºF for 30 minutes.

Nutrition Values
(Calories: 286; Total Fat: 8.6g; Carbs: 44.6g; Sugars: 6.7g; Protein: 9.3g)

Spicy Cauliflower

(Prep Time: 10 Mins |Total Time: 15 Mins |Serves: 3)

Ingredients
- 1 pound cauliflower
- ½ cup vegetable broth
- 1 tablespoon fresh lemon juice
- 1 tablespoon olive oil
- 1 teaspoon red pepper flakes, crushed
- Salt, to taste

Cooking Direction

1. Season the cauliflower with salt and red pepper flakes.
2. Put the olive oil and cauliflowers in the Instant Pot and select "Sauté".
3. Sauté for 4 minutes and add vegetable broth.
4. Set the Instant Pot to "Manual" at high pressure for 6 minutes.
5. Release the pressure naturally and stir in the lemon juice.

Nutrition Values
(Calories: 87; Total Fat: 5.2g; Carbs: 8.6g; Sugars: 3.9g; Protein: 3.9g)

Nutty Brussels Sprouts

(Prep Time: 5 Mins |Total Time: 9 Mins |Serves: 3)

Ingredients

- 1 pound brussels sprouts, trimmed and halved
- ½ tablespoon butter, melted
- ½ cup almonds, chopped
- 1 teaspoon salt

Cooking Direction

1. Place the steamer trivet in the bottom of Instant Pot and add water.
2. Put the brussels sprouts on the trivet.
3. Set the Instant Pot to "Manual" at high pressure for 4 minutes.
4. Release the pressure quickly and remove the trivet.
5. Drizzle with butter and top with almonds.

Nutrition Values
(Calories: 174; Total Fat: 10.4g; Carbs: 17.1g; Sugars: 3.9g; Protein: 8.5g)

Simple Broccoli

(Prep Time: 5 Mins |Total Time: 10 Mins |Serves: 3)

Ingredients

- 1 pound broccoli florets
- 1 cup water
- 2 tablespoons butter, melted
- Salt and freshly ground black pepper, to taste

Cooking Direction

1. Place the steamer trivet in the bottom of Instant Pot and add water.
2. Put the broccoli florets on the trivet.
3. Set the Instant Pot to "Manual" at high pressure for 5 minutes.
4. Release the pressure quickly and remove the trivet.
5. Drizzle with butter and season with salt and black pepper.

Nutrition Values
(Calories: 119; Total Fat: 8.2g; Carbs: 10.1g; Sugars: 2.6g; Protein: 4.3g)

Kale and Carrots Platter

(Prep Time: 5 Mins |Total Time: 22 Mins |Serves: 4)

Ingredients

- 1 cup fresh kale, trimmed and chopped
- 3 medium carrots, peeled and cut into ½-inch slices
- 5 garlic cloves, minced
- 2tablespoons olive oil
- 1 small onion, chopped
- ½ cup vegetable broth
- 1 tablespoon fresh lemon juice
- ¼ teaspoon red pepper flakes, crushed
- Salt and black pepper, to taste

Cooking Direction

1. Put the olive oil, garlic and onions in the Instant Pot and select "Sauté".
2. Sauté for 4 minutes and add carrots.
3. Sauté for 3 minutes and add broth, kale, red pepper flakes, salt and black pepper.
4. Set the Instant Pot to "Manual" at high pressure for 9 minutes.
5. Release the pressure naturally and stir in the lemon juice.

Nutrition Values
(Calories: 103; Total Fat: 7.1g; Carbs: 9.7g; Sugars: 3.4g; Protein: 1.4g

Healthy Spinach Plate

(Prep Time: 5 Mins |Total Time: 19 Mins |Serves: 3)

Ingredients

- 5 cups fresh spinach, chopped
- 1 small onion, chopped
- 1 cup vegetable broth
- 1 tablespoon garlic, minced
- 1tablespoon olive oil
- 1 tablespoon fresh lemon juice
- ½ cup tomatoes, chopped
- ½ cup tomato puree
- ½ teaspoon red pepper flakes, crushed
- Salt and freshly ground black pepper, to taste

Cooking Direction

1. Put the olive oil, garlic and onions in the Instant Pot and select "Sauté".
2. Sauté for 4 minutes and add spinach, red pepper flakes, salt and black pepper.
3. Sauté for 3 minutes and add in the remaining ingredients.
4. Set the Instant Pot to "Manual" at high pressure for 7 minutes.
5. Release the pressure quickly and serve hot.

Nutrition Values

(Calories: 101 ; Total Fat: 5.6g; Carbs: 10.4g; Sugars: 4.4g; Protein: 4.5g

Refreshing Green Beans

(Prep Time: 5 Mins |Total Time: 11 Mins |Serves: 6)

Ingredients

- 2 pounds fresh green beans
- 2 garlic cloves, minced
- 4 tablespoons butter
- 3 cups water
- Salt and freshly ground black pepper, to taste

Cooking Direction

1. Put the fresh green beans and all other ingredients in the Instant Pot.
2. Set the Instant Pot to "Manual" at high pressure for 6 minutes.
3. Release the pressure quickly and serve hot.

Nutrition Values

(Calories: 116; Total Fat: 7.9g; Carbs: 11.1g; Sugars: 2.1g; Protein: 2.9g)

Colorful Veggies

(Prep Time: 5 Mins |Total Time: 18 Mins |Serves: 8)

Ingredients

- 1½ pounds cherry tomatoes
- 8 medium zucchinis, chopped roughly
- 2 tablespoons olive oil
- 3 garlic cloves, minced
- 3 small yellow onions, chopped roughly
- 1½ cups water
- 3 tablespoons fresh basil, chopped
- Salt and black pepper, to taste

Cooking Direction

1. Put the olive oil, garlic and onions in the Instant Pot and select "Sauté".
2. Sauté for 4 minutes and add zucchinis and tomatoes.
3. Sauté for 3 minutes and add remaining ingredients except basil.
4. Set the Instant Pot to "Manual" at high pressure for 6 minutes.
5. Release the pressure naturally and garnish with basil.

Nutrition Values

(Calories: 130; Total Fat: 4.5g; Carbs: 21.6g; Sugars: 12.7g; Protein: 5.5g)

Chapter 8 Snack Recipes

Spiced Nuts

(Prep Time: 10 Mins |Total Time: 30 Mins |Serves: 6)

Ingredients

- 1 cup cashews
- 1 cup almonds
- 1 cup pecans
- 1 cup raisins
- 1 tablespoon butter
- ½ teaspoon brown sugar
- ½ teaspoon black pepper
- 1½ teaspoon chilli powder
- ½ teaspoon sea salt
- ½ teaspoon garlic powder
- ¼ teaspoon cayenne pepper
- ½ teaspoon cumin powder

Cooking Direction

1. Put the butter, almonds, cashews, raisins and pecans in the Instant Pot.
2. Season with all the spices and stir gently.
3. Set the instant pot to "Manual" and cook for 20 minutes at high pressure.
4. Release the pressure naturally and serve.

Nutrition Values

(Calories: 335; Total Fat: 22.4g; Carbs: 31.5g; Sugars: 16.5g; Protein: 8.1g)

Mushroom Spinach Treat

(Prep Time: 10 Mins |Total Time: 22 Mins |Serves: 3)

Ingredients

- ½ cup spinach
- ½ pound fresh mushrooms, sliced
- 2 garlic cloves, minced
- 2 tablespoons fresh thyme, chopped
- 1 onion, chopped
- 1 tablespoon olive oil
- 1 tablespoon fresh cilantro, chopped
- Salt and black pepper, to taste

Cooking Direction

1. Put the olive oil, garlic and onions in the Instant Pot and select "Sauté".
2. Sauté for 4 minutes and add spinach, mushrooms, salt, black pepper and thyme.
3. Set the instant pot to "Manual" and cook for 7 minutes at high pressure.
4. Release the pressure naturally and garnish with cilantro.

Nutrition Values

(Calories: 86; Total Fat: 5.32g; Carbs: 8.1g; Sugars: 3g; Protein: 4gg)

Spicy Roasted Olives

(Prep Time: 10 Mins |Total Time: 17 Mins |Serves: 4)

Ingredients

- 2 cups green and black olives, mixed
- 2 tangerines
- 2 garlic cloves, minced
- 2 tablespoons vinegar
- ½ inch piece of turmeric, finely grated
- 1 fresh red chilli, thinly sliced
- 2 sprigs rosemary
- 1 tablespoon olive oil

Cooking Direction

1. Put all the ingredients except the tangerines in the Instant Pot.
2. Squeeze the tangerines in the Instant Pot over all the ingredients.
3. Set the instant pot to "Manual" and cook for 6 minutes at high pressure.
4. Release the pressure naturally and dish out.

Nutrition Values

(Calories: 163; Total Fat: 13.6g; Carbs: 2.3g; Sugars: 0.5g; Protein: 0.4g)

Cooked Guacamole

(Prep Time: 10 Mins |Total Time: 20 Mins |Serves: 4)

Ingredients

- 1 large onion, finely diced
- 4 tablespoons lemon juice
- ¼ cup cilantro, chopped
- 4 avocados, peeled and diced
- 3 tablespoons olive oil
- 3 jalapenos, finely diced
- Salt and black pepper, to taste

Cooking Direction

1. Put the olive oil and onions in the Instant Pot and select "Sauté".
2. Sauté for 3 minutes and add cilantro, lemon juice, avocados, salt, black pepper and jalapenos.
3. Set the instant pot to "Manual" and cook for 6 minutes at high pressure.
4. Release the pressure naturally and dish out.

Nutrition Values

(Calories: 401; Total Fat: 37.4g; Carbs: 19.4g; Sugars: 2.8g; Protein: 4.18g)

Butternut Squash

(Prep Time: 10 Mins |Total Time: 17 Mins |Serves: 2)

Ingredients

- 1 whole butternut squash, washed
- 1 tablespoon butter
- 1 tablespoon BBQ sauce
- Salt and black pepper, to taste
- ¼ teaspoon smoked paprika

Cooking Direction

1. Season the butternut squash with paprika, salt and pepper.
2. Put the butter and seasoned whole butternut squash in the Instant Pot.
3. Set the instant pot to "Manual" and cook for 6 minutes at high pressure.
4. Release the pressure naturally and top with BBQ sauce.

Nutrition Values

(Calories: 154; Total Fat: 6.6g; Carbs: 19.5g; Sugars: 5.6g; Protein: 3.1g;)

Baked Potato

(Prep Time: 10 Mins |Total Time: 40 Mins |Serves: 2)

Ingredients

- 2medium potatoes, well-scrubbed
- 1 tablespoon olive oil
- 2 sheets aluminium foil
- ¼ cup sour cream
- Salt, to taste

Cooking Direction

1. Arrange the trivet in the Instant Pot.
2. Rub the potatoes with olive oil and salt.
3. Wrap the potatoes tightly in the aluminium foil.
4. Transfer the potatoes on the trivet.
5. Set the instant pot to "Manual" and cook for 30 minutes at low pressure.
6. Release the pressure naturally and fill in the sour cream.

Nutrition Values

(Calories: 269; Total Fat: 13.2g; Carbs: 34.7g; Sugars: 2.5g; Protein: 4.5g)

Cajun Spiced Pecans

(Prep Time: 10 Mins |Total Time: 30 Mins |Serves: 3)

Ingredients

- ½ pound pecan halves
- 1 teaspoon dried basil
- 1 teaspoon dried thyme
- ½ tablespoon chilli powder
- ¼ teaspoon garlic powder
- ¼ teaspoon cayenne pepper
- 1 tablespoon olive oil
- 1 teaspoon dried oregano

- Salt, to taste

Cooking Direction
1. Put all the ingredients in the Instant Pot.
2. Set the instant pot to "Manual" and cook for 20 minutes at low pressure.
3. Release the pressure naturally and serve.

Nutrition Values
(Calories: 345; Total Fat: 33.1g; Carbs: 7.2g; Sugars: 0.1g; Protein: 4.4g)

Creamy Cheese Avocado

(Prep Time: 10 Mins |Total Time: 15 Mins |Serves: 3)

Ingredients
- 3 avocados, peeled, pitted and chopped
- ½ cup cream cheese, softened
- 3 garlic cloves, minced
- 3 tablespoon of fresh lemon juice
- Salt and black pepper, to taste

Cooking Direction
1. Season the avocados with salt and black pepper.
2. Put the seasoned avocados and garlic cloves in the Instant Pot.
3. Set the instant pot to "Manual" and cook for 3 minutes at high pressure.
4. Release the pressure naturally and dish out the avocados.
5. Stir in lemon juice and cream cheese to the avocados.
6. Refrigerate before serving.

Nutrition Values
(Calories: 265; Total Fat: 23.8g; Carbs: 10.3g; Sugars: 2.9g; Protein: 5.5g)

Portobello Mushroom Burger

(Prep Time: 30 Mins |Total Time: 15 Mins |Serves: 3)

Ingredients
- 3 Portobello mushroom caps
- 1 tablespoon garlic, minced
- 1 teaspoon dried oregano, crushed
- 1 teaspoon dried basil, crushed
- ¼ cup balsamic vinegar
- 2 tablespoons olive oil
- 3 (1-ounce) Parmesan cheese slices
- Salt and black pepper, to taste

Cooking Direction
1. Mix together all the ingredients except cheese slices and mushroom caps.
2. Arrange the mushroom caps smooth side up in a baking dish.
3. Top evenly with herb mixture and keep aside for 20 minutes.
4. Place the trivet in the Instant Pot and put the baking dish on it.
5. Set the instant pot to "Manual" and cook for 8 minutes at high pressure.
6. Release the pressure naturally and top with 1 cheese slice each.

Nutrition Values
(Calories: 187; Total Fat: 15.5g; Carbs: 3.9g; Sugars: 0.6g; Protein: 10g)

Energy Booster Cookies

(Prep Time: 10 Mins |Total Time: 20 Mins |Serves: 6)

Ingredients
- 2 large eggs
- 2/3 cup cocoa powder
- 1/3 cup sugar
- 1¼ cups almond butter
- Salt, to taste

Cooking Direction
1. Put all the ingredients in a food processor and pulse.
2. Roll the mixture into 12 equal small balls and press them.
3. Arrange the balls onto a cookie sheet in a single layer.
4. Place the trivet in the Instant Pot and transfer the cookie sheet on it.
5. Set the instant pot to "Manual" and cook for 10 minutes at high pressure.
6. Release the pressure naturally and dish out the cookies.

Nutrition Values
(Calories: 107; Total Fat: 4.8g; Carbs: 17.1g; Sugars: 11.6g; Protein: 4.5g)

Cheese Biscuits

(Prep Time: 10 Mins |Total Time: 20 Mins |Serves: 4)

Ingredients

- ½ cup coconut flour, sifted
- ¼ cup butter, melted and cooled
- ¼ tablespoon baking powder
- 1 teaspoon garlic powder
- 5 eggs
- 1 cup cheddar cheese, shredded
- Salt, to taste

Cooking Direction

1. Mix together garlic powder, baking powder, coconut flour and salt in a bowl.
2. Beat eggs with butter in another bowl and mix with the flour mixture.
3. Add the cheese and place the mixture onto prepared cookie sheets with a tablespoon.
4. Place the trivet in the Instant Pot and transfer the cookie sheet on it.
5. Set the instant pot to "Manual" and cook for 10 minutes at high pressure.
6. Release the pressure naturally and dish out the biscuits.

Nutrition Values

(Calories: 357; Total Fat: 27.9g; Carbs: 11.7g; Sugars: 0.8g; Protein: 16.2g)

Zucchini Sticks

(Prep Time: 10 Mins |Total Time: 15 Mins |Serves: 8)

Ingredients

- 3 zucchini, cut into 3-inch sticks lengthwise
- 3 eggs
- ¾ cup almonds, grounded
- ¾ cup Parmesan cheese, grated
- ¾ teaspoon Italian herb seasoning
- Salt and black pepper, to taste

Cooking Direction

1. Season zucchini sticks with salt and black pepper.
2. Beat the eggs and mix together remaining ingredients.
3. Dip the zucchini sticks in egg and then coat with the cheese mixture.
4. Put the zucchini sticks onto prepared baking sheet.
5. Place the trivet in the Instant Pot and transfer the cookie sheet on it.
6. Set the instant pot to "Manual" and cook for 20 minutes at high pressure.
7. Release the pressure naturally and dish out.

Nutrition Values

(Calories: 127; Total Fat: 9.1g; Carbs: 6.1g; Sugars: 2.4g; Protein: 7.6g)

Grilled Peaches

(Prep Time: 7 Mins |Total Time: 15 Mins |Serves: 5)

Ingredients

- 5 medium peaches
- ¼ teaspoon ground cloves
- ½ teaspoon ground cinnamon
- ½ teaspoon brown sugar
- 2 tablespoons olive oil
- ¼ teaspoon salt

Directions

1. Remove the pits from the peaches and add olive oil on the cut side of the peaches.
2. Sprinkle the peaches with salt, cloves, cinnamon and brown sugar.
3. Place the trivet in the Instant Pot and transfer the peaches on it.
4. Set the instant pot to "Manual" and cook for 7 minutes at high pressure.
5. Release the pressure naturally and dish out.

Nutrition Values

(Calories: 109; Total Fat: 6g; Carbs: 14.6g; Sugars: 14.3g; Protein: 1.4g)

Honey Citrus Roasted Cashews

(Prep Time: 35 Mins |Total Time: 10 Mins |Serves: 2)

Ingredients

- ¾ cup cashews
- ¼ teaspoon salt
- ¼ teaspoon ginger powder
- 1 teaspoon orange zest, minced
- 4 tablespoons honey

Directions

1. Mix together honey, orange zest, ginger powder and salt.
2. Add cashews to this mixture and place it in a ramekin.
3. Place the trivet in the Instant Pot and transfer the cashews on it.
4. Set the instant pot to "Manual" and cook for 20 minutes at high pressure.
5. Release the pressure naturally and dish out.

Nutrition Values

(Calories: 292; Total Fat: 12.3g; Carbs: 43g; Sugars: 34.5g; Protein: 5.2g)

Pumpkin Muffins

(Prep Time: 10 Mins |Total Time: 25 Mins |Serves: 10)

Ingredients

- 2 cups almond flour
- 4 tablespoons coconut flour
- 1½ teaspoons baking soda
- 2 teaspoons pumpkin pie spice
- ¼ teaspoon salt
- 1 cup pumpkin puree
- 3 teaspoons almond butter
- 1½ teaspoons baking powder
- ½ teaspoon ground cinnamon
- 3 large eggs
- ½ cup raw honey
- 2 tablespoon almonds, toasted and chopped

Cooking Direction

1. Whisk together almond flour, coconut flour, cinnamon, baking soda, baking powder, salt and pumpkin pie spice.
2. Whisk together eggs, honey, pumpkin puree and butter.
3. Combine both the wet and dry mixtures.
4. Fill inside the muffin cups and top with almonds.
5. Place the trivet in the Instant Pot and transfer the muffin cups on it.
6. Set the instant pot to "Manual" and cook for 12 minutes at high pressure.
7. Release the pressure naturally and dish out.

Nutrition Values

(Calories: 268; Total Fat: 15.9g; Carbs: 25.7g; Sugars: 15.1g; Protein: 8.7g)

Banana Chips

(Prep Time: 10 Mins |Total Time: 40 Mins |Serves: 3)

Ingredients

- 3 bananas, cut into 1/8 inch slices
- 3 tablespoons lemon juice
- 3 tablespoons nutmeg

Directions

1. Mix together all the ingredients in a bowl.
2. Spread banana slices evenly over baking sheet in one layer.
3. Place the trivet in the Instant Pot and transfer the baking sheet on it.
4. Set the instant pot to "Manual" and cook for 25 minutes at high pressure.
5. Release the pressure naturally and dish out.

Nutrition Values

(Calories: 145; Total Fat: 3.1g; Carbs: 30.7g; Sugars: 16.7g; Protein: 1.8g)

Mustard Flavoured Artichokes

(Prep Time: 10 Mins |Total Time: 25 Mins |Serves: 3)

Ingredients

- 3 artichokes
- 3 tablespoons mayonnaise
- 1 cup water
- 2 pinches paprika
- 2 lemons, sliced in half
- 2 teaspoons Dijon mustard

Cooking Direction

1. Mix together mayonnaise, paprika and Dijon mustard.
2. Place the trivet in the Instant Pot and add water.
3. Put the artichokes upwards and arrange lemon slices on it.
4. Set the instant pot to "Manual" and cook for 12 minutes at high pressure.
5. Release the pressure naturally and put the artichokes in the mayonnaise mixture.

Nutrition Values

(Calories: 147; Total Fat: 5.4g; Carbs: 24.4g; Sugars: 3.6g; Protein: 6g)

Red Potatoes with Chives

(Prep Time: 10 Mins |Total Time: 25 Mins |Serves: 3)

Ingredients

- 1 pound red potatoes, unpeeled
- 1 bay leaf
- 2 tablespoons butter, melted
- ½ cup water
- 1 garlic clove, peeled
- 1 tablespoon cream cheese
- 2 tablespoons chives, minced
- Salt and black pepper, to taste

Cooking Direction

1. Put the butter, bay leaf and garlic in the Instant Pot and select "Sauté".
2. Sauté for 2 minutes and add red potatoes, water, chives, salt and black pepper.
3. Set the Instant Pot to "Manual" at high pressure for 10 minutes.
4. Release the pressure naturally and top with cream cheese.

Nutrition Values

(Calories: 188; Total Fat: 9.1g; Carbs: 24.7g; Sugars: 1.6g; Protein: 3.3g)

Cheesy Polenta Squares

(Prep Time: 10 Mins |Total Time: 30 Mins |Serves: 12)

Ingredients

- 4 cups yellow cornmeal
- 8 cups water
- 1 cup Parmesan cheese
- 1 cup butter
- 2 teaspoons salt
- 1 teaspoon black pepper

Cooking Direction

1. Put the water, yellow cornmeal, 4 tablespoons butter and salt in the Instant Pot.
2. Set the Instant Pot to "Manual" at high pressure for 10 minutes.
3. Release the pressure naturally and stir in Parmesan cheese, black pepper and ½ cup unsalted butter.
4. Put this mixture in the baking dish.
5. Place the trivet in the Instant Pot and transfer the baking dish on it.
6. Set the instant pot to "Manual" and cook for 17 minutes at high pressure.
7. Release the pressure naturally and

Nutrition Values

(Calories: 291; Total Fat: 17.3g; Carbs: 31.5g; Protein: 4.2g; Cholesterol: 42mg)

Cheesy Burrito Bites

(Prep Time: 15 Mins |Total Time: 25 Mins |Serves: 4)

Ingredients

- 4 oz. tofu, browned and chopped
- ¼ cup purple onion
- ¼ cup cilantro, chopped
- ½ teaspoon salt
- ½ cup cooked black beans
- ¼ cup cheddar cheese, shredded
- 1 tablespoon olive oil
- 4 oz. Mexican rice, cooked
- ¼ cup tomatoes, diced
- ¼ cup water
- 2 giant flour tortillas
- ½ avocado, peeled and sliced

Cooking Direction

1. Put the olive oil and tofu in the Instant Pot and select "Sauté".
2. Sauté for 2 minutes and add Mexican rice.
3. Dish out and keep aside.
4. Put the onions, cilantro, tomatoes and salt in the Instant Pot.
5. Set the Instant Pot to "Manual" at high pressure for 6 minutes.
6. Release the pressure naturally and mix with the rice mixture.
7. Put the spoonful of rice mixture, some avocado slices, 1 tablespoon of black beans and shredded cheddar cheese in a tortilla sheet and roll it tightly.
8. Repeat this process with the other tortilla sheet.

Nutrition Values

(Calories: 381; Total Fat: 14g; Carbs: 52.7g; Protein: 14g; Cholesterol: 7mg)

Instant Pot Cashews

(Prep Time: 5 Mins |Total Time: 10 Min| Serves: 6)

Ingredients:

- 2 teaspoons applesauce
- 2 cups cashews
- 1½ teaspoons smoked paprika
- 1 teaspoon olive oil
- ½ teaspoon salt

Cooking Direction

1. Put the oil and cashews in the Instant Pot and select "Sauté".
2. Sauté for 3 minutes and add applesauce, smoked paprika and salt.
3. Set the Instant Pot to "Manual" at high pressure for 3 minutes.
4. Release the pressure naturally and serve in small bowls.

Nutrition Values

(Calories:275; Total Fat: 22.2g; Carbs: 16.2g; Dietary Fiber: 2.1g; Protein: 7.3g)

Black Currant Biscuits

(Prep Time: 5 Mins |Total Time: 25 Min| Serves: 6)

Ingredients:

- 1 cup flour
- 2 tablespoons butter
- ¼ cup currants
- ½ teaspoon baking powder
- 3 tablespoons milk

Cooking Direction

1. Arrange the trivet in the Instant Pot and add water.
2. Combine baking powder and flour in a bowl.
3. Add butter and mix until a coarse mixture is formed.
4. Add milk and currants and mix to form soft dough.
5. Place dough onto a lightly floured surface and roll into ½-inch thickness.
6. Cut ½-inch of circles and arrange circles onto prepared baking sheet.
7. Transfer the baking sheet on the trivet and lock the lid.
8. Set the Instant Pot to "Manual" at high pressure for 15 minutes.
9. Release the pressure naturally and dish out.

Nutrition Values

(Calories:117; Total Fat: 4.2g; Carbs: 17.1g; Dietary Fiber: 0.8g; Protein: 2.5g)

Blackberry Leather

(Prep Time: 5 Mins |Total Time: 40 Min| Serves: 5)

Ingredients:
- 2 cups fresh blackberries
- 1 tablespoon fresh mint leaves
- ¼ teaspoon fresh lemon juice
- 1 teaspoon ground cinnamon
- ¼ cup unsweetened applesauce

Cooking Direction
1. Arrange the trivet in the Instant Pot and add water.
2. Put all the ingredients in a food processor and pulse until smooth.
3. Transfer the mixture on a baking sheet and place it on the trivet.
4. Set the Instant Pot to "Manual" at high pressure for 30 minutes.
5. Release the pressure naturally and cut the leather into equal sized strips.

Nutrition Values
(Calories:32; Total Fat: 0.3g; Carbs: 7.4g; Dietary Fiber: 3.5g; Protein: 0.9g)

Potato Gratin

(Prep Time: 5 Mins |Total Time: 20 Min| Serves: 4)

Ingredients:
- 2 large potatoes, sliced thinly
- 2 eggs
- ½ cup cheddar cheese, grated
- 1 tablespoon plain flour
- 6 tablespoons coconut cream

Cooking Direction
1. Arrange the trivet in the Instant Pot and add water.
2. Mix together coconut cream, eggs and flour in a bowl until a thick sauce forms.
3. Divide and place the potato slices evenly in 4 ramekins and pour the coconut cream mixture.
4. Top with cheddar cheese and transfer the ramekins on the trivet.
5. Set the Instant Pot to "Manual" at high pressure for 10 minutes.
6. Release the pressure naturally and dish out.

Nutrition Values
(Calories:275; Total Fat: 12.4g; Carbs: 32.1g; Dietary Fiber: 5g; Protein: 10.1g)

Apple Chips

(Prep Time: 5 Mins |Total Time: 20 Min| Serves: 2)

Ingredients:
- 1 apple, peeled, cored and thinly sliced
- ½ teaspoon ground cinnamon
- 1 tablespoon sugar
- Pinch of salt
- Pinch of ground ginger

Cooking Direction
1. Arrange the trivet in the Instant Pot and add water.
2. Mix together all the ingredients in a bowl and put on the baking tray.
3. Set the Instant Pot to "Manual" at high pressure for 10 minutes.
4. Release the pressure naturally and dish out.

Nutrition Values
(Calories:82; Total Fat: 0.2g; Carbs: 22g; Dietary Fiber: 3g; Protein: 0.3g)

Risotto Bites

(Prep Time: 5 Mins |Total Time: 20 Min| Serves: 6)

Ingredients:
- 3 cups cooked risotto
- 3-ounce mozzarella cheese, cubed
- 1 egg, beaten
- 1/3 cup Parmesan cheese, grated
- ¾ cup bread crumbs

Cooking Direction
1. Arrange the trivet in the Instant Pot and add water.
2. Mix together risotto, Parmesan and egg in a bowl until well combined.

3. Make medium-sized balls from the mixture and insert a mozzarella cube in the centre.
4. Put the bread crumbs in a dish and coat the balls evenly.
5. Place the balls on the trivet and lock the lid.
6. Set the Instant Pot to "Manual" at high pressure for 10 minutes.
7. Release the pressure naturally and dish out.

Nutrition Values
(Calories:409; Total Fat: 4.3g; Carbs: 84.3g; Dietary Fiber: 0.6g; Protein: 13.2g)

Turmeric Super Bowl

(Prep Time: 5 Mins |Total Time: 20 Min| Serves: 4)

Ingredients:
- 4 cups snack mix
- 1 tablespoon water
- 2 egg whites
- ½ teaspoon turmeric powder
- 1 pinch ginger powder

Cooking Direction
1. Arrange the trivet in the Instant Pot and add water.
2. Mix together egg whites, ginger powder, water and turmeric powder in a bowl.
3. Add snack mix to this mixture until the snack mix is coated with the mixture.
4. Cover the whole mixture with the foil and press into bowl-like shape.
5. Place this bowl on the trivet and lock the lid.
6. Set the Instant Pot to "Manual" at high pressure for 20 minutes.
7. Release the pressure naturally and dish out.

Nutrition Values
(Calories:265; Total Fat: 10.4g; Carbs: 36.4g; Dietary Fiber: 3.9g; Protein: 7.6g)

Green Devilled Eggs

(Prep Time: 5 Mins |Total Time: 20 Min| Serves: 6)

Ingredients:
- 6 large eggs
- 2 teaspoons fresh lime juice
- 1 medium avocado, peeled, pitted and chopped
- 1/8 teaspoon cayenne pepper
- Pinch of salt

Cooking Direction
1. Put the eggs and water in the Instant Pot and lock the lid.
2. Set the Instant Pot to "Manual" at high pressure for 5 minutes.
3. Release the pressure naturally and put in cold water for 5 minutes.
4. Peel the eggs, slice them in half and scoop out the yolks.
5. Mash together yolks, lime juice, avocado and salt in a bowl.
6. Fill the egg halves with avocado mixture and sprinkle with cayenne pepper.

Nutrition Values
(Calories:144; Total Fat: 11.5g; Carbs: 4.5g; Dietary Fiber: 2.3g; Protein: 7g)

Parsnip Fries

(Prep Time: 5 Mins |Total Time: 40 Min| Serves: 6)

Ingredients:
- 2 pounds small parsnips, peeled and quartered
- 1 teaspoon chilli powder
- 3 tablespoons olive oil
- 3 tablespoons fresh ginger, minced
- Salt and black pepper, to taste

Cooking Direction
1. Arrange the trivet in the Instant Pot and add water.
2. Grease the baking dish with olive oil and add rest of the ingredients.
3. Cover the baking dish with foil and transfer on the trivet.
4. Set the Instant Pot to "Manual" at high pressure for 30 minutes.
5. Release the pressure naturally and serve immediately.

Nutrition Values
(Calories:185; Total Fat: 7.7g; Carbs: 29.5g; Dietary Fiber: 8g; Protein: 2.1g)

Kale Chips

(Prep Time: 5 Mins |Total Time: 20 Min| Serves: 4)

Ingredients:
- 1 pound fresh kale leaves, stemmed and torn
- 1 tablespoon olive oil
- 1 lemon, squeezed
- ¼ teaspoon cayenne pepper
- Salt, to taste

Cooking Direction
1. Arrange the trivet in the Instant Pot and add water.
2. Place kale pieces onto prepared baking sheet and top with olive oil, cayenne pepper, salt and lemon juice.
3. Transfer the baking sheet on the trivet and lock the lid.
4. Set the Instant Pot to "Manual" at high pressure for 15 minutes.
5. Release the pressure naturally and serve immediately.

Nutrition Values
(Calories:90; Total Fat: 3.6g; Carbs: 13.3g; Dietary Fiber: 2.1g; Protein: 3.6g)

Cauliflower Poppers

(Prep Time: 5 Mins |Total Time: 15 Min| Serves: 6)

Ingredients:
- 4 cups cauliflower florets
- 2 teaspoons olive oil
- ¼ teaspoon chilli powder
- 2 eggs
- Salt and black pepper, to taste

Cooking Direction
1. Whisk eggs, chilli powder, salt and black pepper in a bowl.
2. Dip cauliflower florets in the mixture and keep aside.
3. Put the olive oil in the Instant Pot and select "Sauté".
4. Add some dipped cauliflower florets and sauté for 3 minutes until golden brown.
5. Set the Instant Pot to "Manual" at high pressure for 5 minutes.
6. Release the pressure naturally and dish out to serve.

Nutrition Values
(Calories:52; Total Fat: 3.1g; Carbs: 3.7g; Dietary Fiber: 1.7g; Protein: 3.2g)

Crème Caramel

(Prep Time: 5 Mins |Total Time: 20 Min| Serves: 4)

Ingredients:
- 1 cup caramel
- 2 cups full fat milk
- 5 eggs
- 1 tablespoon vanilla extract
- ½ cup granulated sugar

Cooking Direction
1. Whisk the eggs until well beaten and keep aside.
2. Mix vanilla extract and sugar in milk and set aside.
3. Put the milk in the Instant Pot and select "Sauté".
4. Cook for 5 minutes and keep aside for cooling.
5. Pour the cool milk into the egg mixture and whisk well.
6. Put the caramel in the ramekins and top with milk mixture and cover with aluminium foil.
7. Arrange the trivet in the Instant Pot and add water.
8. Transfer the ramekins on the trivet and lock the lid.
9. Set the Instant Pot to "Manual" at high pressure for 8 minutes.
10. Release the pressure naturally and dish out to serve.

Nutrition Values
(Calories:290; Total Fat: 6.9g; Carbs: 45.5g; Dietary Fiber: 0g; Protein: 12.2g)

Red Wine Poached Pears

(Prep Time: 5 Mins |Total Time: 25 Min| Serves: 6)

Ingredients:
- 6 firm tart pears
- 1 teaspoon ginger, grated
- 1 cinnamon stick
- 1 bottle red wine
- 2 cups granulated sugar

Cooking Direction
1. Put the red wine, cinnamon stick, ginger, pears and sugar in the Instant Pot.
2. Set the Instant Pot to "Manual" at high pressure for 8 minutes.
3. Release the pressure naturally for 10 minutes and dish out the pears.
4. Select "Sauté" and reduce the sauce by cooking for 3 minutes.
5. Slice the pears and drizzle the wine mixture on them.

Nutrition Values
(Calories:377; Total Fat: 0.3g; Carbs: 99.2g; Dietary Fiber: 6.7g; Protein: 0.8g)

White Chocolate Orange Fondue

(Prep Time: 5 Mins |Total Time: 10 Min| Serves: 3)

Ingredients:
- 100 g Swiss white chocolate
- 1 teaspoon sugar
- 1 teaspoon orange essence
- 100 g fresh cream
- 1 teaspoon fresh orange peel, chopped finely

Cooking Direction
1. Arrange the trivet in the Instant Pot and add water.
2. Put white chocolate, fresh cream, sugar, orange essence and orange peel in a small ceramic pot.
3. Set the Instant Pot to "Manual" at high pressure for 3 minutes.
4. Release the pressure naturally and dish out the fondue.

Nutrition Values
(Calories:274; Total Fat: 18.1g; Carbs: 25.4g; Dietary Fiber: 0.1g; Protein: 3g)

Baked Apples

(Prep Time: 5 Mins |Total Time: 18 Min| Serves: 6)

Ingredients:
- 6 apples, cored
- 1 cup red wine
- 1 teaspoon cinnamon powder
- ¼ cup raisins
- ½ cup sugar

Cooking Direction
1. Arrange the apples in the Instant Pot and top with rest of the ingredients.
2. Set the Instant Pot to "Manual" at high pressure for 8 minutes.
3. Release the pressure naturally and dish out.

Nutrition Values
(Calories:229; Total Fat: 0.4g; Carbs: 53.3g; Dietary Fiber: 5.6g; Protein: 0.8g)

Cherry Pie

(Prep Time: 5 Mins |Total Time: 45 Mins |Serves: 2)

Ingredients:
- ¾ Pie Crust, cut in half
- 2 cups Water
- 1 cup pitted Cherries
- 1 ½ tbsp Quick Tapioca
- 1/3 cup Sugar
- ¼ tsp Vanilla Extract
- Pinch of Salt

Cooking Direction
1. Pour the water into the IP and lower the trivet.

2. In a bowl, combine he cherries, extract, sugar, salt and tapioca.
3. Grease a baking dish and place half of the pie crust at the bottom.
4. Pour the filling over.
5. Cut the other pie crust half into strips and arrange over the filling.

6. Place the baking dish on the trivet and close the lid.
7. Cook on HIGH for 14 minutes.
8. Do a quick pressure release. Serve and enjoy!

Nutrition Values

(Calories 390| Total Fats 12g | Carbs: 70g | Protein 2g| Dietary Fiber: 2g)

Pumpkin Pie

(Prep Time: 5 Mins |Total Time: 30 Mins |Serves: 2)

Ingredients:
- ½ pound Butternut Squash, diced
- 3 tbsp Honey
- 1 tsp Cornstarch
- ¼ tsp Cinnamon
- ¼ cup Coconut Milk
- 1 small Egg
- 1 cup Water

Cooking Direction
1. Pour the water into the Instant Pot. Lower the trivet.
2. Place the squash on the trivet and close the lid.

3. Cook for 4 minutes on HIGH.
4. Transfer the squash to a plate but let the cooking liquid remain in the IP.
5. Combine the squash with the remaining ingredients in a bowl.
6. Grease a baking dish and pour the batter into it.
7. Place on the trivet and cook for 10 minutes on HIGH.
8. Do a quick pressure release. Serve and enjoy!

Nutrition Values

(Calories 173| Total Fats 2g | Carbs: 40g | Protein 3g| Dietary Fiber: 4g)

Stuffed Peaches

(Prep Time: 5 Mins |Total Time: 35 Mins |Serves: 2)

Ingredients:
- 2 Peaches
- 2 tbsp Butter
- ¼ tsp Almond Extract
- Pinch of Cinnamon
- 2 tbsp Cassava Flour
- 2 tbsp Maple Syrup
- 2 tsp chopped Almonds
- 1 ½ cups Water

Cooking Direction
1. Pour the water into the Instant Pot. Lower the rack.

2. Slice the tops off the peaches and discard the pits.
3. Combine the rest of the ingredients in a bowl.
4. Stuff the peaches with the mixture.
5. Place them on the rack and close the lid.
6. Cook for 3 minutes on HIGH.
7. Do a quick pressure release.
8. Serve and enjoy!

Nutrition Values

(Calories 145| Total Fats 5g | Carbs: 25g | Protein 1.5g| Dietary Fiber: 1g)

Stuffed Peaches

(Prep Time: 5 Mins |Total Time: 35 Mins |Serves: 2)

Ingredients:
- 2 Peaches
- 2 tbsp Butter
- ¼ tsp Almond Extract
- Pinch of Cinnamon
- 2 tbsp Cassava Flour

- 2 tbsp Maple Syrup
- 2 tsp chopped Almonds
- 1 ½ cups Water

Cooking Direction
1. Pour the water into the Instant Pot. Lower the rack.

2. Slice the tops off the peaches and discard the pits.
3. Combine the rest of the ingredients in a bowl.
4. Stuff the peaches with the mixture.
5. Place them on the rack and close the lid.
6. Cook for 3 minutes on HIGH.
7. Do a quick pressure release.
8. Serve and enjoy!

Nutrition Values
(Calories 145| Total Fats 5g | Carbs: 25g | Protein 1.5g| Dietary Fiber: 1g)

Chocolate Chip Oat Cookies
(Prep Time: 5 Mins |Total Time: 30 Mins |Serves: 2)

Ingredients:
- ¼ cup Oats
- 2 tbsp Milk
- 1 tbsp Honey
- 2 tbsp Sugar
- 2 tsp Coconut Oil
- ½ tsp Vanilla Extract
- 2 tbsp Chocolate Chips
- ¼ cup Flour
- Pinch of Salt
- 1 ½ cups Water

Cooking Direction
1. Pour the water into the Instant Pot. Lower the trivet.
2. Combine all of the cookie ingredients in a bowl.
3. Line a baking dish with parchment paper.
4. With a cookie scoop, drop the cookies onto the paper.
5. Make sure to flatten them slightly.
6. Place the dish on the trivet and close the lid.
7. Set the IP to MANUAL.
8. Cook on HIGH for 8 minutes.
9. Do a quick pressure release.
10. If they are not crispy for your liking.
11. Cook them on SAUTE for a few extra minutes.
12. Serve and enjoy!

Nutrition Values
(Calories 410| Total Fats 20g | Carbs: 58g | Protein 6g| Dietary Fiber: 1g)

Banana Chocolate Chip Muffins
(Prep Time: 5 Mins |Total Time: 30 Mins |Serves: 2)

Ingredients:
- 1/3 cup Buttermilk
- 1/3 tsp Baking Soda
- 2 tbsp Chocolate Chips
- 1 Banana, mashed
- ½ cup Flour
- 1 cup Water
- 1 tbsp Honey
- Pinch of Cinnamon
- 3 tbsp Butter, melted
- 1 tbsp Flaxseeds

Cooking Direction
1. Pour the water into the Instant Pot. Lower the trivet.
2. Whisk together all of the ingredients.
3. Make sure to get rid of all the lumps.
4. Divide the mixture between two silicone muffin cups.
5. Place the muffin cups on the trivet.
6. Close the lid and set the IP to MANUAL.
7. Cook on HIGH for 15 minutes.
8. Do a quick pressure release.
9. Serve and enjoy!

Nutrition Values
(Calories 230| Total Fats 13g | Carbs: 30g | Protein 3g| Dietary Fiber: 3g)

Simple Vanilla Egg Custard
(Prep Time: 5 Mins |Total Time: 25 Mins |Serves: 2)

Ingredients:
- 2 Eggs
- Pinch of Cinnamon
- ¼ tsp Vanilla Extract
- 1 1/3 cup Milk
- 1 ½ cups Water
- ¼ cup Sugar

Cooking Direction

1. Pour the water into the Instant Pot. Lower the trivet.
2. In a bowl, beat the eggs.
3. Add the rest of the ingredients and whisk to combine.
4. Grease 2 ramekins and divide the mixture between them.
5. Place the ramekins on the trivet and close the lid.
6. Cook on HIGH for 7 minutes.
7. Release the pressure naturally.
8. Serve and enjoy!

Nutrition Values

(Calories 150| Total Fats g | Carbs: 16g | Protein 7g| Dietary Fiber: 1g)

Chocolate Fondue

(Prep Time: 5 Mins |Total Time: 15 Mins |Serves: 2)

Ingredients:

- 5 ounces Chocolate
- Pinch of Cinnamon
- 4 ounces Heavy Cream
- 1 tsp Coconut Liqueur
- Pinch of Salt
- ½ cup Lukewarm Water

Cooking Direction

1. Pour the water into the Instant Pot. Lower the trivet.
2. Melt the chocolate in a microwave, in a heatproof bowl.
3. Add the rest of the ingredients, except the liqueur, and stir to combine.
4. Place the dish on the trivet.
5. Close and seal the lid and set the IP to STEAM.
6. Cook for 4 minutes.
7. Add the liqueur, stir to incorporate.
8. Serve and enjoy!

Nutrition Values

(Calories 215| Total Fats 20g | Carbs: 12g | Protein 2g| Dietary Fiber: 0g)

Cinnamon Apple Bowl

(Prep Time: 5 Mins |Total Time: 15 Mins |Serves: 2)

Ingredients:

- 2 Apples, peeled and diced
- ¼ cup Almond Flour
- ¼ cup Shredded Coconut
- 1 cup Coconut Milk

Cooking Direction

1. Place all of the ingredients in your Instant Pot.
2. Close the lid and set the IP to MANUAL.
3. Cook for 5 minutes on HIGH.
4. Do a quick pressure release.
5. Divide between 4 small bowls.
6. Serve and enjoy!

Nutrition Values

(Calories 140| Total Fats 8g | Carbs: 17g| Protein 2g | Dietary Fiber: 3.5g)

Orange and Raspberry Poached Peaches

(Prep Time: 5 Mins |Total Time: 25 Mins |Serves: 4)

Ingredients:

- ½ cup Raspberries
- 1 cup Fresh Orange Juice
- 4 Peaches, peeled and pitted

Cooking Direction

1. Combine the orange juice and raspberries in a blender.
2. Blend until smooth and pour the mixture into the IP.
3. Place the peaches inside the steamer basket and lower it into the pot.
4. Close the lid and set the IP to MANUAL.
5. Cook on HIGH for 5 minutes.
6. Do a quick pressure release.
7. Serve and enjoy!

Nutrition Values

(Calories 130| Total Fats 1g | Carbs: 8g| Protein 1g | Dietary Fiber: 3g)

Steamed Lime Apples

(Prep Time: 5 Mins |Total Time: 15 Mins |Serves: 2)

Ingredients:
- ½ cup Lime Juice
- 1 cup Water
- 2 Apples, peeled and cut into wedges
- 1 tbsp Almond Butter

Cooking Direction
1. Combine the water and lime juice in the Instant Pot.
2. Place the apple wedges inside the steamer basket.
3. Lower the basket into the pot and close the lid.
4. Set the IP to MANUAL.
5. Cook for 3 minutes on HIGH.
6. Serve the apples drizzled with almond butter.
7. Enjoy!

Nutrition Values
(Calories 144| Total Fats 5g | Carbs: 26g| Protein 2g | Dietary Fiber: 5g)

Fried Cinnamon Bananas

(Prep Time: 5 Mins |Total Time: 15 Mins |Serves: 1)

Ingredients:
- 1 Banana, sliced
- Pinch of Cinnamon
- 2 tbsp Coconut Oil

Cooking Direction
1. Set your Instant Pot to SAUTE.
2. Add the coconut oil and cook until melted.
3. Add the banana slices and cook until they become golden brown on all sides.
4. Transfer to a bowl and sprinkle with cinnamon.
5. Serve and enjoy!

Nutrition Values
(Calories 280| Total Fats 20g | Carbs: 27g| Protein 1.3g | Dietary Fiber: 3g)

Ratatouille Riviera-Style

(Prep Time: 15 Mins |Total Time: 35 Mins |Serves: 4)

Ingredients:
- 1 tbsp. extra-virgin olive oil
- 3 cloves garlic, minced
- 2 onions, chopped
- 500g eggplant, chopped
- 400g squash, diced
- 4 tomatoes, chopped
- 2 tsp. dried basil
- 1 red capsicum, chopped
- 1 green capsicum, chopped
- ½ tsp. ground pepper
- ½ tsp. dried thyme
- 1 tsp salt

Directions:
1. Sauté garlic and onion in your instant pot until softened and fragrant; stir in all veggies, except tomatoes, and cook for a few minutes until tender.
2. Add in the tomatoes and lock lid; cook on high pressure for 5 minutes and then let pressure come down on its own. Serve.

Nutrition Values
(Calories 116| Total Fats 4.5g | Carbs: 20.8g| Protein 4.5g | Dietary Fiber: 8.3g)

Lemon Broccoli

(Prep Time: 5 Mins |Total Time: 7 Mins |Serves: 5)

Ingredients:
- 1 cup water
- 900 g broccoli, tough parts removed and ends scored
- 4 tablespoons lemon juice
- salt and pepper

Directions:

1. Add water to your instant pot and add in broccoli; drizzle with lemon juice and season with salt and pepper.
2. Lock lid and cook on high for 2 minutes and then release pressure naturally. Serve.

Nutrition Values
(Calories 126| Total Fats 4.3g | Carbs: 21.6g| Protein 4.3g | Dietary Fiber: 8.4g)

Instant Pot Baked Potatoes
(Prep Time: 5 Mins |Total Time: 25 Mins |Serves: 4)

Ingredients:
- 2 pounds medium potatoes
- 1 cup water

Directions:
1. Add the potatoes in your instant pot and poke each potato facing up with a knife several times;
2. Add water and lock the lid.
3. Cook on high pressure for 10 minutes and then release pressure naturally.
4. Transfer the potatoes onto an oven rack and bake for about 15 minutes or until crispy, but fluffy.

Nutrition Values
(Calories 156| Total Fats 0.2g | Carbs: 35.6g| Protein 3.8g | Dietary Fiber: 5.4g)

Instant Pot Olive & Eggplant Spread
(Prep Time: 5 Mins |Total Time: 23 Mins |Serves: 5)

Ingredients:
- 2 pounds eggplant, sliced in big chunks
- 1 cup water
- 3-4 garlic cloves, skin on
- 1 tablespoons tahini
- ¼ cup freshly squeezed lemon juice
- 4 tablespoons olive oil
- 1 tbsp. chopped fresh thyme
- ¼ cup black olives, pitted
- 1 teaspoon salt

Directions:
1. Add olive oil to your instant pot and set it on sauté mode; add the eggplants and sauté for 5 minutes or until caramelized.
2. Add the garlic and stir in salt and water. Lock lid and cook on high pressure for 3 minutes.
3. Release the pressure naturally and pour out most of the brown liquid; take out the garlic cloves and remove the skin.
4. transfer to a blender and add lemon juice, tahini, and olives; blend until very smooth.
5. Serve sprinkled with more black olives, thyme and drizzled with olive oil. Enjoy!

Nutrition Values
(Calories 145| Total Fats 11.7g | Carbs: 10.8g| Protein 2.2g | Dietary Fiber: 6g)

Tasty Roasted Garlic
(Prep Time: 9 Mins |Total Time: 15 Mins |Serves: 1)

Ingredients:
- 3 large garlic bulbs, tops trimmed off
- 1 cup water
- 1 tsp. extra virgin olive oil

Directions:
1. Add water to your instant pot and insert a steamer basket.
2. Add the garlic bulbs to the steamer basket and lock lid; cook on high pressure for about 6 minutes and then let pressure come down on its own.
3. Carefully remove the steamer basket from the pot and transfer the garlic bulbs to a dish.
4. Drizzle with olive oil and season with salt and pepper; broil for about 5 minutes or until caramelized and golden. Serve.

Nutrition Values
(Calories 40| Total Fats 4.7g | Carbs: 3g| Protein 0.6g | Dietary Fiber: 0.2g)

Instant Pot Hot Sauce

(Prep Time: 5 Mins |Total Time: 11 Mins |Serves: 4)

Ingredients
- 1¼ cup apple cider vinegar
- 12 oz. fresh hot peppers, stems removed, roughly chopped
- 2 teaspoons sea salt

Directions
1. Add the hot peppers to an instant pot and add the remaining ingredients; lock lid and cook on high pressure for 1 minute.
2. Let pressure come down on its owns and then puree the mixture with an immersion blender until smooth.
3. Strain the pureed pepper mixture into a clean bottle and refrigerate up to three months.

Nutrition Values
(Calories 69| Total Fats 0.4g | Carbs: 9g| Protein 1.6g | Dietary Fiber: 1.3g)

Raspberry Curd

(Prep Time:2 Mins |Cook Time 6 Mins |Servings: 4)

Ingredients:
- 2 cups fresh raspberries
- 1 cup of swerve or erythritol sweetener
- 2 egg yolks
- 2 Tablespoons ghee or coconut oil
- 1 Tablespoon fresh orange juice
- 2 Tablespoons fresh lemon juice
- ½ teaspoon lemon zest
- Pinch of salt

Cooking Direction
1. Add listed ingredients to Instant Pot, except egg yolks and ghee. Stir well.
2. Lock, seal the lid. Press "Manual" button. Cook on HIGH 1 minute.
3. When done, naturally release pressure 5 minutes, then quick release remaining pressure. Remove the lid.
4. Using an immersion blender, puree raspberry mixture until smooth.
5. Press "Sauté" function. Stir in egg yolks and ghee to raspberry mixture.
6. Transfer raspberry mixture to covered bowl, or glass jar. Refrigerate.
7. Serve over non-dairy ice cream, or yogurt.

Nutrition Values
Calories: 115, Fat: 1.8g, Carbohydrates: 24.5g, Dietary Fiber: 3.2g, Protein: 1.63g

Chapter 9 Dessert Recipes

Coconut Cake

(Prep Time: 5 Mins |Total Time: 55 Mins |Serves: 2)

Ingredients:

- 1 Egg, yolk and white separated
- ½ cup Coconut Flour
- 1 tbsp melted Coconut Oil
- ¼ tsp Coconut Extract
- ¾ cup warm Coconut Milk
- ¼ cup Coconut Sugar
- 1 cup Water

Cooking Direction

1. Beat the white until soft form peaks.
2. Bea tin the sugar and yolk.
3. Add the coconut oil and extract and stir to combine.
4. Fold in the coconut flour.
5. Line or grease a small baking dish an pour the batter into it.
6. Pour the water into the IP and lower the trivet.
7. Place the dish on the trivet.
8. Cook for 40 minutes on HIGH.
9. Do a quick pressure release.
10. Serve and enjoy!

Nutrition Values

(Calories 350| Total Fats 14g | Carbs: 47g | Protein 7g| Dietary Fiber: 7g)

Yogurt Vanilla Lighter Cheesecake

(Prep Time: 5 Mins |Total Time: 6 hours and 60 Mins |Serves: 2)

Ingredients:

- 1 small Egg
- ½ cup Yogurt
- ¼ tsp Vanilla
- 2 tbsp melted Butter
- ½ cup Graham Cracker Crumbs
- 2 ounces Cream Cheese, softened
- 1 tbsp Sugar
- 1 cup Water

Cooking Direction

1. Pour the water into the Instant Pot and lower the trivet.
2. Combine the butter and crackers and press the mixture into the bottom of a greased small baking dish.
3. Bea the yogurt, vanilla, sugar, and cream cheese.
4. Beat in the egg.
5. Pour over the crust.
6. Place the baking dish on the trivet and close the id.
7. Cook on HIGH for 20 minutes.
8. Do a quick pressure release.
9. Let cool to room temperature then place it in the fridge for 5-6 hours.
10. Serve and enjoy!

Nutrition Values

(Calories 280| Total Fats 9g | Carbs: 26g | Protein 6g| Dietary Fiber: 1g)

Molten Lava Cake

(Prep Time: 5 Mins |Total Time: 20 Mins |Serves: 2)

Ingredients:

- 1 tbsp Butter, melted
- 3 tbsp Almond Flour
- ½ cup chopped Dark Chocolate
- 1 cup Water
- 1 Egg, beaten
- ¼ tsp Vanilla
- ¼ cup Coconut Sugar

Cooking Direction

1. Pour the water into the Instant Pot. Lower the trivet.
2. Combine all of the remaining ingredients in a bowl.
3. Grease two ramekins and divide the batter among them.
4. Place them on the trivet and close the lid.

5. Cook for 9 minutes on HIGH.
6. Do a quick pressure release.
7. Serve and enjoy!

Nutrition Values

(Calories 414| Total Fats 23g | Carbs: 48g | Protein 8g| Dietary Fiber: 2.6g)

Stuffed Peaches

(Prep Time: 5 Mins |Total Time: 35 Mins |Serves: 2)

Ingredients:
- 2 Peaches
- 2 tbsp Butter
- ¼ tsp Almond Extract
- Pinch of Cinnamon
- 2 tbsp Cassava Flour
- 2 tbsp Maple Syrup
- 2 tsp chopped Almonds
- 1 ½ cups Water

Cooking Direction
1. Pour the water into the Instant Pot. Lower the rack.
2. Slice the tops off the peaches and discard the pits.
3. Combine the rest of the ingredients in a bowl.
4. Stuff the peaches with the mixture.
5. Place them on the rack and close the lid.
6. Cook for 3 minutes on HIGH.
7. Do a quick pressure release.
8. Serve and enjoy!

Nutrition Values

(Calories 145| Total Fats 5g | Carbs: 25g | Protein 1.5g| Dietary Fiber: 1g)

Blueberry Jam

(Prep Time: 5 Mins |Total Time: 30 Mins |Serves: 2)

Ingredients:
- ¼ cup Honey
- ½ cup Blueberries

Cooking Direction
1. Combine the honey and blueberries in the IP.
2. Set it to KEEP WARM and let it sit until the honey turns liquid.
3. When the honey becomes liquid, set the IP to SAUTE and bring it to a boil.
4. Cover, press CANCEL, and set to MANUAL.
5. Cook on HIGH for 2 minutes.
6. Do a natural pressure release.
7. Serve and enjoy!

Nutrition Values

(Calories 180| Total Fats 0g | Carbs: 40g | Protein 1g| Dietary Fiber: 1g)

Vanilla Rice Pudding

(Prep Time: 5 Mins |Total Time: 30 Mins |Serves: 2)

Ingredients:
- 1/3 cup Basmati Rice
- ½ tsp Vanilla Extract
- ¼ cup Heavy Cream
- 2/3 cup Milk
- 1 ½ tbsp Maple Syrup
- Pinch of Salt

Cooking Direction
1. Combine everything in the Instant Pot, except the cream.
2. Close the lid and set the IP to PORRIDGE.
3. Cook for 17 minutes.
4. Do a natural pressure release.
5. Stir in the heavy cream.
6. Serve and enjoy!

Nutrition Values

(Calories 240| Total Fats 7g | Carbs: 38g | Protein 5g| Dietary Fiber: 7g)

Pressure Cooked Brownies

(Prep Time: 5 Mins |Total Time: 45 Mins |Serves: 2)

Ingredients:
- 1 tbsp Honey
- 2 cups Water
- ½ cup Sugar
- 1 Egg
- 2 tbsp Cocoa Powder
- Pinch of Salt
- ¼ cup melted Butter
- 2/3 cup Flour
- 1/3 cup Baking Powder

Cooking Direction
1. Pour the water into the Instant Pot. Lower the trivet.
2. Whisk the wet ingredients in one bowl.
3. Stir together the dry ones in another.
4. Combine the two mixtures gently.
5. Grease a baking dish with some cooking spray.
6. Pour the batter into it.
7. Place the dish on the trivet and close the lid.
8. Cook on HIGH for 25 minutes.
9. Do a quick pressure release.
10. Serve and enjoy!

Nutrition Values
(Calories 525| Total Fats 25g | Carbs: 75g | Protein 8g| Dietary Fiber: 3g)

Almond Tapioca Pudding

(Prep Time: 5 Mins |Total Time: 30 Mins |Serves: 2)

Ingredients:
- 2/3 cup Almond Milk
- ¼ cup Tapioca Pearls
- 2 tbsp Sugar
- ½ tsp Almond Extract
- ½ cup Water
- Pinch of Cinnamon

Cooking Direction
1. Pour the water into the Instant Pot. Lower the trivet.
2. Take a heat –proof bowl and place all of the ingredients into it.
3. Stir well to combine.
4. Cover with a foil and place the bowl on the trivet.
5. Close the lid and set the IP to MANUAL.
6. Cook on HIGH for 7-8 minutes.
7. Do a natural pressure release.
8. Serve and enjoy!

Nutrition Values
(Calories 190| Total Fats 2.5g | Carbs: 39g | Protein 2.5g| Dietary Fiber: 5.2g)

Blondies with Peanut Butter

(Prep Time: 5 Mins |Total Time: 55 Mins |Serves: 2)

Ingredients:
- 1 ½ cups Water
- ¼ cup Brown Sugar
- 2 tbsp White Sugar
- 1/3 cup Oats
- 1/3 cup Flour
- 1 Egg
- 2 tbsp Peanut Butter
- 3 tbsp Butter, softened
- Pinch of Salt

Cooking Direction
1. Pour the water into the Instant Pot. Lower the trivet.
2. Grease a baking dish with cooking spray and set aside.
3. Cream together the sugars, egg, butter, peanut butter, and salt, in a mixing bowl.
4. Fold in the dry ingredients.
5. Pour the batter into the greased pan.
6. Place the pan on the trivet and close the lid.
7. Cook on POULTRY for 26 minutes.
8. Wait 10 minutes before doing a quick pressure release.
9. Let it cool for 15 minutes before inverting onto a plate and slicing.
10. Serve and enjoy!

Nutrition Values
(Calories 550| Total Fats 18g | Carbs: 61g | Protein 8g| Dietary Fiber: 1.5g)

Gingery Applesauce

(Prep Time: 5 Mins |Total Time: 15 Mins |Serves: 2)

Ingredients:
- 1 ½ pounds Apples, chopped
- 1 ½ tbsp Crystalized Ginger
- ½ cup Water

Cooking Direction
1. Pour the water into the Instant Pot.
2. Add the apples and ginger and stir to combine.
3. Close the lid and set the IP to MANUAL.
4. Cook on HIGH for 4 minutes.
5. Wait 10 minutes and then release the pressure naturally.
6. Msh with a potato masher.
7. Serve and enjoy!

Nutrition Values
(Calories 260| Total Fats 1g | Carbs: 66g | Protein 5g| Dietary Fiber: 5g)

Peach Crumb

(Prep Time: 5 Mins |Total Time: 55 Mins |Serves: 2)

Ingredients:
- ¼ cup Breadcrumbs
- 2 small Peaches, sliced
- 2 tbsp Lemon Juice
- ¼ tsp Lemon Zest
- ¼ cup melted Butter
- ¼ tsp ground Ginger
- Pinch of Cinnamon
- 2 tbsp Sugar
- 1 ½ cups Water

Cooking Direction
1. Pour the water into the Instant Pot. Lower the trivet.
2. Grease a baking dish with cooking spray and arrange the peach slices in it.
3. Combine the remaining ingredients in a bowl and spread over the peaches.
4. Place the dish on the trivet and close the lid.
5. Cook on HIGH for 20 minutes.
6. Do a natural pressure release.
7. Serve and enjoy!

Nutrition Values
(Calories 505| Total Fats 25g | Carbs: 70g | Protein 2.5g| Dietary Fiber: 4g)

Pear Ricotta Cake

(Prep Time: 5 Mins |Total Time: 30 Mins |Serves: 2)

Ingredients:
- 2 tbsp Sugar
- 1 Egg
- 1 Pear, diced
- ½ cup Ricotta
- ½ cup Flour
- ½ tsp Baking Soda
- ½ tsp Vanilla
- 1 ½ tbsp Oil
- 1 tbsp Lemon Juice
- 1 tsp Baking Powder
- 2 cups Water

Cooking Direction
1. Pour the water into the Instant Pot. Lower the trivet.
2. Whisk together all of the ingredients in a large bowl.
3. Stir well to avoid leaving any lumos.
4. Grease a baking dish that fits inside the IP, with some cooking spray.
5. Pour the batter into the dish and then place it on the trivet.
6. Close the lid of the IP and set it to MANUAL.
7. Cook on HIGH for 15 minutes.
8. Release the pressure quickly.
9. Serve and enjoy!

Nutrition Values
(Calories 452| Total Fats 20g | Carbs: 60g | Protein 13g| Dietary Fiber: 4g)

Lemon and Blackberry Compote

(Prep Time: 5 Mins |Total Time: 135 Mins |Serves: 2)

Ingredients:
- Juice of ½ Lemon
- Pinch of Lemon Zest
- 1 cup Frozen Blackberries
- 5 tbsp Sugar
- 1 tbsp Cornstarch
- 1 tbsp Water

Cooking Direction
1. Combine the lemon juice, sugar, zest, and blackberries, in your IP.
2. Close the lid and set the IP to MANUAL.
3. Cook for 3 minutes on HIGH.
4. Do a natural pressure release.
5. Whisk together the water and cornstarch and stir the mixture into the compote.
6. Cook on SAUTE until slightly thickened.
7. Place in the fridge for 1 ½ - 2 hours.
8. Serve and enjoy!

Nutrition Values
(Calories 220 | Total Fats 0g | Carbs: 60g | Protein 1g| Dietary Fiber: 4g)

Poached Gingery Orange Pears

(Prep Time: 5 Mins |Total Time: 20 Mins |Serves: 2)

Ingredients:
- 2 Pears
- 1 cup Orange Juice
- 1 tsp minced Ginger
- Pinch of Nutmeg
- Pinch of Cinnamon
- 2 tbsp Sugar

Cooking Direction
1. Pour the juice into the IP.
2. Stir in the sugar, ginger, cinnamon, and nutmeg.
3. Peel the pears and cut in half.
4. Place the inside the IP.
5. Close the lid and cook for 7 minutes on HIGH.
6. Do a natural pressure release.
7. Serve drizzled with the sauce.
8. Enjoy!

Nutrition Values
(Calories 170| Total Fats 1g | Carbs: 43g | Protein 1g| Dietary Fiber: 5g)

Caramel Flan

(Prep Time: 5 Mins |Total Time: 30 Mins |Serves: 2)

Ingredients:
- 1 Egg
- 4 ounces Condensed Milk
- ½ cup Coconut Milk
- ½ tsp Vanilla Extract
- 1 ½ cups plus 3 tbsp Water
- 5 tbsp Sugar

Cooking Direction
1. Combine the sugar and water in the IP on SAUTE.
2. Cook until caramelized.
3. Divide the caramelized sugar (immediately otherwise it will harden) between 2 greased ramekins.
4. Bea the remaining ingredients in a bowl and then pour on top of the caramel.
5. Cover with aluminum foil.
6. Pour the water into the Instant Pot. Lower the trivet.
7. Place the ramekins on the trivet and close the lid.
8. Cook on HIGH for 5 minutes.
9. Do a natural pressure release.
10. Allow to cool before inverting onto a plate.
11. Serve and enjoy!

Nutrition Values
(Calories 108| Total Fats 3g | Carbs: 16g | Protein 3g| Dietary Fiber: 0g)

Strawberry Cream

(Prep Time: 5 Mins |Total Time: 4 hours and 20 Mins |Serves: 2)

Ingredients:
- 1 cup Strawberry Halves
- 1 cup Coconut Milk

Cooking Direction
1. Combine the ingredients in your IP.
2. Close the lid and set the IP to MANUAL.
3. Cook on HIGH for 2 minutes.
4. Do a quick pressure release.
5. Let the mixture cool completely.
6. Blend with a hand blender and divide between two glasses.
7. Refrigerate for 4 hours.
8. Serve and enjoy!

Nutrition Values

(Calories 63| Total Fats 3g | Carbs: 9g| Protein 1g | Dietary Fiber: 2g)

Berry Compote

(Prep Time: 5 Mins |Total Time: 2 hours and 30 Mins |Serves: 4)

Ingredients:
- 2 tbsp Arrowroot
- 1 cup Raspberries
- 1 cup halved Strawberries
- 1 cup Blackberries
- 1 cup Blueberries
- Juice of 1 Orange
- ½ cup Water

Cooking Direction
1. Place the berries, water, and orange juice, in the Instant Pot.
2. Close the lid and set the IP to MANUAL.
3. Cook on HIGH for 3 minutes.
4. Do a quick pressure release.
5. Whisk in the arrowroot and set the IP to SAUTE.
6. Cook until thickened.
7. Let cool completely and transfer to an airtight container.
8. Refrigerate for 2 hours before serving.
9. Enjoy!

Nutrition Values

(Calories 95| Total Fats 0.5g | Carbs: 23g| Protein 1g | Dietary Fiber: 6.7g)

Creamy Coconut Peach Dessert

(Prep Time: 5 Mins |Total Time: 2 hours and 20 Mins |Serves: 4)

Ingredients:
- 3 Peaches, peeled and chopped
- ½ cup shredded Coconut
- ½ cup Coconut Milk
- Pinch of Cinnamon

Cooking Direction
1. Combine all of the ingredients in the IP.
2. Close the lid and set the IP to MANUAL.
3. Cook on HIGH for about 4 minutes.
4. Do a quick pressure release.
5. Mash with a fork and let cool.
6. Divide between 4 bowls, cover, and refrigerate for 2 hours.
7. Serve and enjoy!

Nutrition Values

(Calories 50| Total Fats 1g | Carbs: 9g| Protein 0.5g | Dietary Fiber: 1.5g)

Banana and Almond Butter Bars

(Prep Time: 5 Mins |Total Time: 20 Mins |Serves: 2)

Ingredients:
- ½ cup Almond Butter
- 3 Bananas
- 2 tbsp 100% Cocoa Powder
- 1 ½ cups Water

Cooking Direction
1. In a bowl, mash together the bananas and almond butter.
2. Stir in the cocoa powder.
3. Grease a baking dish and pour the banana mixture into it.

4. Pour the water into the IP and lower the rack.
5. Place the baking dish on the rack and close the lid.
6. Set the IP to MANUAL and cook on HIGH for 15 minutes.
7. Do a quick pressure release.

8. Remove the baking dish from the IP.
9. Let cool and cut into bars.
10. Serve and enjoy!

Nutrition Values
(Calories 141| Total Fats 10g | Carbs: 14g| Protein 3g | Dietary Fiber: 2g)

Fruity Sauce with Apples

(Prep Time: 5 Mins |Total Time: 15 Mins |Serves: 2)

Ingredients:
- 2 Apples, peeled and cubed
- 1 cup mixed Berries
- 1 cup Pineapple chunks
- ¼ cup Fresh Orange Juice
- 2/3 cup Water
- ¼ cup chopped Almonds
- 1 tbsp Coconut Oil

Cooking Direction
1. Combine all of the ingredients, except the almonds, in the Instant Pot.

2. Close the lid and set the IP to MANUAL.
3. Cook for 5 minutes on HIGH.
4. Release the pressure quickly.
5. Open the lid and blend the mixture with a hand blender.
6. Stir in the almonds.
7. Serve and enjoy!

Nutrition Values
(Calories 120| Total Fats 4g | Carbs: 15g| Protein 1g | Dietary Fiber: 4g)

Stewed Pears with Coconut Butter

(Prep Time: 5 Mins |Total Time: 15 Mins |Serves: 3)

Ingredients:
- 2 Large Pears, peeled and cut into wedges
- 2 tbsp Coconut Oil
- 3 tbsp Coconut Butter, melted
- 1 tsp Cinnamon
- 1 cup Water

Cooking Direction
1. Pour the water into the IP.
2. Place the pears inside the steamer basket and lower the basket into the pot.
3. Close the lid and cook for 2 minutes.
4. Quickly release the pressure and open the lid.

5. Transfer the bowl to a plate and discard the water from the pan.
6. Melt the coconut butter in the IP on SAUTE and add the pears inside.
7. Sprinkle with cinnamon and cook until they become browned.
8. Serve drizzled with the melted coconut butter.
9. Enjoy!

Nutrition Values
(Calories 240| Total Fats 17g | Carbs: 22g| Protein 1g | Dietary Fiber: 6g)

Green Beans w/ Lemon Juice

(Prep Time: 5 Mins |Total Time: 10 Mins |Serves: 2)

Ingredients:
- 4 ounces trimmed green beans
- 1 teaspoon fresh lemon juice
- ½ teaspoon extra-virgin olive oil
- Pinch of sea salt

Directions:

1. Steam the green beans in your instant pot for about 5 minutes for until crisp-tender.
2. Drizzle with fresh lemon juice, olive oil and sprinkle with sea salt. Enjoy!

Nutrition Values
(Calories 28| Total Fats 1.3g | Carbs: 4.1g| Protein 1.1g | Dietary Fiber: 1.9g)

Peppermint Cheesecake

(Prep Time: 15Mins |Cook Time 35Mins |Servings: 3)

Ingredients

- 1 cups organic cream cheese, softened, ¼ cup sour cream
- 1 large organic eggs
- ½ cup swerve or erythritol sweetener
- 1/2 Tablespoon coconut, Pinch of salt
- 1 teaspoons pure vanilla extract, ½ teaspoons pure peppermint extract
- Chocolate Ganache:
- 3-ounces unsweetened chocolate chips, melted
- ⅓ cup organic heavy cream, Pinch of salt
- Crust:
- 1/2 cup almond flour
- 1 Tablespoons swerve or erythritol sweetener
- 1 Tablespoons ghee or goat butter, melted

Cooking Direction

1. Combine ingredients for crust. Press down in a spring form pan; choose pan suitable for Instant Pot. Place in freezer for 10 minutes.
2. In a large bowl or blender, combine filling ingredients. Stir well.
3. Pour cheesecake filling in spring form pan. Cover with aluminum foil.
4. Add 1 cup of water, and trivet to Instant Pot. Place spring form pan on top.
5. Close, seal the lid. Press "Manual" button. Cook on HIGH 35 minutes.
6. When done, naturally release pressure 15 minutes, then quick release remaining pressure. Remove the lid.
7. Remove pan from pot. Cool on counter 30 minutes, then refrigerate 4 hours.
8. In a bowl, combine chocolate ganache ingredients. Microwave 30 seconds. Stir. Repeat until smooth.
9. Transfer cheesecake to platter. Drizzle over ganache. Serve.

Nutrition Values

(Calories: 453, Fat: 33.3g, Carbohydrates: 30g, Dietary Fiber: 0.8g, Protein: 9g)

Maple Flan

(Prep Time:7 Mins| Cook Time: 1 hour and 30 mins |Servings: 4)

Ingredients:

- ½ cup maple syrup
- 3 large organic eggs
- 1½ cups coconut milk
- 1½ cups organic heavy cream
- 1 Tablespoon pure vanilla extract
- ½ teaspoon salt

Cooking Direction

1. Add half of maple syrup to bottom of Instant Pot soufflé dish.
2. In a bowl, whisk eggs, and quarter cup of maple syrup
3. In a medium saucepan, combine coconut milk, heavy cream, vanilla extract, salt. Simmer on low 5 minutes.
4. Temper hot cream to eggs: Drizzle in small amount of hot cream slowly to beaten eggs. Stir well. Pour in rest of hot cream. Stirring constantly.
5. Using a fine mesh strainer, strain ingredients into soufflé dish. Cover with aluminum foil.
6. Add 3 cups of water, and trivet to Instant Pot. Place soufflé dish on trivet.
7. Lock, seal the lid. Press "Slow Cook" button. Cook on HIGH 75 minutes.
8. When done, quick release pressure. Remove the lid.
9. Transfer soufflé dish to a wire rack. Allow to cool 60 minutes.
10. Refrigerate 4 hours. Serve with non-dairy cream, fresh berries.

Nutrition Values

(Calories: 247, Fat: 18g, Carbohydrates: 18.63g, Dietary Fiber: 1.3g, Protein: 4.09g)

Apple Cake

(Prep Time:10 Mins |Cook Time: 1 hour|Servings: 3)

Ingredients:

- 2 cups fresh red or green apples, peeled, cored, chopped
- ½ cup homemade applesauce
- 1 teaspoon ground cinnamon powder
- ¼ teaspoon ground nutmeg
- 1½ cups almond flour
- ¼ cup goat butter or ghee, melted
- ¼ cup coconut oil
- 2 large eggs
- ½ cup swerve or erythritol sweetener
- ½ cup almonds, roughly chopped
- ½ teaspoon pure vanilla extract
- Pinch of salt

Cooking Direction

1. In a large bowl, combine listed ingredients, except the almonds. Stir well.
2. Grease a 7-inch cake pan for Instant Pot with non-stick spray.
3. Pour in batter. Top with almonds. Cover pan with foil.
4. Add 1 cup of water, and trivet to Instant Pot. Place cake pan on trivet.
5. Close, seal the lid. Press "Manual" button. Cook on HIGH 60 minutes.
6. When done, naturally release pressure. Remove the lid.
7. Transfer pan to a wire rack. Allow to cool slightly before slicing. Serve.

Nutrition Values

(Calories: 313, Fat: 27g, Carbohydrates: 22g, Dietary Fiber: 3g, Protein: 5g)

Lavender Crème Brulée

(Prep Time: 4 Mins |Cook Time:9 Mins |Servings: 4)

Ingredients:

- 8 egg yolk
- 2 cups unsweetened coconut cream
- ⅓ cup swerve sweetener
- 1 teaspoon pure vanilla extract
- 1 Tablespoon dried culinary lavender
- 1½ cups water

Cooking Direction

1. In a bowl, combine coconut cream, and sweetener. Stir well.
2. Whisk in egg yolks. Stir in vanilla extract and lavender.
3. Grease ramekins with nonstick spray. Divide batter evenly between ramekins.
4. Add water and, trivet to Instant Pot. Place ramekins on trivet.
5. Lock, seal the lid. Pres "Manual" button. Cook on HIGH 9 minutes.
6. When done, naturally release pressure. Remove the lid.
7. Transfer ramekins to cool rack. Allow to cool 1 hour at room temperature. Chill in refrigerator 4 hours. Serve with fresh berries.

Nutrition Values

(Calories: 382, Fat: 36.3g, Carbohydrates: 13g, Dietary Fiber: 2g, Protein: 4.3g)

Almond Butter Chocolate Cake

(Prep Time:6 Mins| Cook Time: 2 Mins |Servings: 1)

Ingredients:

- 1 Tablespoon almond butter, melted
- 1 teaspoon ghee, melted
- ½ teaspoon pure vanilla extract
- 1 Tablespoon unsweetened coconut cream
- 1 large organic egg
- 2 Tablespoons swerve sweetener
- 2 Tablespoons cocoa powder

Cooking Direction

1. In a large bowl, combine listed ingredients, except the almond butter. Stir well.
2. Grease a ramekin with non-stick spray. Pour in batter.
3. Pour 1 cup of water, and trivet to Instant Pot. Place ramekin on trivet.
4. Lock, seal the lid. Press "Manual" button. Cook on HIGH 2 minutes.

5. When done, quick release pressure. Remove the lid.
6. Drizzle melted almond butter over ramekin cake. Serve.

Nutrition Values
(Calories: 257, Fat: 22.6g, Carbohydrates: 20.1g, Dietary Fiber: 5.2g, Protein: 11.2g)

Stuffed Peaches

(Prep Time: 17 Mins| Cook Time: 3Mins |Servings: 3)

Ingredients:
- 3 organic fresh peaches, tops removed, pitted
- ¼ cup organic coconut flour or organic almond flour
- ¼ cup Swerve sweetener
- 1 Tablespoons ghee or coconut oil
- 1 teaspoon organic ground cinnamon powder
- ½ teaspoon pure almond extract
- Pinch of salt

Cooking Direction
1. In a bowl, combine flour, swerve, oil, cinnamon, almond extract, and salt. Stir well.
2. Divide mixture evenly between the peaches.
3. Add 1 cup of water, and steamer basket to Instant Pot.
4. Place stuffed peaches on top of steamer basket.
5. Lock, seal the lid. Press "Manual" button. Cook on HIGH 3 minutes.
6. When done, quick release pressure. Remove the lid.
7. Transfer peaches to platter. Top with non-dairy ice cream. Serve.

Nutrition Values
(Calories: 172, Fat: 14.21g, Carbohydrates: 1.76g, Dietary Fiber: 0.9g, Protein: 9.11g)

Chocolate Avocado Muffin Bites

(Prep Time:7 Mins| Cook Time:8 Mins| Servings: 3)

Ingredients:
- 1 large organic eggs
- 1 cup apple juice
- ½ cup coconut oil, melted
- 1 Tablespoons organic cocoa powder
- 1 cup coconut flour
- ½ teaspoon baking powder
- ½ teaspoon baking soda
- 1 teaspoon organic cinnamon powder
- 1 teaspoons organic vanilla extract
- Pinch of salt
- 1 cup ripe avocados, peeled, pit removed, mashed
- ⅓ cup unsweetened dark chocolate chips

Cooking Direction
1. In a large bowl, combine listed ingredients. Stir well.
2. Grease ramekins or silicone muffin cups with non-stick cooking spray. Divide and fill with the chocolate avocado mixture.
3. Add 1 cup of water, and trivet to Instant Pot.
4. Place ramekins/ muffin cups on top of trivet.
5. Lock, seal the lid. Press "Manual" button. Cook on HIGH 8 minutes.
6. When done, naturally release pressure. Remove the lid.
7. Transfer to wire rack to cool. Serve.

Nutrition Values
(Calories: 272 , Fat: 25g, Carbohydrates: 10g, Dietary Fiber: 3g, Protein: 4g)

Lemon Tapioca Pudding

(Prep Time: 5 Mins |Total Time: 20 Min| Serves: 2)

Ingredients:
- ½ cup tapioca pearls, rinsed
- 1 cup milk
- ½ cup water
- ½ cup sugar
- ½ lemon zest

Cooking Direction
1. Arrange the trivet in the Instant Pot and add water.
2. Mix tapioca pearls, lemon zest, milk, sugar and water in a heatproof bowl.

3. Place the bowl on the trivet and lock the lid.
4. Set the Instant Pot to "Manual" at high pressure for 8 minutes.
5. Release the pressure naturally and dish out in glasses.

Nutrition Values
(Calories:339; Total Fat: 2.5g; Carbs: 78.7g; Dietary Fiber: 0.1g; Protein: 4.1g)

Glazed Banana

(Prep Time: 5 Mins |Total Time: 10 Min| Serves: 2)

Ingredients:
- 1 tablespoon olive oil
- 1 under-ripened banana, peeled and sliced
- 1 tablespoon water
- 1 tablespoon unsweetened applesauce
- 1/8 teaspoon of ground cinnamon

Cooking Direction
1. Beat together applesauce and water in a bowl.
2. Put the oil and banana slices in the Instant Pot and select "Sauté".
3. Sauté for 2 minutes on each side and transfer the banana slices onto a serving plate.
4. Pour applesauce mixture over banana slices evenly and sprinkle with cinnamon.

Nutrition Values
(Calories:119; Total Fat: 7g; Carbs: 13.5g; Dietary Fiber: 1.7g; Protein: 0.5g)

Grilled Peaches

(Prep Time: 5 Mins |Total Time: 14 Min| Serves: 3)

Ingredients:
- 3 medium peaches, halved and pitted
- ½ cup coconut cream
- 1 teaspoon vanilla extract
- ¼ cup walnuts, chopped
- 1/8 teaspoon ground cinnamon

Cooking Direction
1. Mix together coconut cream and vanilla extract in a bowl.
2. Arrange the trivet in the Instant Pot and add water.
3. Place the peach slices on the trivet, cut-side down.
4. Set the Instant Pot to "Manual" at high pressure for 5 minutes.
5. Release the pressure naturally and spoon the coconut cream over each peach half.
6. Top with walnuts and cinnamon and serve.

Nutrition Values
(Calories:220; Total Fat: 16.1g; Carbs: 17.5g; Dietary Fiber: 3.9g; Protein: 4.8g)

Banana Custard

(Prep Time: 5 Mins |Total Time: 30 Min| Serves: 4)

Ingredients:
- 14-ounce almond milk
- 2 ripe bananas, peeled and finely mashed
- 3 eggs
- ½ teaspoon vanilla extract
- ½ cup sugar

Cooking Direction
1. Arrange the trivet in the Instant Pot and add water.
2. Mix together all the ingredients in a bowl and divide the banana mixture in prepared glasses evenly.
3. Put the glasses on the trivet and lock the lid.
4. Set the Instant Pot to "Manual" at high pressure for 20 minutes.
5. Release the pressure naturally and dish out.

Nutrition Values
(Calories:423; Total Fat: 27.1g; Carbs: 44.3g; Dietary Fiber: 3.7g; Protein: 7.1g)

Chocolate Peanut Butter Cups

(Prep Time: 5 Mins |Total Time: 25 Min| Serves: 6)

Ingredients:
- ¼ cup heavy cream
- 2 ounces chocolate
- ½ cup sugar
- 1 cup butter
- ¼ cup peanut butter, separated

Cooking Direction
1. Arrange the trivet in the Instant Pot and add water.
2. Melt the peanut butter and butter, and add chocolate, sugar and heavy cream.
3. Stir gently and transfer the mixture in a baking mould.
4. Put the baking mould on the trivet and lock the lid.
5. Set the Instant Pot to "Manual" at high pressure for 15 minutes.
6. Release the pressure naturally and dish out.

Nutrition Values

(Calories:465; Total Fat: 40.7g; Carbs: 24.6g; Dietary Fiber: 1g; Protein: 3.8g)

Chocolate Cheesecake

(Prep Time: 5 Mins |Total Time: 30 Min| Serves: 8)

Ingredients:
- 4 eggs
- 4 cups cream cheese, softened
- 1 cup sugar
- 4 tablespoons cocoa powder
- 2 teaspoons vanilla extract

Cooking Direction
1. Arrange the trivet in the Instant Pot and add water.
2. Put cream cheese and eggs in a blender and blend until smooth.
3. Add rest of the ingredients and pulse until mixed well.
4. Transfer the mixture into 4 (8-ounce) mason jars evenly.
5. Put the mason jars on the trivet and lock the lid.
6. Set the Instant Pot to "Manual" at high pressure for 20 minutes.
7. Release the pressure naturally and refrigerate to chill for at least 5 hours before serving.

Nutrition Values

(Calories:539; Total Fat: 43g; Carbs: 29.9g; Dietary Fiber: 0.8g; Protein: 12g)

21 Days Meal Plan

Meal Plan	Breakfast	Lunch	Dinner	Snacks / Dessert
Day-1	Diced Turmeric Eggs	Instant Rotisserie Chicken	Steak Soup with Vegetables	Spiced Nuts
Day-2	Veggie Quiche	Slow-Cooked Turkey	Thai Peanut Chicken	Baked Potato
Day-3	Apple and Almond Porridge	Green Chicken	Corn Soup	Cheese Biscuits
Day-4	Tomato Poached Eggs	Vegetarian Chili Potato Stew	Lemon Chicken	Grilled Peaches
Day-5	Carrot and Pecan Muffins	Thai Goose with Basil	Easy Vegetarian Spring Soup	Apple Chips
Day-6	Easy Breakfast Casserole	Pork and Mushroom Stew	Tomato Brisket	Crème Caramel
Day-7	Korean Steamed Eggs	Garlic Drumsticks	Sloppy Joes	Parsnip Fries
Day-8	Berries Compote	Beef Brisket with Veggies	Coconut Cabbage	Pear Ricotta Cake
Day-9	Cauliflower Pudding	Pulled Pork Soup	Mushroom Stir-Fry	Chocolate Fondue
Day-10	Egg and Asparagus Frittata	Basil Beef with Yams	Chestnut Soup	Lemon Broccoli
Day-11	Hard Boiled Egg Loaf	Tomato Soup	Chicken Chili	Raspberry Curd
Day-12	Oysters and Eggs Frittata	Chicken Curry	Veggie Patties	Coconut Cake
Day-13	Breakfast Simple Pancakes	Turkey Patties	Pork Tacos	Molten Lava Cake
Day-14	Ham Muffins	Instant Pot Italian Beef	Turkey Casserole	Stuffed Peaches
Day-15	Breakfast Quinoa with Berries	Pork Fried Rice	Caprese Pasta	Gingery Applesauce
Day-16	Apple Streusel	Easy Taco Meat	Manchow Soup	Peach Crumb
Day-17	Egg & Ham Casserole	Beef Bourguignon	Chicken Paprikash	Stuffed Peaches
Day-18	Sausage Hash	Pork Chops with Red Cabbage	Colorful Veggies	Creamy Coconut Peach Dessert
Day-19	Simple Bread	Shrimp Scampi	Eggplant Burgers	Maple Flan
Day-20	Eggs with Spinach	Beef Taco Pie with Cheese	Crab Cakes	Caramel Flan
Day-21	Apple Breakfast Quinoa	Orange and Gingery Fish	Crunchy Tuna	Glazed Banana

Appendix 1: Measurement Conversion Chart

Volume Equivalents(Liquid)

US STANDARD	US STANDARD(OUNCES)	METRIC(APPROXIMATE)
2 TABLESPOONS	1 fl.oz.	30 mL
1/4 CUP	2 fl.oz.	60 mL
1/2 CUP	4 fl.oz.	120 mL
1 CUP	8 fl.oz.	240 mL
1 1/2 CUP	12 fl.oz.	355 mL
2 CUPS OR 1 PINT	16 fl.oz.	475 mL
4 CUPS OR 1 QUART	32 fl.oz.	1 L
1 GALLON	128 fl.oz.	4 L

Volume Equivalents (DRY)

US STANDARD	METRIC (APPROXIMATE)
1/8 TEASPOON	0.5 mL
1/4 TEASPOON	1 mL
1/2 TEASPOON	2 mL
3/4 TEASPOON	4 mL
1 TEASPOON	5 mL
1 TABLESPOON	15 mL
1/4 CUP	59 mL
1/2 CUP	118 mL
3/4 CUP	177 mL
1 CUP	235 mL
2 CUPS	475 mL
3 CUPS	700 mL
4 CUPS	1 L

Weight Equivalents

US STANDARD	METRIC (APPROXIMATE)
1/2 OUNCE	15g
1 OUNCE	30g
2 OUNCE	60g
4 OUNCE	115g
8 OUNCE	225g
12 OUNCE	340g
16 OUNCES OR 1 POUND	455g

Temperatures Equivalents

FAHRENHEIT (F)	CELSIUS(C) (APPROXIMATE)
250	121
300	149
325	163
350	177
375	190
400	205
425	218
450	232

Appendix 2: Recipes Index

Printed in Poland
by Amazon Fulfillment
Poland Sp. z o.o., Wrocław

53202390R00105